A History
of the ICC

THE NORTON ESSAYS IN AMERICAN HISTORY

Under the general editorship of

HAROLD M. HYMAN

William P. Hobby Professor of American History
Rice University

A History
of the ICC

From Panacea to Palliative

Ari and Olive Hoogenboom

New York W · W · NORTON & COMPANY · INC ·

FIRST EDITION

Library of Congress Cataloging in Publication Data
Hoogenboom, Ari Arthur, 1927–
    A history of the ICC.
    (The Norton essays in American history)
    Bibliography: p.
    1. United States. Interstate Commerce Commission—
History. I. Hoogenboom, Olive, joint author.
II. Title.
HE2757. 1976.H66   353.008'75   75–28497
ISBN   0–393–05565–5
ISBN   0–393–09204–6 pbk.

1 2 3 4 5 6 7 8 9 0

For Lynn
and all 1975 college graduates

Contents

Foreword

~~~~~~

NEARLY EVERYONE agrees that the Interstate Commerce Commission (ICC) has failed. The disintegration of freight and passenger service; the dependence on highways, interstate trucking, and automobiles in the midst of a growing energy shortage and an ecology movement; the chaos of rates and regulations bearing little or no relation to costs all contribute to a massive transportation crisis that wastes billions of dollars annually. Established in 1887 as the first independent regulatory agency— and becoming the model of subsequent ones—the ICC did not fulfill its founders' hopes that it solve the railroad problem. Despite having been charged further in the 1920s with building up a system "prepared to handle promptly all interstate traffic of the country," the ICC planned nothing.[1]

While few dispute its lack of success, how and why the ICC failed is hotly debated. There are roughly five viewpoints on the ICC. Standing apart from the current debate is the classic, and no longer accepted, position, expressed best by I. L. Sharfman, that the ICC has generally maintained a proper balance between the interests of powerful, monopolistic railroads and the public, insuring moderate profits and adequate service at a reasonable cost. The most prevalent view today is that the ICC did not live up to its promise because it was captured and manipulated by

1. Chief Justice William Howard Taft in Dayton-Goose Creek Ry. v. U.S., 263 U.S. 456, 478 (1924), in I. L. Sharfman, *The Interstate Commerce Commission: A Study in Administrative Law and Procedure,* 5 vols. (New York, 1931–37), 1:179.

the very industry it was created to regulate. A group of Ralph Nader's raiders, led by Robert C. Fellmeth, energetically apply this hypothesis to the contemporary transportation crisis, while Gabriel Kolko argues that railroads not only dominated the commission from its inception but wanted regulation and worked for the passage of the Interstate Commerce Act. The Kolko hypothesis has been sharply challenged by Albro Martin, who argues that the ICC did not succeed because in the critical decade prior to World War I it was captured by "archaic," railroad-hating Progressive politicians. ICC regulation, Martin maintains, starved railroads, lost would-be investors to better-paying enterprises, and started railroads on their long decline. Adherents of a fourth view argue that failure of the ICC is rooted in its structure. Marver H. Bernstein discerns that independent regulatory commissions have a life cycle of hopeful gestation, vigorous youth, devitalized maturity, and debilitating old age, while George W. Hilton says that having created in the ICC an "incomplete cartel"—the most undesirable way to organize an industry—Congress should abolish this commission. Finally, others suggest, and we agree, that the ICC is not predestined by bureaucratic or economic law to fail but that commissioners and their staffs have chosen failure. The combination of weak commissioners—whom presidents appoint—and an entrenched, unimaginative bureaucracy, anxious to preserve the status quo, has caused the ICC's problems. Our text is provided by Judge Learned Hand, who observed that commissions tend to "fall into grooves . . . and when they get into grooves, then God save you to get them out of the grooves."[2]

This book has benefited from the help and criticism of colleagues and friends. To Charles H. Hession and Jerome L. Sternstein of Brooklyn College, we owe our greatest debt for their meticulous reading and searching criticism of the entire manuscript. In addition, Sternstein made available to us his extensive notes on Gilded Age and Progressive era politicians.

2. Henry J. Friendly, *The Federal Administrative Agencies: The Need for Better Definition of Standards* (Cambridge, Mass., 1962), p. 25.

Harold M. Hyman of Rice University and James L. Mairs of W.
W. Norton patiently awaited, cordially read, and pointedly criti-
cized this study. Gerald G. Eggert of the Pennsylvania State
University generously shared with us his research on Thomas
M. Cooley and Richard Olney. Two old friends, Grady Mc-
Whiney of the University of Alabama and W. Patrick Strauss of
Oakland University, helped develop some of these ideas by ar-
ranging for the history departments of Wayne State and Oakland Universities to listen to our conclusions on the ICC and to
discuss with us its problems. We wish to thank Allis Wolfe,
Jason Berger, John Knowlton, Jacqueline Balk, and Theodore
Lauer for helping us in our research. We acknowledge our dependence on the Brooklyn College Library, the New York Public Library, and the Library of Congress and thank their staffs
for aid and hospitality. We are also grateful to all those past and
present who have studied the ICC and this nation's transportation problems and have recorded their findings. Our many individual debts to them are acknowledged in our bibliography and
footnotes.

ARI HOOGENBOOM
OLIVE HOOGENBOOM

Brooklyn
4 June 1975

A History
of the ICC

1

Much Hope and Little Power: The Late Nineteenth Century

RAILROADS revolutionized American transportation, economy, and society and confronted the United States with enormous problems. Competition, which regulated farmers, merchants, and manufacturers to the satisfaction of nineteenth-century Americans, not only failed to regulate railroads but led them to discriminate among shippers according to their size and location. When state efforts to regulate railroads proved inadequate, Americans established the Interstate Commerce Commission amid high hopes that it would eliminate discrimination.[1]

The Railroad Problem

In 1830 there were twenty-three miles of railroads in the United States; by 1869 piecemeal and haphazard rail systems had been joined and expanded to cross the continent and to crisscross the more populous, industrialized northeastern and midwestern states. To better handle long-distance freight, railroads standardized their rolling stock, developed a standard automatic coupler, and moved toward a gauge of 4 feet 8½

1. Henry C. Adams, "A Decade of Federal Railway Regulation," *Atlantic Monthly* 81 (April 1898):433–35.

inches, which accounted for 78 percent of railroad mileage by 1880. In 1883 railroads converted the fifty-four different times they observed into four time zones.[2]

Rates, however, were not uniform, and only rail service itself was of greater concern to shippers. If cheap, bulky products—such as ore, coal, grain, and lumber—were to be hauled, rates would have to be low. Furthermore, loading and unloading costs were the same for local and transcontinental shipments, making it impossible to set rates by a simple weight and mileage formula. With tremendous investments in roadbeds, rolling stock, and stations, railroads had high fixed costs whether they ran one or a hundred trains daily. Since the cost differential between underutilized and utilized equipment was virtually the same, railroads lowered rates where freight was needed to fill empty cars. Hoping to reap freight harvests from regions they served, many railroads also set low rates on strategic items to encourage economic growth. Railroads charged what the traffic would bear and related their rates to the value, rather than the cost, of the service performed. While economically rational when monopoly prevailed, value-of-service ratemaking proved economically irrational and difficult to regulate when competition existed.[3]

The fact that railroads competed in some areas and monopolized other areas made rate rationalization difficult. By the mid-1880s two or more competing railroads served most cities, while one road served most hinterland sections. Though bitter in certain areas, rail competition is often exaggerated. In the late 1870s St. Louis and Atlanta had twenty rail routes between them, varying from 526 to 1,855 miles, but many of these routes were so circuitous and time-consuming that they were not competitive. The toughest rivalry was in Trunk Line terri-

2. See John F. Stover, *American Railroads* (Chicago, 1961) for a survey of American railroads.
3. Edward C. Kirkland, *Industry Comes of Age: Business, Labor, and Public Policy, 1860–1897* (New York, 1961), pp. 75–76.

tory, handling long-distance through traffic between the midwestern cities of Chicago and St. Louis and the major northeastern seaports, where the Grand Trunk, New York Central, Erie, Pennsylvania, and Baltimore & Ohio railroads belligerently competed. Intermittent rate cutting culminated in the disastrous 1876 to 1877 depression rate war. Eastbound, first-class freight rates dropped from a dollar to 15 cents per hundred pounds, while westbound rates dropped from 75 to 25 cents. Fluctuating rates left shippers, who preferred calculation to guesswork, almost as frustrated as they left railroad managers and investors. To increase freight and to stabilize costs for large shippers, railroads rebated up to half of published rates to companies guaranteeing substantial shipments.[4]

To maintain their rates when competition increased and rebates grew costly, railroads formed pools and assigned member roads a portion of the traffic. For example, the Iowa Pool (an unwritten understanding among the Chicago, Burlington & Quincy, the North Western, and the Rock Island railroads, which lasted from 1870 to 1885) allowed member roads to retain 45 percent of passenger income and half of freight income while equally dividing the remainder. In 1877, following the rate war, the New York Central, Pennsylvania, Erie, and Baltimore & Ohio railroads formed a pool administered by the Eastern Trunk Line Executive Committee; western roads formed a Western Executive Committee; and Albert Fink, the nation's leading advocate and practitioner of pooling, chaired the Joint Executive Committee. With power to decide and interpret, Fink enforced agreed-upon pooling rates and divided traffic and receipts among participants. Though they helped stabilize rates, pools themselves were unstable. Unscrupulous managers cheated participants, and, despite Fink's efforts, the courts re-

4. Ibid., pp. 76–81; Gabriel Kolko, *Railroads and Regulation, 1877–1916* (Princeton, 1965), pp. 7–8; Robert W. Harbeson, "Railroads and Regulation, 1877–1916: Conspiracy or Public Interest," *Journal of Economic History* 27 (1967):231–32.

fused to enforce agreements. By improving rates, pools also encouraged entrepreneurs to construct competing roads.[5]

Railroad managers preferred consolidation to pools. Powerful roads—such as the Pennsylvania, which eventually combined 600 roads—built their systems by leasing feeder and competing lines. During the two decades prior to 1873, many short lines combined end to end to form trunk lines, and during the two decades following 1873 these trunk lines acquired feeder lines and became large railroad systems. Railroad barons frequently acquired or neutralized a needed or troublesome road by purchasing enough stock to control its management. Personal holdings and interlocking directorates circumvented recently enacted state-regulatory legislation prohibiting railroads from buying competing properties. During and after the 1880s, restrictions on combinations began to disappear. The consolidation movement peaked during a sixteen-month period in 1899 and 1900 when a sixth of the nation's rail mileage was absorbed by other lines.[6]

Though pools and consolidations helped eliminate competition, from 1865 to 1885 rates dropped by a third to a half, a considerable reduction even allowing for the deflationary trend of the times. With technological advances enabling them to move freight more cheaply and with fuel and steel-rail costs dropping more rapidly than freight rates, railroads were able to sustain these falling rates, which nevertheless remained discriminatory. Farmers, merchants, and industrialists served by a single railroad paid higher rates than those served by competing roads. The Pennsylvania Railroad, with its Pittsburgh monopoly, charged Andrew Carnegie's steel company proportionately higher freight rates than those paid by his rivals. In contrast, competing railroads gave John D. Rockefeller rebates (partial

5. Kirkland, *Industry*, pp. 86–88; Kolko, *Railroads and Regulation*, pp. 8–20; George W. Hilton, "The Consistency of the Interstate Commerce Act," *Journal of Law and Economics* 9 (1966):88–93.

6. U.S., Congress, Senate, Committee on Commerce, *National Transportation Policy*, 87th Cong., 1st sess., 26 June 1961, S. Rept. 445, pp. 229–32; Kirkland, *Industry*, pp. 91–93.

refunds on paid freight rates) and drawbacks (rebates on a competitor's freight rates) for his Cleveland-based Standard Oil Company. The Pennsylvania also charged more to ship grain from Chicago to Pittsburgh than from Chicago to New York, and local rates were proportionately higher than through rates. Railroads destroyed individual businessmen and stunted entire areas; discriminatory freight rates on Minneapolis flour ruined New York State millers, while rates on Chicago-bound Iowa grain and livestock starved Iowa river-town markets.[7]

Although many farmers, merchants, manufacturers, and railroad men opposed discrimination, they could not agree on how to eliminate it. The problem was complex. Railroads were the first large American business and were absolute monopolies in large areas, yet fiercely competitive at many points. The fact that railroads appeared to be prospering more than they actually were—since their total costs were greater than their short-run marginal costs indicated—accentuated misunderstandings. Confused by the economics of railroad management and pricing, most contemporaries looked for simple remedies. Many wistfully thought that abuses would disappear if informed stockholders would overrule powerful railroad barons, a few favored public ownership, some yearned for stabilized pools, others wanted to consolidate all roads into a few privately controlled systems, while still others called for increased competition. The 1874 Windom report, "Transportation-Routes to the Seaboard," advocated that the federal government build one or more trunk lines to "regulate all the others on fair business principles, remedy the abuses that now exist, check combinations, and thereby reduce the cost of transportation to reasonable rates." Rejecting privately controlled, consolidated systems as well as publicly owned railroads, many Americans thought that government regulation compelling railroads to compete

7. Kirkland, *Industry*, pp. 93–101; Joseph Frazier Wall, *Andrew Carnegie* (New York, 1970), pp. 506–19; Allan Nevins, *Study in Power: John D. Rockefeller, Industrialist and Philanthropist*, 2 vols. (New York, 1953), 1:60–70, 86–94; George H. Miller, *Railroads and the Granger Laws* (Madison, Wis., 1971), pp. 99–100.

would eliminate abuses. But competition, while lowering rates for some, increased the discrimination many assumed it would end. Regulation could also stabilize rates and reduce competition by promoting collusion and pools among railroads. Perplexed by the problems railroads created, the nation revived the mercantilist tradition it had never really abandoned. Without any clear notion of how to solve railroad problems, it embraced the idea of regulation for the common good.[8]

State Regulation

To deal with railroads, states established railroad commissions. In 1832 Connecticut created a commission to see that a railroad charter was complied with; in 1844 New Hampshire established the first commission assigned safety inspection; and in that same year Rhode Island set up a commission to prevent rate-and-service discrimination. There were only four state commissions in 1860, but their number grew rapidly from 1869 to 1887. Although the Massachusetts commission (1869) could use only publicity to enforce its decisions, noising abroad unpopular practices and rates by its energetic chairman, Charles Francis Adams Jr., stabilized rates and reformed practices. By 1887 fourteen states, including all of New England except New Hampshire, had copied this advisory commission, but often lacked its dynamic leadership.[9]

Stronger commissions originated in the Midwest, where railroad overdevelopment and merchant and farmer discontent were rampant. The railroad rate-fixing structure, which favored major collecting points (Chicago, in particular) over interior collecting points, blighted business in whole areas and infuriated local merchants. To prevent trains loaded with hinterland pro-

8. John R. Meyer et al., *The Economics of Competition in the Transportation Industries* (Cambridge, Mass., 1959), p. 6; Kirkland, *Industry*, pp. 101–12; Hilton, "Consistency of the Interstate Commerce Act," pp. 94–103.
9. Robert E. Cushman, *The Independent Regulatory Commissions* (New York, 1941), pp. 20–25; Kirkland, *Industry*, pp. 117–19; Hilton, "Consistency of the Interstate Commerce Act," pp. 101–2.

duce from passing nonstop through their towns, these merchants in the 1860s originated and backed antidiscriminatory, antirailroad, antimonopoly legislation. By the 1870s they were joined by farmers whose expectations of cheap transportation had been bitterly disappointed by railroads, often made unscrupulous by financial difficulties. To attract railroads, many farmers had helped finance them. Thirteen hundred farmers in eight Wisconsin counties, for example, had mortgaged their farms for $1.5 million to invest in railroad stock. Growing out of farmer resentment of barefaced discrimination, the Granger movement made further demands for regulation. Setting maximum rates, Illinois furnished the model for nine other states and the precedent for national regulation. Beginning in 1873 the Illinois commission divided railroads into five categories, based on their earnings, and fixed rates accordingly. By 1881 consolidations made only two categories necessary. Recognizing the higher proportionate cost of a short haul, the commission computed rates on all shipments by utilizing 5-mile units for the first 150 miles, 10-mile units for the next 50 miles, and 20-mile units for mileage beyond 200 miles. Rates for a long haul were still cheaper per mile, but on identical shipments local rates could no longer exceed through rates.[10]

Railroads soon challenged state rate regulation. In the early 1870s state and lower federal courts in Illinois, Iowa, and Wisconsin upheld state regulation, and in 1876 the United States Supreme Court resoundingly declared state regulation constitutional. In *Munn* v. *Illinois* the Supreme Court maintained that railroads were "engaged in a public employment affecting the public interest" and could "charge only a reasonable sum." Courts could determine reasonable rates until state legislatures acted; and in the absence of federal legislation state legislatures could regulate even interstate railroads. State regulation, however, had disadvantages. Differing from state to state, rates were

10. Miller, *Railroads and Granger Laws*, passim; Stover, *American Railroads*, pp. 120–21; Cushman, *Independent Regulatory Commissions*, pp. 25–27; Kirkland, *Industry*, pp. 119–22.

often complex and contradictory, railroads frequently recouped money lost on regulated local traffic by raising unregulated through rates, and commissions were often accused of favoring railroads. By 1886 the Supreme Court's *Wabash* v. *Illinois* decision reflected the dissatisfaction of shippers and railroad managers with state regulation. Denying the right of Illinois to regulate interstate rates between points in Illinois and New York, the Court concluded that if interstate commerce were regulated it must be by "general rules and principles, which demand that it should be done by the Congress of the United States under the commerce clause of the Constitution."[11]

Demands for Federal Regulation

By 1886 it was obvious that Americans wanted the federal government to regulate railroads. Less obvious now are what groups pressed most for regulation, what regulating schemes they espoused, and what influence they had in shaping and enacting the Interstate Commerce Act (ICA). Historians differ sharply over who was responsible for the ICA. Solon J. Buck champions the farmer, Lee Benson the merchant, Gerald D. Nash the independent oil producer, while Gabriel Kolko, in a strikingly novel hypothesis, accuses railroad men of fighting for the ICA to regulate in their behalf an industry they were unable to control. In fact, all four of these groups exerted influence on the ICA. Working through clubs and later through the National Grange (the Patrons of Husbandry), midwestern farmers had seconded merchant demands and helped secure state Granger laws regulating rates and creating commissions to enforce them. By 1878, however, Granger laws in Minnesota, Wisconsin, and Iowa had been repealed. The Grange had spent its force, and neither it nor the growing Farmers Alliances had a direct influence on the passage of the ICA. Nevertheless, Granger laws—

11. Munn v. Illinois, 94 U.S. 113 (1876) and Wabash Ry. Co. v. Illinois, 118 U.S. 557 (1886), in I. L. Sharfman, *The Interstate Commerce Commission: A Study in Administrative Law and Procedure*, 5 vols. (New York, 1931–37), 1:16, 19 (hereafter cited as Sharfman, *ICC*); Kirkland, *Industry*, pp. 124–26.

particularly the Illinois law—were important precedents for architects of federal legislation and made congressmen realize that farmers wanted to end railroad abuses.[12]

Merchants were more articulate than farmers and in many states more effective in demanding railroad regulation. Not only had midwestern merchants originated the Granger laws, but, after the late 1870s when New York farmers joined metropolitan merchants in their fight against railroads, merchant-dominated pressure groups spoke for both interests and became the most influential organizations in the railroad-regulation movement. Eager for freight-rate advantages over their competitors in rival seaboard or interior cities, New York merchants established in 1873 the New York Cheap Transportation Association (later known as the Board of Trade and Transportation). Led by Francis B. Thurber, a prominent wholesale grocer, and Simon Sterne, its legislative representative, and supported by farmers for its lip service to nondiscriminatory rates proportioned to services, the Board of Trade and Transportation was the chief instigator of New York State's 1879 Hepburn committee investigation, which Sterne conducted. That searching, eight-month inquiry subpoenaed the books of the New York Central Railroad; placed its president, William H. Vanderbilt, on the witness stand, where he refused to answer basic questions; and revealed that in 1879 the New York Central had more than 6,000 discriminatory contracts and that half of its traffic to and from New York City paid special rates. In addition the investigation exposed the enormous power wielded by Standard Oil in extracting rebates and revealed that 50 to 78 percent of the Central's $90 million in stock represented water. Stock watering —a common Gilded Age railroad sin—increased the nominal value of a property represented by its stock without increasing

12. Solon J. Buck, *The Granger Movement . . . , 1870–1880* (Cambridge, Mass., 1913), pp. 123–237; Solon J. Buck, *The Agrarian Crusade: A Chronicle of the Farmer in Politics* (New Haven, 1920), pp. 43–59; Fred A. Shannon, *The Farmer's Last Frontier: Agriculture, 1860–1897* (New York, 1945), pp. 176–78, 310–11; Miller, *Railroads and Granger Laws*, pp. 116, 138, 160–71.

its actual worth. As a result, management had more funds to play with but also had more pressure to squeeze out excessive profits, since dividends had to be paid on watered stock. Although railroads defeated a state antidiscrimination bill proposed by the Hepburn committee, New York merchants succeeded in 1882 when legislation, which Sterne drafted, created the New York Board of Railroad Commissioners. Utilizing his New York experience on the national level, Sterne subsequently helped draft the ICA.[13]

Manufacturers and producers also suffered from railroad discrimination and swelled the outcry for federal regulation. Charles Pratt, a New York oil refiner, bitterly opposed the rebates enjoyed by Standard Oil until he joined its group and shared its rebates. Outside the Standard group and unable to negotiate similar rebates, independent Pennsylvania producers and refiners asked help from the government. Generated by these independents, state and federal pressure forced Standard Oil to abandon its 1872 South Improvement Company scheme to facilitate rebates, but by 1875 the Standard group had organized the Central Association to handle its rebates with the Pennsylvania, Erie, and New York Central railroads. Prodded by the independents' spokesman, Congressman James H. Hopkins of Pittsburgh, the House of Representatives called in 1876 for an inquiry by its Committee on Commerce. With an incompetent chairman and a dominant member partial to Standard Oil, the committee soon abandoned its investigation; railroad officials had ignored its subpoenas, and the little testimony taken had disappeared. Hopkins also introduced an interstate commerce bill, reportedly drawn by counsel for the Reading Railroad, which did not share in Standard's traffic. This bill prohibited rebates and discrimination, required that railroads post rate schedules, and relied on the courts for enforcement. The bill died in the Commerce Committee and Hopkins failed to win

13. Lee Benson, *Merchants, Farmers, & Railroads: Railroad Regulation and New York Politics, 1850–1887* (Cambridge, Mass., 1955), pp. 57, 115–38, 143–44, 204–46.

reelection, but in 1877 he urged the new chairman of the Commerce Committee, John H. Reagan of Texas, to work for federal railroad regulation.[14]

When in the fall of 1877 Standard Oil acquired a major pipeline from the Pennsylvania Railroad as well as rebates on its oil shipments, independents formed a producer's union to press for regulatory legislation. Hastily drafting an imprecise elaboration of the Hopkins measure (adding a strong prohibition of higher rates for short hauls), this producer's union got a fellow oilman, Pennsylvania Congressman Lewis F. Watson, to introduce its measure in January 1878. During the summer of 1878 Reagan clarified and enlarged this bill to prohibit pooling, and that December it passed the House (139 to 104) despite opposition from westerners who benefited from cheap long-haul rates. The Reagan bill, however, died in the Senate; and in 1880 independent oilmen surrendered to Standard Oil. Keeping up the fight, Reagan reintroduced his bill in every Congress until much of its content and phraseology was incorporated in the Interstate Commerce Act of 1887.[15]

With the disintegration of pools in the early 1880s and the return of cutthroat competition, many railroad officials accepted in theory the principle of federal regulation, but Reagan's bill, prohibiting pooling and relying on the courts—rather than a commission—for enforcement, was not what they had in mind. They found legislation proposed by Senator Shelby M. Cullom of Illinois less objectionable than Reagan's bill. Both bills outlawed discrimination and rebates and called for reasonable and publicized rates. Although neither bill provided for rate regulation, Cullom's bill, which did not outlaw pooling, had a more flexible long-short-haul clause and set up a commission which conceivably could serve as the mechanism to enforce pool rates. William K. Ackerman, a former president of the Illinois Central Railroad who preferred a weak, advisory, statistics-collecting

14. Ibid., p. 68; Gerald D. Nash, "Origins of the Interstate Commerce Act of 1887," *Pennsylvania History* 24 (1957):181–85.
15. Nash, "Origins of the Interstate Commerce Act," pp. 185–90.

commission to a strong, ratesetting board concluded that the
Cullom bill was "one of the best that has been offered, for the
simple reason that it does not undertake to do too much." On
the other hand, Charles E. Perkins, president of the Chicago,
Burlington & Quincy, was hostile to railroad regulation and
doubted the wisdom of legislation. Though able to postpone
legislation, Perkins and other stanch laissez faire advocates realized they could not prevent it. Perkins had predicted in 1878
that "the public *will* regulate us to some extent & we must make
up our minds to it."[16]

In January 1885 the House again passed the Reagan bill
(161 to 75), while in February the Senate approved the Cullom
bill (43 to 12). The Forty-eighth Congress expired, however,
before reaching an agreement on these measures. For many the
Supreme Court's 1886 Wabash decision transformed a need for
legislation into a necessity by creating a twilight zone in which
states could not and the federal government did not regulate
railroads. During the next Congress, the Senate voted the Cullom bill (47 to 4) and the House the Reagan bill (192 to 41).
Managers from both houses, including Cullom and Reagan,
compromised their differences. Reagan both annoyed Grangers,
by accepting a commission, and aroused opposition from railroads and their friends, by insisting on the antipooling section
and stiffening Cullom's long-short-haul clause.[17]

If not enthusiastic, railroad leaders were prepared to accept
the Cullom bill, but, contrary to the Kolko hypothesis, they
found the compromise bill abhorrent. John P. Green, a vice-
president of the Pennsylvania Railroad, urged Senator John
Sherman to reshape the compromise bill before it became law.

16. Kolko, *Railroads and Regulation*, pp. 34–41; U.S., Congress,
Senate, Select Committee on Interstate Commerce, *Report*, 49 Cong., 1st
sess., 18 January 1886, S. Rept. 46, pt. 2:620; ibid., Appendix, pt. 1:213–
25 (cited below as S. Rept. 46); Thomas C. Cochran, *Railroad Leaders,
1845–1890: The Business Mind in Action* (Cambridge, Mass., 1953),
p. 197.

17. *Congressional Record*, 48th Cong., 2d sess., 8 January 1885, 554–
55; ibid., 4 February 1885, 1254; ibid., 49 Cong., 1st sess., 12 May 1886,
4422–23; ibid., 30 July 1886, 7752–57; S. Rept. 46, pt. 2:1284.

The long-short-haul clause, he argued, would either bankrupt "a great many of the railroads" or force them to abandon through-traffic to water carriers, while "pools instead of being prohibited ought to be legalized and encouraged." Colgate Hoyt, who advised Sherman on railroad securities, warned:

All persons interested in railroad investments & enterprises of any kind and they form a very large part of our community, are very much exercised over the passage of the Interstate Commerce bill in the shape in which it now stands. I sincerely hope you will do everything in your power to prevent its passage, for should any such measure as this proposed become a law, we do not any of us want any investments in railroad enterprises. I know the delicacy politicians have about opposing openly any measure which is so popular with the ignorant portion of the community, but it seems to me that if it should not be deemed wise to defeat the bill or kill it the whole matter can at least be indefinitely postponed.[18]

The Interstate Commerce Bill Becomes Law

Obviously farmers, merchants, industrialists, and railroad men helped shape the interstate commerce bill. The question, which of these groups impelled Congress to pass the bill, is best answered by noting what congressmen said at the time and by tallying their votes. Senator after senator and congressman after congressman testified that they were legislating, as Senator Nelson Aldrich of Rhode Island put it, "in obedience to the general desire that Congress should exercise its unquestioned power over interstate commerce." Senator Sherman marveled at the bill's "general support" and observed that all classes of people wanted some kind of regulation, while Senator James F. Wilson of Iowa exclaimed that the "people" and more specifically "business men and farmers" demanded legislation. Congressmen, furthermore, realized that railroad men did not like the interstate commerce bill in general and the antipooling and long-

18. Green to Sherman, 23 December 1886, and Hoyt to Sherman, 18 December 1886, Sherman Papers, Library of Congress, Washington; Edward A. Purcell, Jr., "Ideas and Interests: Businessmen and the Interstate Commerce Act," *Journal of American History* 54 (1967):575–78. For an opposing view, see Kolko, *Railroads and Regulation*, pp. 3, 43–46.

short-haul clauses in particular.[19] Well aware of who supported and who opposed the bill, congressmen—except perhaps for some tied directly to railroads—reflected the interests of their constituents and gave the debate a sectional cast.

Opponents of the bill clustered in the Northeast (particularly in New England) and scattered elsewhere. Some thought the bill would harm railroads, but, in addition, others thought the bill would hurt their section. Living both at the end of the line and close to unregulated Canadian competition, New Englanders were convinced that the long-short-haul clause, with its emphasis on proportional charges, would damage their competitive position. Those friendly to railroads predicted that, if passed, this crude, experimental bill would make railroads bankrupt and would stop railroad construction while the act was tested. Concerned both for railroads and his section, Senator Aldrich wailed that the bill gave a five-man commission "the power . . . to make or unmake States, to build up or destroy communities, and to increase or extinguish the earnings of railroad companies." A few—antagonistic to either railroads or Republicans—opposed the bill because they favored the more stringent, Democratic Reagan bill. These diehard Reagan bill supporters, who were almost all Democrats, damned the compromise bill as a prorailroad bill despite the fact that railroads opposed it. James B. Weaver, an Iowa Greenbacker elected with Democratic support, when asked by a colleague if he did "not know that this city has been swarming with agents of railroad corporate power in order to defeat this bill," admitted, "They, of course, do not want any bill to pass." He then added, "but if one must pass they want, in my opinion, just such provisions as are in this bill."[20]

Ardent supporters of the compromise bill—in the main, midwesterners—recognized that railroads did not want the bill to pass. Congressman Richard W. Guenther, an Oshkosh, Wis-

19. *Congressional Record*, 49th Cong., 2d sess., 14 January 1887, 641, 648, Appendix, p. 15.
20. Ibid., Appendix, p. 21; ibid., 19 January 1887, 822.

consin, druggist, bitterly attacked "the power, the greed, the avarice, the extortion, the iniquity, the injustice, the tyranny of these railroad corporations," noted that "year after year, session after session, the railroad magnates, through their attorneys and lobbyists, have succeeded in defeating all legislation upon the subject of interstate commerce," and declared "the passage of this bill will be the greatest triumph the people have achieved in many years." Although Guenther as well as his freshman colleague Robert M. La Follette of Wisconsin and Republican Senator George F. Edmunds of Vermont thought that railroads would be better off with the bill, they spoke of railroad opposition to it. La Follette alluded to the "fear and alarm expressed in railway circles concerning this bill," while Edmunds believed that if the bill passed the railway system would "find itself compelled (for that is what it is) against its will, against its opinion, against its inspiring fears and discontent on the part of business people all over the United States, to be subject to the force of this act." Those favoring the measure considered that its postponement or defeat would be a railroad victory. Cullom warned that lack of action equaled "letting it go out to the country that the railroads are still masters of the situation," and Edmunds wondered, if the bill were defeated, "how many years will it be before the people of the United States can emancipate themselves from the tyranny of this corporate management and corporate combination that now exists."[21]

21. Ibid., p. 814; ibid., 20 January 1887, Appendix, p. 187; ibid., 14 January 1887, 645–46, 659. Edmunds's stand is a puzzle. A few years later, Charles Francis Adams Jr., president of the Union Pacific, labeled him "the most thoroughly corrupt and dishonest, and the most insidiously dangerous man, when balked of his bribes, that there is today in Washington." Adams noted that Edmunds did not take bribes directly but took retainers from Jay Gould, Collis P. Huntington, and Henry Villard to represent their railroads in court and guard their interests in the Senate. Although there are several possible explanations for Adams's accusation, Edmunds's support of the ICA, and his attack on railroads, we suggest that though Adams might have exaggerated Edmunds's activities, he did not fabricate them and that if Edmunds were obeying the railroads in supporting the ICA, he would not have attacked them. We suspect that Edmunds may have considered that his retainers merely obligated him to look after

Although loquacious congressmen have been accused of talking bills into law, it is their votes that pass laws. Thirty senators were sufficiently dissatisfied on 14 January 1887 to want to recommit the conference bill, but 41 senators opposed that move. A few moments later, the Senate approved the bill with 50 senators either voting for or paired in favor while 20 were opposed. Of the 20 ardent opponents, 15 were Republican or allied to Republicans; 12 were from New England, New York, and Pennsylvania; and at least five were or had been railroad presidents. Although California's senators (one of whom was Leland Stanford of the Southern Pacific Railroad) both opposed the bill, no other senators from states west of Ohio and Alabama voted against the interstate commerce bill. Indeed only two senators from states not bordering the Atlantic or Pacific oceans voted against the bill. Senators from seacoast terminals were hostile to the long-short-haul clause. Eight of the 10 additional senators who wished to recommit the bill but did not oppose its passage were Republicans, five were from New England and New Jersey and five were personally involved with railroads. So strong was northeastern opposition in the Senate that Edmunds of Vermont was the bill's only enthusiastic supporter north of Mason and Dixon's line and east of Ohio.[22]

Similiar conclusions can be drawn from the 21 January House vote. A total of 231 supported the conference bill, while 48 were opposed; but eight of the 48 had earlier supported the more rigorous Reagan bill, leaving 40 congressmen (30 of whom were Republican) who opposed the compromise bill and opposed or did not vote for the Reagan bill. Of these, 11 came from New England, 11 from New York and Pennsylvania, three from Ohio, and three from California. All of the 17 representa-

the narrow interests of specific railroads, leaving him free to act upon questions of national railroad policy, such as the ICA. Edward Chase Kirkland, *Charles Francis Adams, Jr., 1835–1915: The Patrician at Bay* (Cambridge, Mass., 1965), pp. 109–11.

22. *Congressional Record*, 49th Cong., 2d sess., 14 January 1887, 664–66. Excluding paired senators, the actual final vote was 43 to 15.

tives who opposed both the compromise bill and the Reagan bill were Republican and were from the Northeast. Among consistent opponents to regulation were Edward D. Hayden, a director of the Boston & Albany Railroad, and James S. Negley of Pittsburgh, who also engaged in railroading.[23]

This debate and vote reveal what various interests and sections thought of the interstate commerce bill. Congressmen were convinced that "the people," particularly farmers, merchants, and businessmen in the interior of the nation, demanded legislation. Contrary to Kolko's hypothesis, congressmen were also aware of widespread railroad opposition to the compromise bill. Those most opposed to it were those involved with railroads and shipping at terminal points in the Northeast and California. Although independent Pennsylvania oil producers and New York merchants helped originate the interstate commerce bill, when the chips were down, their senators opposed it; and in both houses those states along with New England provided the only significant pocket of resistance. The Midwest and the South muscled the bill through; the Northeast and the railroads could not block legislation which had been demanded for nearly two decades. During those years more than 150 bills for federal railroad regulation had been introduced in Congress; this time the momentum could not be stopped.[24]

Establishing the ICC

On 4 February 1887 after study and hesitation, President Grover Cleveland signed the bill into law. Creating a five-man commission, the Interstate Commerce Act outlawed pools and rate discrimination—whether by special rates, rebates, drawbacks, or long-short-haul abuses—and demanded that rates be

---

23. Ibid., 21 January 1887, 881. Those representatives who indicated how they were paired are included. The actual vote was 219 to 41.

24. Cushman, *Independent Regulatory Commissions*, pp. 40–41. Also see Purcell, "Ideas and Interests," pp. 561–78, and Albro Martin, "The Troubled Subject of Railroad Regulation in the Gilded Age—A Reappraisal," *Journal of American History* 61 (1974):339–71.

"reasonable and just" and be published. Presidentially appointed commissioners were to serve staggered six-year terms. No more than three commissioners were to belong to the same political party, and none were to have railroad connections. The act authorized the commission to investigate any railroad engaged in interstate commerce and empowered it to compel witnesses to testify and to secure relevant books and papers. If a railroad, however, ignored the ICC's orders or decisions, the commission had to petition the appropriate United States circuit court "to hear and determine the matter." Finally, the ICC could require railroads to submit annual reports and to use a uniform accounting system.

Attacks on the imprecise nature of the law, however, were not empty rhetoric. Pooling traffic and earnings was illegal but collective ratemaking was neither legalized nor outlawed. Vaguely calling for "reasonable and just" charges, the ICA also outlawed the long-short-haul abuse but only "under substantially similar circumstances and conditions," a qualification which Jordan Jay Hillman rightly calls "the triumph of cultivated ambiguity." With the value-of-service rate system (based on a railroad manager's guess of what the traffic could afford, rather than on his computation of what the service cost) left undisturbed by the new act, reasonable-and-just rates were difficult to define. No one could accurately prophesy the impact of the ICA. Would it like the British law create a commission with "power enough to annoy the railroads" but "not power enough to help the public"?[25]

Though no one could predict its future, the Interstate Commerce Commission had potential power. The new law provided a framework to abolish railroad abuses, but its effectiveness depended on the commissioners and ultimately on the courts. Would presidents appoint able, energetic, and dedicated com-

25. Hilton, "The Consistency of the Interstate Commerce Act," pp. 105–10; A. T. Hadley, *Railroad Transportation* (1885), p. 173, cited by Cushman, *Independent Regulatory Commissions*, p. 35; Jordan Jay Hillman, *Competition and Railroad Price Discrimination: Legal Precedent and Economic Policy* (Evanston, Ill., 1968), pp. 7–43.

missioners, would the Supreme Court back their decisions, and would those decisions eliminate abuses and ultimately shape a rational transportation system?

Cleveland pleased both railroad managers and the public by appointing Thomas M. Cooley, a Republican, chairman of the new commission. A University of Michigan law professor, a justice of the Michigan Supreme Court, and a distinguished student of the Constitution—particularly of its limits on state legislative power and its protection of individual liberty—Cooley provided the basis for many anti-state-intervention and pro-property-rights decisions made by late-nineteenth-century courts. Cooley tempered his laissez faire notions, however, with an overriding commitment to equal rights and a belief in judicial restraint. Having grown up in New York State as a loco-foco, or anti-bank-monopoly, Democrat, Cooley later moved west and in 1848 helped organize the Michigan Free Soil party. He favored free schools and free trade and denounced class legislation and monopolies, such as railroads and banking. Cooley wished to curtail state legislative power because he identified it with special privileges for a class or a corporation, but in practice he accepted a fairly wide exercise of regulatory power. In short, the rise of powerful monopolistic corporations left Cooley by the 1880s still rejecting unlimited state interference with private property but accepting state regulation of profits where competition had been eliminated. Cooley, who had opposed railroad land grants, was familiar with railroad affairs. He had arbitrated disputes for Albert Fink's Joint Executive Committee, which enforced pooling rates, and when appointed to the ICC was serving as receiver of the bankrupt Wabash lines east of the Mississippi.[26]

26. Lewis G. Vander Velde, "Thomas McIntyre Cooley," in *Michigan and the Cleveland Era* . . . , ed. Earl D. Babst and Lewis G. Vander Velde (Ann Arbor, Mich., 1948). pp. 77–106; *Dictionary of American Biography*, s.v. "Cooley, Thomas McIntyre" (hereafter cited as *DAB*); Alan Jones, "Thomas M. Cooley and the Interstate Commerce Commission: Continuity and Change in the Doctrine of Equal Rights," *Political Science Quarterly* 81 (1966):602–27; Alan Jones, "Thomas M. Cooley

Even with the promise of a $7,500 salary (higher than that of any United States judge excepting Supreme Court members), it took Cleveland until the end of March to persuade four other qualified individuals to serve on the new commission. His second appointment was William R. Morrison, a recently defeated Democratic congressman from Illinois renowned for futile attacks on the protective tariff. Conspicuous but not successful, Morrison manifested neither administrative nor deliberative talents and knew little of railroad affairs, but he was both honest and fearless and usually supported beneficial reforms. Cleveland also named his political associate Augustus Schoonmaker, a lawyer without railroad experience who as attorney general and civil service commissioner of New York had become known for his ability and his impeccable character. Aldace F. Walker and Walter Bragg, the two remaining appointees, had grappled with the problem of railroad regulation. A railroad lawyer and a state senator who had long opposed the "corrupt and greedy ring" controlling the Central Vermont Railroad, Walker had written the Vermont Railroad Commission Act. President of the Alabama railroad commission and an authority on regulation, Bragg had helped shape the ICA. Although Albert Fink and F. B. Thurber questioned the commission's lack of practical experience, they joined the enthusiastic chorus applauding Cleveland's selections, which indeed were good. Possessing among them experience with politics, railroads, and regulatory commissions, the first ICC members were neither blindly hostile to railroads nor their pliant tools.[27]

---

and 'Laissez-Faire Constitutionalism': A Reconsideration," *Journal of American History* 53 (1967): 751–71; Clarence Atha Miller, *The Lives of the Interstate Commerce Commissioners and the Commission's Secretaries* (Washington, 1946), pp. 15–19; Sidney Fine, *Laissez Faire and the General-Welfare State: A Study of Conflict in American Thought, 1865–1901* (Ann Arbor, Mich., 1956), pp. 128–30, 142–43, 152.

27. *New York Times* 23 and 24 March 1887; *DAB*, s.v. "Morrison, William Ralls"; Miller, *Interstate Commerce Commissioners*, pp. 21–28. For a negative view of Cleveland's appointees, see Kolko, *Railroads and Regulation*, pp. 47–49.

Early Decisions

Shortly after the law went into effect on 5 April 1887, over a thousand complaints, grievances, and questions swamped the ICC. Dominated by Cooley and his equal-rights notions, the commission strove to achieve "equality and justice" in its decisions. The most vexing immediate problem was what exceptions, if any, should be made to the long-short-haul clause, or section 4 of the ICA. Long-short-haul abuse was particularly common in the South, where competing water transportation often forced low rates. Loath to demand compliance without an investigation, the ICC temporarily suspended section 4 for the twenty-seven members of the Southern Railway & Steamship Association (a former pool which after the ICA had reorganized as a rate association). Suspension for all railroads south of the Ohio and east of the Mississippi aroused resentment and fear for the future of section 4. John H. Reagan told Morrison that suspension would defeat the purpose of the act and insisted that the ICC lacked power to suspend section 4. To allay fears, Cooley on 18 May reiterated that suspension was temporary to permit an investigation and insisted that no general exceptions would be made, that exceptional cases would be established by investigation, and that an incidental injury to a party or interest was not grounds for an exception. One month later, on 15 June, in its key Louisville & Nashville decision, the ICC through Cooley unanimously declared that railroads—not the ICC with its small staff—would have to decide initially whether the "circumstances and conditions" of their long-haul and short-haul traffic were sufficiently dissimilar to justify charging less for a long haul than for a short one. For guidelines, the ICC stated that exceptions to section 4 were justified only when competing either with unregulated traffic (water transportation or foreign or intrastate railroads) or in "rare and peculiar" cases. If a railroad opted for rate discrimination and was challenged, it would have to prove that circumstances warranted discrimination or suffer the consequences (a $5,000 fine). Judge Henry J.

Friendly in 1962 called Cooley's opinion a "model for administrators" because it provided guidance, not "vacuous and weasel-
worded utterances characteristic of our day," because it offered
"meat, not gelatin." While railroad officials were pleased by this
decision, it also benefited many shippers who would be hurt by
rigid application of the long-short-haul principle. Where competition from water routes and Canadian railroads existed, strict
adherence to section 4 would raise, not lower, both long-haul
and short-haul rates by diverting through-traffic revenue to unregulated competitors.[28]

The Louisville & Nashville decision led many railroads to
continue long-short-haul discrimination. Acting within the
ICC's guidelines, the Pacific Coast Association of Transcontinental Railroads decided in July to maintain higher rates for
interior California points than for Pacific terminals. Cooley's
successor as receiver of the Wabash eastern railroad, John Mc-
Nulta, boldly defied section 4 and ICC guidelines by justifying
discrimination favoring Peoria's eastern traffic to meet the competition of a stronger, regulated railroad. Railroad managers
were delighted by McNulta's pluck, which would force the
courts to determine the strength of section 4. Aware of numerous section 4 violations, the ICC moved in October to compel
compliance with the law even if shippers had not complained
and even though—with only eleven staff members—the commission did not have time to ferret out damning data from its
mountainous file of rate schedules. To railroad managers' con-
sternation, the ICC ordered them to justify their exceptions to
the long-short-haul principle. The *Chicago Tribune*'s exuberant
reaction that "the Interstate Commerce Act is working wonders

28. U.S., Interstate Commerce Commission, *1st Annual Report*,
1887, pp. 122–25 (hereafter cited as *Annual Report*); Re Southern Railway & Steamship Association, 1 ICR 278 (1887), in Sharfman, *ICC*,
1:29–30, n. 26, 3B:545–50; *New York Times*, 16 and 19 May 1887;
Henry J. Friendly, *The Federal Administrative Agencies: The Need for
Better Definition of Standards* (Cambridge, Mass., 1962), pp. 28–31;
Kolko, *Railroads and Regulation*, pp. 49–52.

and the railroad magnates are trembling," Cooley thought, was "sheer bosh." Committed to equality tempered by justice for both shippers and railroads, Cooley observed, "The law is working as it has been all the while; slowly but surely in one steady direction; working a quiet reform and not a destructive revolution." Section 4 was not a dead letter in 1887, but by 1892 the ICC ruled that carriers themselves could no longer decide exceptions when competing with other regulated carriers because they tended to view that competition as "rare and peculiar" and rendered the "exceptional ruling . . . inoperative, delusive, and opened the door to many evasions of the statute." Section 4 did have an effect; after the 1887 ICA and the 1892 ruling, railroads reduced short-distance rates.[29]

Besides indicating short-haul discrimination, complaints to the ICC noted discrimination against individual passengers and shippers. Having purchased a first-class ticket from the Western & Atlantic Railroad, William H. Councill, a black minister and principal of the Alabama State Normal School at Huntsville, would not leave a first-class car, was beaten on the head with a lantern, evicted, and forced to ride in the filthy "darkies" car. William H. Heard, an African Methodist Episcopal minister, lodged a similar complaint against the Georgia Central Railroad. After the commission ruled against such blatant discrimination but maintained that "separate but equal" facilities would be acceptable, Cooley admitted in his diary that "the only way to have equal accommodations was to have identical accommodations." Southern railroads ignored these commission rulings. The Georgia Central again discriminated against Heard, he again complained, the commission again condoned segregation

29. Jones, "Cooley and the ICC," p. 614; *New York Times*, 3, 9, and 10 July and 25 October 1887; *1st Annual Report*, 1887, p. 229; Trammell v. Clyde Steamship Co., 4 ICR 120 (1892), in Sharfman, *ICC*, 3B:550–52; Paul W. MacAvoy, *The Economic Effects of Regulation: The Trunk-Line Railroad Cartels and the Interstate Commerce Commission Before 1900* (Cambridge, Mass., 1965), p. 201. For a less charitable view of Cooley and section 4, see Kolko, *Railroads and Regulation*, pp. 49–53.

but insisted that all purchasers of first-class tickets receive first-class accommodations, and the railroad again refused to comply.[30]

More sensitive to freight than to passenger discrimination, the commission soon tackled John D. Rockefeller's Standard Oil Company. Prior to the ICA, no other company had exceeded Standard Oil in extracting rebates from railroads. The commission noted, however, that when the ICA outlawed rebates carriers continued the large shipper's unfair advantage by reducing carload rates without reducing less-than-carload rates. The excuse for this discrimination was that railroads could handle a full carload (with one destination and one bill of lading, loaded and unloaded by the shipper) more cheaply than a carload comprising more than one shipment. Balancing equality for those making small shipments and justice for less-numerous, large, efficient shippers, the ICC recognized the carload as a unit but refused to permit extreme rate differences between carload and less-than-carload lots. In effect, the commission limited but did not eliminate the advantages of Standard Oil and other large shippers over small rivals.[31]

In subsequent decisions, the commission continued its middle course. When in 1890 Francis B. Thurber and the New York Board of Trade and Transportation requested the elimination of lower rates for carload shipments, the ICC refused, arguing that it would be an "impracticable" and "retrograde movement" that would "seriously demoralize classification and business" and would be "detrimental in many respects to the public interests." The commission, on the other hand, "repeatedly and without exception" refused lower rates for entire trainloads. The ICC reasoned that by 1887 the carload was already

30. Councill v. Western & Atlantic R.R. Co., 1 ICR 638 (1887), in *1st Annual Report*, 1887, p. 93, and *New York Times*, 1 June and 24 July 1887; Heard v. Georgia R.R. Co., 1 ICR 719 (1888), in *2d Annual Report*, 1888, pp. 107–8; Heard v. Georgia R.R. Co., 2 ICR 508 (1889), in *3d Annual Report*, 1889, pp. 131, 162–63; Jones, "Cooley and the ICC," p. 614, n. 43.

31. Scofield v. Lake Shore & Michigan Southern R. Co., 2 ICR 67, 74 (1888), in Sharfman, *ICC*, 3B:398–99, n. 148.

established in rate structure and could be utilized by "a great part of the country's shippers" while only a few economic giants could ship trainloads.[32]

The Cooley Style

At times following and at times resisting Cooley, the ICC narrowed its jurisdiction and power. Retreating in December 1887 from an earlier position, it exempted express companies, unless railroad controlled, from the ICA. More important, the commission had already begun its traditional case-by-case approach, which kept it aloof from the economic policies of the party in power but also kept the ICC from developing its own railroad policy. With its judicial stance and its limited staff and resources, the commission could not create the reasonable-and-just rates demanded by the ICA. Rather than creating reasonable-and-just rates, Cooley hoped to secure them through national rate control without interference from state commissions. Cooley, furthermore, was reluctant to coerce railroads by following rulings with damages. Even after Congress in 1889 paved the way for injured parties to collect ICC-awarded damages from railroads, Cooley preferred that damages be awarded by a jury in court. Circuit court decisions forced the commission by 1892 to consider damages, but Cooley's attitude on that question reveals his philosophy of regulation. "The less coercive power we have," he wrote, "the greater, I think, will be our moral influence." Refusing to think of the ICC as a police court enforcing its will by punishment, Cooley preferred to rely on the "gradual education of the public in the matter of railway transportation, the quiet work we can perform in the improvement of the law and the unification of a railway system." Recognizing that the ICC's case-by-case approach narrowed its scope, Cooley sought to broaden its influence by initiating a "campaign of education and policy reform." Despite his failing health, he

32. Thurber v. New York Central and Hudson River R. Co., 2 ICR 742 (1890), ibid., p. 397, n. 145, American Round Bale Press Co. v. A., T. & S. F. Ry. Co., 32 ICC 463–64 (1914), ibid., p. 398, n. 146.

traveled and spoke extensively to support his program of rate control (as distinct from rate creation). By urging a group of western railroad managers in 1888 to pay attention "to the prevailing sensitiveness of public opinion," the banker J. P. Morgan attested that Cooley was making some headway. Other contemporaries, however, complained that Cooley failed to realize that an occasional "cut and slash" at the railroads would make them more aware of his regulation philosophy and more alert to the public interest.[33]

Although Cooley was largely responsible for the ICC's passive, judicial stance, he perceived that the commission should also play a positive administrative role. In February 1888 the Brotherhood of Locomotive Engineers (BLE) struck the Chicago, Burlington & Quincy (CB&Q), and in March, with the strike going badly (thanks largely to strikebreaking engineers belonging to the rival Knights of Labor), the BLE ordered its members not to handle CB&Q cars. While eastern roads refused to boycott CB&Q cars, western roads—hating and fearing the rate-slashing Burlington as a bully attempting to establish a midwestern railroad trust—generally complied until the CB&Q secured injunctions against these secondary boycotts. With the strike tying up Chicago-area traffic and threatening to spread, Cooley on 9 March contemplated an ICC investigation of the strike and its background quarrels and rate wars.

By the end of March, the "very bad" Burlington management exasperated Cooley, and he belatedly urged the ICC to investigate the strike. Although realizing that an investigation might be too late to settle the strike, he feared that the public would condemn the commission for ignoring such a serious interruption of interstate commerce. Cooley urged the ICC to get to "the very bottom" of the affair and to "place the blame where it belonged." When Morrison and Walker agreed with

33. Marver H. Bernstein, *Regulating Business by Independent Commission* (Princeton, 1955), pp. 29, 134; Albro Martin, *Enterprise Denied: Origins of the Decline of American Railroads, 1897–1917* (New York, 1971), p. 174; Jones, "Cooley and the ICC," pp. 615–16; Sharfman, *ICC*, 3B:336–38; Kirkland, *Adams*, p. 119.

Cooley but Schoonmaker and Bragg opposed him "in very strong, and almost violent language," the commission postponed action. By late April, at the behest of the striking engineers, Cooley resolved to investigate, but Morrison and Walker, thinking Congress might investigate, were by then reluctant, and Schoonmaker and Bragg, arguing that the commission had no authority, adamantly refused. Both "annoyed" and "disgusted," Cooley wrote in his diary:

I did say that I had not the slightest doubt either of our authority or of our duty. We had no business to await the action of one of the houses of Congress, & to do so was belittling our functions & would justly make us contemptible. To construe the law as narrowly as Bragg & Schoonmaker seemed inclined to do, would emasculate it. It was our duty, I thought to strengthen the law by vigorous action under it: we ought to make ourselves more felt by the railroads: be masters of the situation: be the authority in railroad matters, & by asserting authority, take leadership. Much more I said to the same effect, for I felt strongly that our office was about to be rendered ridiculous.

The ICC postponed its decision until the next morning; Cooley worked late that evening, took a chill, and developed pneumonia. By the time he had recovered in early June, it was too late for action, but with the backing of the ICC he asked both the CB&Q and the strikers to submit their version of the strike. When the highhanded CB&Q management resented Cooley's request, he seized the opportunity to reiterate to its president, Charles E. Perkins, that the ICC should have investigated the strike. Had Cooley been endowed with both a more vigorous constitution and commission, the fact-finding investigation he envisioned might have enhanced the ICC's power and helped settle this and subsequent strikes.[34]

34. Diary of Thomas M. Cooley, 26 April 1888, Cooley Papers, Michigan Historical Collections, University of Michigan, Ann Arbor; Gerald G. Eggert, *Railroad Labor Disputes: The Beginnings of Federal Strike Policy* (Ann Arbor, Mich., 1967), pp. 81–107; Donald L. McMurry, *The Great Burlington Strike of 1888: A Case History in Labor Relations* (Cambridge, Mass., 1956), pp. 170–72; Jones, "Cooley and the ICC," pp. 616–18.

Cooley wished to enhance the commission's power in order to protect the public interest. Ratecutting in 1888—particularly by lines west of Chicago—led railroads to urge repeal of the ICA's antipooling section 5. Opposing repeal, Cooley also rejected the notion that the commission maintain minimum rates, which would achieve the objective of pools by eliminating competitive rate slashing. "It may be affirmed with entire confidence," he emphasized, "that the Act was not passed to protect railroad corporations against the misconduct or the mistakes of their officers, or even primarily to protect such corporations against each other." The term reasonable and just was "employed to establish a maximum limitation for the protection of the public, not a minimum limitation for the protection of reckless carriers against their own action." Cooley chose what he conceived to be the public interest over the railroad interest.[35]

Railroad presidents vigorously disapproved of the ICA and were unhappy with Cooley; and he in turn disapproved of their actions. By 2 December 1888, Cooley was privately convinced that "the great need of the day was to reform railroad managers," and ten days later in Chicago he lectured them on the evils of rate wars and urged them to "stand before the community in some other light than lawbreakers." Railroad officials hardly needed to be told of the evils of railroad warfare. To avoid that warfare they were prepared to obey, evade, or break the law. After protracted negotiations from November 1888 to February 1889, western railroad presidents and a group of bankers led by J. P. Morgan organized the Interstate Commerce Railway Association (ICRA) to maintain "reasonable uniform and stable rates." Cooley regarded these developments with suspicious and occasionally hostile eyes. On 8 January 1889 he defended the ICA's short-haul and antipooling provisions as just, claimed the ICA was obeyed and working well, attacked railroad men who "were giving more attention to contrivances

35. In Re Chicago, St. Paul & Kansas City R. Co., 2 ICR 137 (1888), in Sharfman, *ICC*, 3B:599, n. 492; Jones, "Cooley and the ICC," p. 619.

for evading the spirit of the law than they were to obeying it," and stated his particular dread of a railroad trust, national or regional in scope, "with irresistible power to divide business and make rates." A few days later, however, Cooley gave measured approval to the grand design of Charles Francis Adams Jr., Union Pacific president. Adams envisioned non-ICA-violating railroad rate-and-traffic agreements that the ICC would both approve in advance and enforce. Encountering opposition from the CB&Q and other roads, Adams's plan was not adopted, and the ICRA (with former ICC member Aldace F. Walker at its head) turned out to be a relatively ineffectual body that only succeeded in stabilizing rates through the first half of 1889.

When in the summer of 1889 a new rate war broke out, Cooley denounced railroad men who had broken their agreement, who had cut long-distance rates but had left local rates unchanged. "The officials of the Northwestern Roads," he exclaimed, "are acting like a parcel of fools. Of course, Canadian Pacific competition has eaten deeply into their earnings, but that is no reason why illegal tariffs should be made to meet the situation." Cooley and other commissioners were hostile both to a railroad monopoly and to rate wars. The commission favored some competition and would not uphold minimum rates, yet it did not oppose agreements such as the ICRA, and Cooley evidently guardedly approved a scheme whereby the ICC would enforce such an agreement. The commission apparently wished to reap public benefits from competition while avoiding disastrous rate wars and to lead railroads to promulgate reasonable-and-just rates by enunciating guiding principles for their bafflingly detailed rate agreements.[36]

36. On the evolution of the ICRA and Cooley's reaction to it, see Julius Grodinsky, *Transcontinental Railroad Strategy, 1869–1893: A Study of Businessmen* (Philadelphia, 1962), pp. 338–53, particularly pp. 342–47; Kolko, *Railroads and Regulation*, pp. 57–62; Kirkland, *Adams*, pp. 119–20; and Jones, "Cooley and the ICC," pp. 619–21. Grodinsky and Kolko think Cooley favorable to the evolution of the ICRA, while Kirkland considers him moderately favorable and Jones considers him hostile to it.

To lead railroads, Cooley realized that the ICC had to be an effective body. He jealously guarded and attempted to enhance its power. In September 1889 he tried to convince Cullom to amend the ICA to include intrastate as well as interstate railroads. Cooley also defended the commission against onslaughts by the federal courts. In the first ICC decision to be appealed— in January 1889—federal circuit Judge Howell E. Jackson in the *Kentucky and Indiana Bridge* case rejected the ICC's decision and ordered that the facts of the case be reconsidered. Furthermore, in 1890 the Supreme Court declared that the Minnesota Commission's attempt to set reasonable rates violated the due process clause of the Fourteenth Amendment and that such rates had to be determined by the courts. Despite pronounced feebleness, from his own serious illness, and the death of his wife, Cooley counterattacked in late 1890. He predicted that, if the courts continued insisting on fresh evaluation of evidence in appeals of ICC decisions, the railroads would ignore ICC rulings, new evidence would be introduced, delays would result, and the regulatory system would be destroyed.[37]

Congress, however, did not amend the law—as Cooley wished—to make ICC findings final as far as facts were concerned. Cooley also argued that determining a reasonable rate was an administrative and legislative, not a judicial, matter. Keenly aware of the needs of the ICC and anticipating those of future administrative agencies, Cooley suggested that due process of law did not refer exclusively to judicial procedure. Due process could also be secured from administrative agencies without violating the Constitution, and Cooley suggested that Congress institute a procedure of "administrative due process of law." Congress, however, did not listen, Cooley's health grew worse, and in September 1891 he resigned.[38]

37. Kentucky and Indiana Bridge Co. v. Louisville & Nashville Ry. Co., 37 Fed. 567 (1889), overruling 2 ICR 162 (1888), and Chicago, Milwaukee & St. Paul Ry. Co. v. Minnesota 134 U.S. 418 (1890), in Jones, "Cooley and the ICC," pp. 623–25.
38. Ibid., pp. 625–27.

Cooley's illness, Henry Carter Adams exclaimed, was a "national calamity." Cooley had brought Adams—the first Johns Hopkins Ph.D., a founder of the American Economic Association, a critic of laissez faire, and an advocate of collective bargaining—to Washington to head the ICC's statistical bureau. Adams believed that Cooley's program of authoritative opinions (which he hoped would evolve into a body of administrative railroad law) and public education based on statistical analysis would solve the railway problem. Indeed during its first seven years, the ICC—as a result of prosperity and Cooley's leadership—was reasonably effective. Discrimination, which destroyed both stability and profits, appeared on the wane. Published trunk-line rates on long-distance grain shipments were relatively stable (as compared to rates before federal regulation and after the panic of 1893) and trunk-line net receipts and common-stock prices were up. On the other hand, average ton-mile rates declined on all railroads more than 12 percent from 1888 to 1893 and more than 14 percent over the next five years. Legally or illegally, rates were obviously cut, but it would seem that until the panic of 1893 large through shippers did not receive their customary share of these cuts. It was the small shipper, seeking limited service, who owed most to early regulation. In both 1887 and 1893, short-distance rates were reduced not by market conditions, but by ICC rules. Aware of accelerating rate instability and mounting judicial attacks on the ICC in the late 1890s, Adams had ample reason to mourn Cooley's departure. Had his health not broken, Cooley's concept of administrative due process, backed by his impressive credentials as a constitutional authority, might have mitigated the effects of the panic and withstood the onslaughts of the Supreme Court. After Cooley's departure, the Court reduced the commission to performing Adams's chief task—that of collecting statistics.[39]

39. Ibid., p. 627; *DAB*, s.v. "Adams, Henry Carter"; Marvin B. Rosenberry, "Henry Carter Adams," in *Michigan and the Cleveland Era*, pp. 23–41; Adams, "Decade of Federal Railway Regulation," pp. 433–43; MacAvoy, *Economic Effects of Regulation*, pp. 193–204; Martin, "Troubled Subject of Railroad Regulation," pp. 364–65; U.S., Bureau of

Attack by the Courts

Before Cooley resigned, the tug-of-war between the Supreme Court and the ICC had begun. The impact of the commission depended upon the support it received from the courts. Decisions in the *Kentucky and Indiana Bridge* case and the *Minnesota Commission* case had hurt the ICC; railroads no longer developed their cases fully before it, and the Supreme Court declared that the courts, not a state commission, could determine reasonable rates. With the courts continuing to reject the spirit of the ICA after Cooley left office, prosecution for carrier violations became less likely, and illegal acts, which initially had fallen off, increased. Subsequent decisions further hampered the commission. In 1892 the Supreme Court upheld a shipper who, citing the Fifth Amendment, had refused in 1890 to testify whether he had received rebates on interstate grain shipments. Congress responded with the 1893 Compulsory Testimony Act (compelling testimony before the commission but prohibiting prosecution on the basis of that testimony), which in 1896 the Supreme Court upheld in a five-to-four decision. Though finally winning its point, the ICC had been restricted to voluntary testimony during the six years of litigation over witnesses' right to refuse to give self-incriminating testimony. The Supreme Court also begrudgingly allowed the ICC to subpoena witnesses.[40]

Not satisfied that the ICC had merely been weakened, Charles E. Perkins of the CB&Q in December 1892 set out to abolish it. His lawyer Richard Olney, who would soon become Grover Cleveland's attorney general, shrewdly advised Perkins

---

the Census, *Historical Statistics of the United States, Colonial Times to 1957* (Washington, 1960), p. 431 (hereafter cited as *Historical Statistics*). MacAvoy stresses that ICC regulation was effective until 1893, while Martin says it was ineffective.

40. MacAvoy, *Economic Effects of Regulation*, p. 125, n. 55; Counselman v. Hitchcock, 142 U.S. 547 (1892), Brown v. Walker, 161 U.S. 591 (1896), and Interstate Commerce Commission v. Brimson, 154 U.S. 447 (1894), in Sharfman, *ICC*, 1:23–24, n. 19; Adams, "Decade of Federal Railway Regulation," pp. 436–37, 442–43.

that "the part of wisdom is not to destroy the Commission but to utilize it." Olney stressed that an attempt to destroy the ICC would probably fail and might backfire by inspiring efforts to strengthen the commission. Since the ICC had recently been limited by the courts, he emphasized that its supervision was "almost entirely nominal" while it satisfied the "popular clamor" for regulation and could be useful to railroads. As the commission grew older, Olney further suggested it would "take the business and railroad view of things" and protect railroad corporations from "hasty and crude legislation" as well as from the people. Three observations, however, can be made. Perkins —who was the boss—did try to utilize the commission, but he continued his efforts to kill it. Furthermore, Olney, who also represented the Boston & Maine and the Santa Fe railroads, apparently had not convinced himself of the soundness of his advice. Not only had he lobbied against the ICA in 1887, but subsequent to his oft-quoted 1892 letter he worked both to abolish the ICC and to limit its power. Finally, though Olney's prediction that the ICC would take a railroad view was fulfilled in the 1920s, Perkins's prophecy that the ICC, if not destroyed, would be strengthened and would not protect railroads was realized earlier in the Progressive era.[41]

Despite the wishes of Perkins and even with the Court whittling ICC power, Congress increased commission responsibilities. In 1889 an ICC-sponsored conference of state railroad commissioners urged the ICC to recommend national safety legislation to Congress. The commission investigated and weighed the need for automatic couplers and train brakes (driving wheel brakes on locomotives and power brakes on cars) against the difficulties of government interference. It passively and typically—as ensuing years would show—decided that it was "not prepared to recommend a national law prescribing

41. Perkins to Olney, 22 December 1892, and Olney to Perkins, 28 December 1892, Richard Olney Papers, Library of Congress; Gerald G. Eggert, *Richard Olney: Evolution of a Statesman* (University Park, Pa., 1974), pp. 26–32.

appliances," but submitted the whole question to "the wisdom of Congress." The ICC, which Congress created to regulate railroads, wanted Congress to act but would not tell it what to enact. The Senate Committee on Interstate Commerce after investigating discovered that in 1890 "out of every 105 men directly engaged in the handling of trains one was killed, and out of every twelve men so employed one was injured." Continued pressure, particularly by labor organizations, led Congress in the Safety Appliance Act (1893) to require that railroads eliminate the hand coupler and hand brake by 1 January 1898 and that the ICC administer these safety requirements and, if necessary, allow railroads more time to comply. Although safety conditions improved under the new act (2,660 railroad employees out of 784,000 died in 1891, while ten years later 2,675 out of 1,071,000 died), employee mortality rates were still tragically high.[42]

The year 1893 is renowned, however, not for the Safety Appliance Act but for the panic leading to a severe economic depression, which devastated railroads. Major systems went bankrupt, and construction virtually ceased. From 1893 to 1897, one-sixth of the nation's trackage and one-fourth of its total railroad capitalization went into receivership; new mileage in 1895 was 1,519 compared to 11,569 in 1882. Desperately needing revenue, railroads abandoned their cartel agreements, slashed rates, and offered rebates to attract traffic. Any inclination railroad officials may have had to obey either the ICC or their traffic associations was stopped by the depression. Even the consolidation movement (aided by the reorganization of bankrupt lines by bankers, such as J. P. Morgan) failed to halt falling rates and sharp competition. The depression brought decline to the ICC both by encouraging competing railroads to defy it and by keeping politicians so preoccupied that they ig-

---

42. Sharfman, *ICC*, 1:245–51. The ICC granted railroads extensions until 1 August 1900. Ibid., p. 250, n. 9; E. Pendleton Herring, *Public Administration and the Public Interest* (New York, 1936), p. 187; *Historical Statistics*, p. 437.

nored it. Presidents paid little attention beyond appointing commissioners, and Congress showed little desire to strengthen the ICC's administrative machinery. In its 1896 annual report, the ICC pleaded in vain with Congress to enact nine proposed amendments "to make the substance of the law mean what it was supposed to mean at the time of its passage."[43]

At the end of its first decade, the ICC suffered disastrous defeats at the hands of the Supreme Court. Having extracted from a reluctant Court the means to extract evidence from reluctant witnesses, the ICC lost to the courts its fundamental power to fix rates. Assuming it could set the reasonable-and-just rates the ICA demanded, the commission for almost a decade had decided on replacements for rates it found unfair. Having already showed its own proclivity for ratesetting, the Supreme Court in its *Maximum Freight Rate* decision (1897) flatly declared that Congress did not grant the commission "the power to prescribe rates or fix any tariff." The ICC ceased setting rates and dropped attempts to enforce its earlier ratesetting.[44]

The Supreme Court in 1897 not only denied the ICC the power to determine rates but in the *Trans-Missouri* case declared that rate and tonnage agreements among railroads restrained trade and violated the Sherman Antitrust Act. The ICC had accepted the cartel agreements of railroad traffic associations, which set rates but did not apportion freight; from 1887 to 1893—years of strong ICC regulation and effective cartelization of trunk-line railroads—rates remained relatively stable and railroads relatively prosperous. Most of these agreements, however, broke down in the depression following the panic of 1893. After experiencing in March and April 1895 the most extensive rate disruption since federal regulation, trunk-line railroads organized the Joint Traffic Association, which

43. William Z. Ripley, *Railroads: Finance & Organization* (New York, 1915), pp. 108, 376–77; Kirkland, *Industry*, p. 6; Kolko, *Railroads and Regulation*, pp. 64–67; MacAvoy, *Economic Effects of Regulation*, pp. 153–76; Adams, "Decade of Federal Railway Regulation," pp. 442–43.

44. Interstate Commerce Commission v. Cincinnati, N.O.&T.P.R. Co., 167 U.S. 479 (1897), in Sharfman, *ICC*, 1:26.

began operating 1 January 1896. The ICC opposed this agreement because in dividing traffic it clearly violated the ICA's antipooling section 5, but thanks to those violations grain rates were maintained throughout 1896. The Joint Traffic Association—very similar to the Trans-Missouri Freight Rate Association—collapsed after the March 1897 *Trans-Missouri* decision and was dissolved by the Supreme Court in October 1898 not because the ICC protested, not because the association violated the ICA, but because the association violated the Sherman Act. Clearly the Court wished to regulate railroads by competition, rather than ICC rules or traffic-association agreements. Ironically the Court's *Trans-Missouri* and *Joint Traffic* decisions encouraged railroads to eliminate competition through consolidation. As the century ended, the consolidation movement was in full swing, traffic associations had revived, prosperity had returned, and rates rose sharply.[45]

In 1897 the Supreme Court also destroyed the ICA's section 4, which outlawed the long-short-haul abuse. The commission had in 1887 exempted those railroads competing with unregulated carriers (foreign and intrastate railroads and water carriers) but insisted that other exceptions must be rare and peculiar. After railroads began to assume that whatever they willed was rare and peculiar, the ICC in 1892 plugged that loophole. Thereafter while most of the nation's railroads accepted section 4, long-short-haul violations remained common south of the Ohio and east of the Mississippi. In the *Alabama Midland* case, the ICC insisted that regulated-railroad competition was no justification for lower westbound freight-rates to Montgomery than to Troy, which on the Alabama Midland Railway was fifty-two miles east of Montgomery and without competing rail facilities. On appeal, however, the courts accepted the railroad's contention that railroad competition created dissimilarities between

45. MacAvoy, *Economic Effects of Regulation*, pp. 110–92, particularly pp. 187–88, 201–4; United States v. Trans-Missouri Freight Association, 166 U.S. 290 (1897), and United States v. Joint Traffic Association, 171 U.S. 505 (1898), in Sharfman, *ICC*, 1:34, n. 29; Kirkland, *Industry*, pp. 132–34; Cushman, *Independent Regulatory Commissions*, p. 68.

Troy and Montgomery justifying an exception to section 4. Since under the new interpretation no two points were similar, the ICC stopped trying to enforce section 4. The fact that carriers immediately filed thousands of increases for intermediate points, which were once again at the carrier's mercy, demonstrates that section 4 had been effective. In his sharp dissent, Justice John Marshall Harlan attacked specifically the *Alabama Midland* decision, which would "build up favored centers of population at the expense of the business of the country at large" and generally protested:

The Commission was established to protect the public against the improper practices of transportation companies engaged in commerce among the several states. It has been left, it is true, with power to make reports and to issue protests. But it has been shorn, by judicial interpretation, of authority to do anything of an effective character.

Committed to laissez faire, the Supreme Court had found enough weaknesses in the ICA to destroy effective regulation for a decade.[46]

Emasculated by the courts, ignored by the railroads, and unaided by Congress, the ICC in the 1890s also suffered from mediocre leadership. Although warmly sympathetic toward shippers, William Morrison, Cooley's successor as chairman of the ICC, was expert neither in jurisprudence nor in railroads. As chairman of the House Ways and Means Committee, he had led the futile effort to reduce the protective tariff, and, as chairman of the ICC, he led the equally futile effort to eliminate discriminatory rates and rebates. With the departure of Cooley and the evaporation of ICC powers, Henry Carter Adams—the outstanding statistician on the ICC's small staff (between 104 and 133 throughout the 1890s)—emerged as the commission's

46. Trammell v. Clyde Steamship Co., 4 ICR 120 (1892), in Sharfman, *ICC*, 3B:550–52; Board of Trade of Troy, Ala. v. Ala. Mid. Ry. Co., 6 ICR 1 (1893), and Interstate Commerce Commission v. Alabama Midland Ry. Co., 69 Fed. 227 (1895), 74 Fed. 715 (1896), 168 U.S. 144 (1897), ibid., 1:30–32; Martin, "Troubled Subject of Railroad Regulation," p. 365, n. 57.

key man. Mediocre leadership weakens an agency, stifles innovation, and divides the residue of power among strong-willed
subordinates. Adams, one of the nation's leading economists,
fortunately had a broad perspective; in the future powerful ICC
staff members tended to be bound by the traditions and interests
of their agency. Neither the top of the ICC organization chart
nor the faceless bureaucracy at its base automatically made
decisions. Who decided issues depended on the strength and
ability of individual commissioners and staff members. Strong
staff members, however, cannot redeem weak leaders; the
agency is bound to suffer. Cooley, a forceful man steeped in
jurisprudence, might have withstood the attacks of both the
courts and the railroads in the depression-ridden 1890s, but
Morrison could not. When his term expired in the ICC's nadir
year of 1897, William McKinley did not reappoint him.

2

Power to Negate:
The Progressive Era

THE ICC REQUIRED a decade to recover from the blows it sustained in the mid-1890s. During the early years of the twentieth century, it was an axiom of political and economic life that the ICC was without authority. "Regarding the powers and duties of the Interstate Commerce Commission," a member of the Industrial Commission queried in 1901, "is it not a fact that the commission is without power to enforce its decision?" The reply by Thomas F. Woodlock, railroad editor of the *Wall Street Journal*, was a simple, direct, unequivocal yes. In reference to freight increases, the ICC admitted in 1903, "At present this Commission can investigate and report. It has no power to determine what rate is reasonable, and such orders as it can make have no binding effect." Within the few years the situation would change; Congress would endow the ICC with enormous power to supervise and control the railroads.[1]

The Changing Railroad Problem

While the ICC remained quiescent during the decade following 1897, feverish activity by Progressive politicians and the railroad industry affected the ICC. The Progressive movement

---

1. U.S., Industrial Commission, *Report* . . . (19 vols.; Washington, 1900–2), 9:465. Woodlock wanted to keep the ICC powerless and tried his best to do so a generation later when he became a commissioner. U.S., Interstate Commerce Commission, *17th Annual Report*, 1903, p. 17 (hereafter cited as *Annual Report*).

converted many Americans to the idea that federal regulation of industry—particularly of railroads—was necessary, that nineteenth-century laissez faire notions were obsolete, and that the Sherman Act and the ICA must be strengthened and enforced. While Progressives were whipping up support for increased regulation, the railroad problem was changing. By the time they had convinced the public that action was needed, their solution no longer fitted the railroad situation, which differed radically from the late nineteenth to the early twentieth century.

Though the railroad industry had changed, neither Congress nor the ICC seemed aware of that fact. While 1897, with its adverse judicial decisions, marks the nadir of the ICC, it also marks the beginning of a new railroad era. Before the depression of the 1890s, Albro Martin remarks, railroads were "overbuilt, financially undernourished, divided into hundreds of poorly integrated corporate entities, and ridden by rate wars which reduced the profits of the best-situated roads drastically and drove the weaker ones to the wall of bankruptcy." Gilded Age railroad problems—"rebating, long-haul-short-haul discrimination, poor and unsafe service, daredevil financial gymnastics . . . were the symptoms of a railroad network built in a new country ahead of a consistently profitable volume of traffic." The change was wrought both by the depression following the panic of 1893 and by the subsequent prosperity. Railroads owning a third of the nation's mileage defaulted on their bonds and were reorganized, principally by bankers, on a sounder basis, shaking out many reckless, speculative managers. Railroad men also sought to eliminate rebates and ratecutting which the depression engendered and prosperity did not end.[2]

Alexander J. Cassatt, who in 1899 became president of the Pennsylvania Railroad, introduced the community of interest idea. With pools outlawed and traffic associations weak (rebates were also outlawed by the ICA, but that regulation was difficult to enforce) and with large shippers, such as the Rocke-

2. Albro Martin, *Enterprise Denied: Origins of the Decline of American Railroads, 1897–1917* (New York, 1971), pp. 17, 354–55.

feller oil interests, playing railroads against each other, Cassatt proposed that the New York Central and the Pennsylvania acquire stock in competing roads to prevent ratecutting. By 1902 the Pennsylvania had large investments in the Baltimore & Ohio, the Chesapeake & Ohio, and the Norfolk & Western, while the Baltimore & Ohio and the New York Central bought into the Reading. Presenting a united front to shippers, these railroads refused further rebates. Cassatt's plan succeeded. Other communities of interest came to fruition almost simultaneously in the South, Southwest, Northwest, and New England.[3]

In the late 1890s as business recovered from the recent economic panic and depression, enormous consolidation and expansion took place. By the first decade of the new century railroads had to deal with more powerful combinations shipping more and more goods. No longer overbuilt, railroads found their nineteenth-century network rickety and unable to handle twentieth-century demands. With major railroad lines being repaired and updated while carrying record traffic, accidents increased to the point that more passengers (610) and employees (4,534) were killed in 1907 than in any other year of American railroading. Besides increasing accidents, rebuilding increased capital needs. In their search for investors, railroad officials found that capital flows to the more profitable enterprises and that other businesses were more lucrative than railroads. Although by 1900 railroad consolidations and communities of interest halted rate declines, in the late 1890s the dollar's purchasing power—which in preceding decades had appreciated—began a twenty-five-year decline. Freight rates stabilized (revenue per ton-mile which had dropped from .941 cents in 1890 to .724 in 1899 rose only to .780 in 1904 and then declined slowly to the all-time low of .719 in 1916) while inflationary pressures increased operating costs. As the twentieth century opened, the railroad problem could no longer be solved simply

3. Ibid., pp. 17–21; *Dictionary of American Biography*, s.v. "Cassatt, Alexander Johnston" (hereafter cited as *DAB*).

by eliminating discrimination. During the Progressive era, railroads moved to establish and raise general rate levels while shippers wished to maintain existing individual rates.[4]

Wrestling unsuccessfully with the railroad problem, the impotent, turn-of-the-century commission had three relatively effective members. Its leading spirit was Martin A. Knapp, whom Benjamin Harrison appointed in 1891 and Cleveland and Theodore Roosevelt reappointed. Knapp's five-foot frame and quiet, pleasant nature belied his strength of character and force of will. As corporation counsel of Syracuse, New York, and in his subsequent law practice, he acquired expertise in railroad matters. Influential on the commission even before he succeeded William Morrison as chairman in 1898, Knapp wished to strike a "stable equilibrium" between shippers and railroads, favored legalized pooling with ICC rate control, wanted judicial review limited to evidence heard by the commission, and thought railroads should finance improvements out of current earnings. Knapp's sympathetic and understanding attitude toward railroads led to occasional conflicts first with Morrison and ultimately with other commissioners during the last years of Knapp's leadership.[5]

Scarcely less impressive than Knapp was Charles A. Prouty, a Republican appointed by Cleveland in 1896 and twice reappointed by Theodore Roosevelt. A prominent Vermont politician who ran for the Senate in 1914 as a Progressive, and a lawyer who had often represented railroads, Prouty had a technical mind that could master the intricacies of applied science as well as the details of railroad accounting. Testy, witty, and caustic, Prouty became an ardent supporter of Roosevelt's rail-

4. Martin, *Enterprise Denied*, pp. 78, 355; U.S., Bureau of the Census, *Historical Statistics of the United States, Colonial Times to 1957* (Washington, 1960), pp. 431, 437 (hereafter cited as *Historical Statistics*).

5. *DAB*, s.v. "Knapp, Martin Augustine"; Gabriel Kolko, *Railroads and Regulation, 1877–1916* (Princeton, 1965), pp. 70–71, 73, 113–14; Martin, *Enterprise Denied*, pp. 175–77; Clarence Atha Miller, *The Lives of the Interstate Commerce Commissioners and the Commission's Secretaries* (Washington, 1946), pp. 31–32.

road policies, tried to hold down railroad rates, and became convinced that until railroad properties were definitively valued it was impossible to determine if rates were just and reasonable.[6]

Although less influential than Knapp or Prouty, Judson C. Clements was a formidable commissioner. Appointed by Cleveland in 1892, Clements was reappointed four times and served twenty-five years before dying in office. A Confederate veteran, lawyer, and congressman from Georgia who helped shape the ICA, Clements as a commissioner—despite having been connected with the Rome & Northern Railway Company—championed shippers, opposed rate increases, and advocated more control over railroad rates, capitalization, and valuation.[7]

Despite its strong trio, the ICC was powerless in the early 1900s to regulate a railroad system that was creating communities of interest to counteract shipper oligopolies, that was rebuilding to handle unprecedented freight, that needed more income to pay the rising price of money, materials, and labor. Congress and President William McKinley seemed content to have the ICC remain powerless. Shelby M. Cullom in December 1899 attempted to strengthen it with a bill (written primarily by Prouty) granting the commission power to set maximum and minimum rates on complaint and to fix a uniform freight classification. The Committee on Interstate Commerce, which Cullom chaired, was so hostile that to keep the bill off the Senate floor it refused even to report it negatively. At least four committee members had significant railroad interests (Stephen B. Elkins, John Kean, John H. Gear, and Edward Wolcott), while a fifth, Nelson W. Aldrich, had traction interests and was favorably inclined toward railroads. Clearly the committee was not interested in further railroad legislation; in 1901 Cullom experienced delays in assembling a committee quorum (Aldrich, for one,

6. *DAB*, s.v. "Prouty, Charles Azro"; Martin, *Enterprise Denied*, p. 177; Miller, *Interstate Commerce Commissioners*, pp. 43–44.
7. *DAB*, s.v. "Clements, Judson Claudius"; Martin, *Enterprise Denied*, pp. 177, 288, 300; Kolko, *Railroads and Regulation*, p. 178; Miller, *Interstate Commerce Commissioners*, pp. 37–39.

claimed to be too busy) to approve mild legislation requiring monthly accident reports. Discouraged, Cullom in December 1901 relinquished his chairmanship to Stephen B. Elkins.[8]

One of the late nineteenth century's most successful businessmen-politicians, Elkins made a fortune by combining politics, law, lobbying, and land and mineral speculation. Renowned for skillfully utilizing business connections and for daring leadership at national conventions in James G. Blaine's behalf, Elkins by 1901 had abandoned both president-making and the national outlook that pursuit entails and manifested a characteristically senatorial concern over the political situation in West Virginia and his business interests there. Though he had railroad interests, Elkins was a mine operator who shipped huge quantities of coal. He declared in 1906, "My interest on the side of the shipper is ten times greater than on the side of the railroads, and . . . my interest in railroads is confined to my own state." Perhaps thinking that an ineffectual enemy was preferable to an undependable friend, J. P. Morgan preferred that Cullom remain chairman of the committee rather than risk the potentially dangerous leadership of Elkins, a railroad man, to be sure, but also a daring, adventurous, skillful politician with substantial shipping interests.[9]

Fourteen months after Elkins took over the Committee on Interstate Commerce, Congress passed the first significant ICA amendment. The Elkins Antirebating Act (1903) made the published rate (filed with the ICC) the legal rate; any departure —rebates, drawbacks, other concessions, or even general rate-cutting—constituted a criminal violation with fines up to $20,000 for both shippers and railroads. The Elkins Act was

8. James W. Neilson, *Shelby M. Cullom: Prairie State Republican* (Urbana, Ill., 1962), pp. 206–13.

9. On Elkins as a president-maker, see Robert D. Marcus, *Grand Old Party: Political Structure in the Gilded Age, 1880–1896* (New York, 1971); pp. 64–67, 85–88, 104–25. See also *DAB*, s.v. "Elkins, Stephen Benton"; Martin, *Enterprise Denied*, p. 146; Kolko, *Railroads and Regulation*, pp. 90–92; Neilson, *Cullom*, p. 211.

Progressive—it relied upon a federal regulatory agency (the ICC) to eliminate railroad discrimination—but it was written by James A. Logan of the Pennsylvania Railroad, along with Knapp, Prouty, and Elkins, and was part of Alexander Cassatt's design to prevent ratecutting.

Rebates, however, were just a part, albeit a significant part, of the railroad problem. The traffic manager of a major system told the ICC that rebates and similar concessions amounted to 10 percent of gross freight revenues. Cassatt hoped the principle of legal rates would reinforce the stabilizing influence of the communities of interest and would keep major shippers and minor railroads in line. The bill originally would legalize pooling and would allow the ICC upon complaint to set a new rate for a year, subject to judicial review, but Logan and Cassatt dropped these propositions when small shippers and merchants objected through the Interstate Commerce Law Convention. Most railroads also disliked this early version. Cassatt told Roosevelt in 1902 that the Pennsylvania's desire to make the ICA "more effective and to strengthen" the ICC differed "radically from that of railroad managers generally" and protested that "our motives have been misrepresented to you by certain railroad interests violently opposed to any measure increasing the powers of the Commission." Unlike most railroad men, Cassatt thought it better "to assist in framing and passing a reasonable measure now than to have a more drastic and perhaps seriously injurious one forced upon us by public clamor" in a subsequent depression. The revised Elkins bill, Theodore Roosevelt remarked, was openly opposed by "no respectable railroad or respectable business." It passed the Senate unanimously and received only six negative votes in the House. The Elkins Act, however, was "not even a preliminary skirmish" over the railroad problem but a "truce of the principals to abolish piracy." Rebates, though "greatly diminished," did survive. But even when railroads did not deviate from published rates, there was no assurance that published rates were reasonable, just, and nondiscriminatory. The central problem of securing fair rates for both shippers and railroads remained. The commission could not solve the problem unless Congress would strengthen the ICA.[10]

Reviving the ICC

Unlike McKinley, Theodore Roosevelt gave the ICC powerful support. He called for increased federal control of railroads and rejected the notion of self-regulation through consolidation. Beginning in February 1902, he attacked the Northern Securities Company. That holding company grew out of the truce ending the May 1901 fight between James J. Hill (backed by J. P. Morgan) and Edward H. Harriman (backed by Kuhn, Loeb & Company and ultimately the Rockefeller interests) for the Northern Pacific, which controlled the Chicago, Burlington & Quincy and its Chicago connections needed by Harriman's Union Pacific and Hill's Great Northern. Controlled by both the Hill-Morgan and the Harriman-Kuhn-Loeb interests, the Northern Securities Company directed the Great Northern, Northern Pacific, and the Chicago, Burlington & Quincy railroads. Called by George E. Mowry the "first true holding company," Northern Securities went far beyond the community of interest concept, and its creation proved that rival railroad leaders could compromise their differences and cooperate and regulate— rather than destroy—themselves. But the government espoused what Balthasar H. Meyer, a Wisconsin expert on railroads who would later become a commissioner, called the "impossible doctrine of protection of the public by railway competition," which he insisted, "we should have cast away more than fifty years ago." While most people hailed the Supreme Court decision destroying the Northern Securities Company (1904), he lamented that decision and called for "some legislation which will

10. Kolko, *Railroads and Regulation*, pp. 94–101; Cassatt to Roosevelt, 1 April 1902, Theodore Roosevelt Papers, Library of Congress, Washington; I. L. Sharfman, *The Interstate Commerce Commission: A Study in Administrative Law and Procedure*, 5 vols. (New York, 1931–37), 1:35–38 (hereafter cited as Sharfman, *ICC*).

enable companies to act together under the law, as they now do quietly among themselves outside of the law."[11]

Destruction of the Northern Securities Company had great economic impact. Competition increased, but railroad competition—even when flourishing—occurred only where two or more roads were available. More important, the consolidation movement, fostered by men like Harriman, Hill, and Morgan, declined and would not revive again for sixty years, and then with dubious results. Morgan and Charles S. Mellen did try with some success to monopolize New England transportation by acquiring railroad, trolley, and steamship lines, but by 1913—thanks to maladministration and outraged public opinion—they had failed. In addition, the threat of action under the Sherman Act unsettled the financial climate in which railroad expansion had taken place. The *Northern Securities* case also notified railroads that their power to regulate themselves through consolidations was limited, that the federal government could dissolve them and other trusts, and that Roosevelt as president wielded enormous economic and political power. Alexander Cassatt, for one, received the message. By 1906 he reported that since rates had stabilized and the roads the Pennsylvania Railroad had bought into were able to stand alone, it had sold its holdings in rival roads.[12]

Having destroyed the Northern Securities combination and having secured his 1904 election, Roosevelt moved to strengthen the commission. His December 1904 message—reiterating the ICC's request—asked Congress to empower the commission to set reasonable rates if shippers complained that published rates were unfair. Railroads, with their monopolistic power over many shippers, became even more unpopular. In the Midwest Governors Robert M. La Follette and Albert B. Cummins, among

11. George E. Mowry, *The Era of Theodore Roosevelt and the Birth of Modern America, 1900–1912* (New York, 1958), pp. 130–31; Martin, *Enterprise Denied*, p. 181.
12. Martin, *Enterprise Denied*, pp. 100–2, 116; Mowry, *Era of Theodore Roosevelt*, pp. 130—34; Kolko, *Railroads and Regulation*, pp. 156–61; *DAB*, s.v. "Mellen, Charles Sanger."

others, were making political capital by attacking railroads, regulating intrastate roads, and urging Roosevelt to regulate effectively interstate rates. From the Mississippi River to the Rocky Mountains and from the Ohio River to the Gulf of Mexico, victorious politicians called for effective railroad regulation. In the 1902 California gubernatorial campaign the anti-railroad candidate Franklin K. Lane nearly defeated the Southern Pacific's man, and in the Northeast the *Wall Street Journal*, equating railroad consolidation with efficiency, conceded that sooner or later railroads would "have to surrender their rate-making power to the government." Roosevelt gave rate reform his highest priority. He regarded the popular issue of effective railroad regulation a "matter of principle," while he thought tariff revision a "matter of expediency." John Morton Blum argues that Roosevelt used the threat of tariff revision to secure conservative, standpat support for railroad legislation. The low-tariff antirailroad men would get a strengthened ICC, while the high tariff prorailroad men would keep the Dingley tariff. Blum's thesis, which rests more on a brilliant argument than on hard evidence, is not convincing. Enormous pressure on Congress made railroad regulation a popular unifying issue that hardly required manipulative tactics to secure a law. Furthermore, some standpatters, especially in the Senate, did not automatically oppose either railroad legislation or reopening the tariff question; and, finally, Roosevelt's quick retreats and statements on tariff revision suggest a fear of opening that divisive issue rather than a cool, clever use of it as a threat. Avoiding the perilous course of tariff revision, Roosevelt followed the line of least resistance leading to railroad rate regulation, but then fought hard and effectively for it.[13]

The House of Representatives quickly approved rate regula-

13. George E. Mowry, *The California Progressives* (Berkeley, 1951), p. 21; Mowry, *Era of Theodore Roosevelt*, pp. 71–78, 198–99; John Morton Blum, *The Republican Roosevelt* (Cambridge, Mass., 1954), pp. 77–85. We are indebted to Jerome L. Sternstein for this analysis of the Blum thesis.

tion. Ignoring the first Hepburn bill (written in the main by Roosevelt's Attorney General William H. Moody), the House in February 1905 passed by a thumping 326-to-17 bipartisan vote the more sweeping Esch-Townsend bill, which would make the ICC more powerful than Roosevelt had planned by allowing it to fix rates, rather than merely to consider contested rates. Getting the Esch-Townsend bill, or any rate-regulation bill, through the Senate was more difficult. Having begun public hearings on rate regulation in December 1904, the Senate would not be rushed, and when the Fifty-eighth Congress ended on 3 March 1905 the bill expired.[14]

Pressure for railroad legislation seems to have been generated more by interaction between constituents and politicians, particularly in rural areas, than by businessmen's organizations. Although the Interstate Commerce Law Convention (representing small shippers and merchants) agitated for federal rate regulation in 1903 and 1904—when it was joined by the powerful National Association of Manufacturers (NAM)—the New York Board of Trade and Transportation and California merchants opposed rate-regulating legislation, and in 1905 the Interstate Commerce Law Convention collapsed and the NAM reversed its stand. Viewed nationally, small merchants and businessmen presented a divided front, while midwestern shippers applied intense pressure on Congress for rate regulation. Though railroads had favored antirebating legislation, they campaigned in 1905 both in and out of Congress against rate regulation. Railroad executives, mobilized by J. P. Morgan's man Samuel Spencer, descended on the Senate hearings and denounced the Esch-Townsend bill in particular and government ratesetting in general. James J. Hill, who had done his mightiest to monopolize northwestern railroads, rejected federal ratesetting. Presumably with a straight face, he intoned in January 1905, "Competition is the test which proves the survival of

14. Mowry, *Era of Theodore Roosevelt*, p. 199; Martin, *Enterprise Denied*, p. 112.

the fittest. The laws of trade are as certain as the laws of gravity."[15]

No politician was more important than Roosevelt in securing further railroad legislation. Throughout 1905 he campaigned extensively. Addressing enthusiastic audiences in the West and South, Roosevelt called railroads both crazy and shortsighted in their hostility to rate regulation since its defeat would bring government ownership nearer. Declaring both the reasonableness and righteousness of his regulatory policy, he insisted it would give a square deal to railroads and shippers, to rich and poor. By mid-November, Roosevelt, who had never backed the Esch-Townsend bill, agreed with his attorney general that it was unconstitutional and favored instead a maximum-rate law. On the evening of 27 November 1905, Roosevelt, some of his advisers—cabinet members Elihu Root, William Howard Taft, William H. Moody, Charles J. Bonaparte, Commissioner of the Bureau of Corporations James R. Garfield, and Senator Philander C. Knox—and Knapp and Prouty of the ICC discussed the bill proposed by the commission and agreed on general principles. Garfield noted, however, that it was "understood that neither it nor any other bill should be an administration measure—that the Pres. is of course entirely free to favor any measure that he may finally deem wise." Spelling out his general principles in his annual message (5 December 1905), Roosevelt declared that the most pressing need was legislation eliminating unjust rates. Specifically he

15. Kolko, *Railroads and Regulation*, pp. 102–7; Blum, *Republican Roosevelt*, p. 82; Mowry, *Era of Theodore Roosevelt*, p. 199; Henry F. Pringle, *Theodore Roosevelt: A Biography* (New York, 1931), p. 293. Martin, *Enterprise Denied*, pp. 112–13, n. 42, disputes Kolko's contention that railroads did not mount an antiregulatory campaign. Kolko, *Railroads and Regulation*, pp. 118–19, n. 41, and pp. 128–29, n. 6. For evidence that railroads started "a publication bureau at enormous expense" in order "to resolutely oppose any form of regulation," see John W. Midgley (Manager, Railway Clearing House Bureau) to John C. Spooner, 27 November 1905, Spooner Papers, Library of Congress. Midgley thought his employers' campaign unwise and that it would have been wiser for railroads to "join cordially in efforts to correct" abuses.

wished to empower the ICC to fix maximum rates upon shippers' complaints (subject to judicial review), to eliminate rebates more effectively by regulating private-car lines, to prevent
railroads from issuing free tickets and passes, and to inspect
railroad account books. Beginning in December 1905, the
Roosevelt administration's vigorous prosecution of rebate givers
and takers added to the demand in early 1906 for railroad
legislation, as did muckraking articles attacking railroads and
their senatorial allies and disclosure that some railroads had
attempted to sway public opinion by bribing newspaper ed-
itors.[16]

When Congress assembled in December 1905, both houses
recognized that railroad-rate legislation was unavoidable.
"Many prominent railroad men," John W. Midgley, manager of
the Railway Clearing House Bureau, confided to a senator, "do
not want any legislation, but they are mistaken as it will surely
come." Midgley was right, and railroad officials soon prepared
to accept ICC maximum-rate regulation with as much judicial
review as possible. Republicans abandoned the Esch-Townsend
bill for a revised Hepburn bill, incorporating Roosevelt's main
ideas. Aware of public pressure and Roosevelt's desires, the
House in February 1906 passed the Hepburn bill 346 to 7.
Prouty exulted to Roosevelt that the bill was "an advance so
extraordinary that he had never dared to suppose it would be
possible to pass it." While realizing legislation was inevitable,
several senators led by Nelson Aldrich attempted to weaken the
Hepburn bill by concentrating on securing the broadest possible
judicial review of ICC rates. The bill passed by the House man-
aged to avoid the issue of judicial review by allowing the courts
to determine its breadth. Narrow judicial review—determining
the ICC's right to set a rate and the methods used but not

16. Diary of James R. Garfield, 27 November 1905, James R. Garfield Papers, Library of Congress; Mowry, *Era of Theodore Roosevelt*,
pp. 200–3; Pringle, *Theodore Roosevelt*, pp. 294–96; Kolko, *Railroads
and Regulation*, pp. 112–15; Robert E. Cushman, *The Independent Regulatory Commissions* (New York, 1941), p. 70. For the ICC's bill, see
19th Annual Report, 1905, pp. 177–83.

second-guessing the rate's reasonableness—would convert the ICC into an independent regulatory commission with quasi-legislative, executive, and judicial powers, while a broad review of the facts would lodge the ratesetting power in the courts. In the end, the Senate (by passing the compromise Allison amendment, which Aldrich may have written) also left the extent of judicial review undetermined. The Allison amendment gave circuit courts jurisdiction and allowed them to determine the breadth of their review; it permitted the courts to enjoin ICC orders but provided for a quick appeal to the Supreme Court. Remarkably close to what Roosevelt had initially advocated, the final bill gave the ICC power to set rates on complaint and gave the courts undefined, but potentially broad, review power (power, Roosevelt reasoned, they already had). With only three negative votes, the bill passed on 18 May 1906. By orchestrating enormous public support, Roosevelt had extracted with an overwhelming majority a fundamental law from a reluctant Senate, but the ICC had helped make his victory possible. Since 1896 the commission had publicized its weaknesses and called for strengthening measures in its annual reports. In 1905 it had drawn up a model bill for the benefit of Roosevelt, Congress, and the public; and the ICC—particularly Knapp and Prouty—had consulted with Roosevelt on legislation.[17]

The Hepburn Act and the ICC

The Hepburn Act brought strength to the ICC. Explicitly giving it power upon complaint and after full hearing to replace an existing rate with a just-and-reasonable maximum rate, the Hepburn Act specified that the ICC's orders were binding on promulgation, that the courts were to compel obedience, and

17. Midgley to John C. Spooner, 25 January 1906, Spooner Papers; Frank H. Dixon, *Railroads and Government: Their Relations in the United States, 1910–1921* (New York, 1922), p. 3. On the complex course of Roosevelt and the Hepburn bill in the Senate, see Blum, *Republican Roosevelt*, pp. 92–105; Kolko, *Railroads and Regulation*, pp. 129–44; Mowry, *Era of Theodore Roosevelt*, pp. 203–6.

that the railroads must obey or contest the order in court. Widening the ICC's jurisdiction to include express and sleeping car companies, oil pipe lines, switches, spurs, yards, depots, and terminals, the act also gave the commission power to prescribe a uniform system of accounting, to require standardized reports, and to inspect railroad accounts. To cope with its new duties, the commission was empowered to appoint examiners and agents and was increased from five to seven members, whose terms of office were lengthened to seven years. The ICC's employees, who rose from 104 in 1890 to 178 in 1905, jumped to 330 in 1907 and 527 in 1909. The Hepburn Act also eliminated the latest wrinkle in rebating—charges, frequently excessive, made by private car lines and industrial railroads for services rendered to common carriers—and required railroads not to discriminate in providing shippers with freight cars and with switches for their sidings. To keep railroads from competing with other producers, the act prohibited railroads after 1 May 1908 from hauling, except for their own use, any product that they produced or mined, except lumber. The act also required a thirty-day notification period before rate changes, restored imprisonment as a punishment for giving or taking rebates, and abolished free passes for those not employed by railroads.[18]

The Hepburn Act made the ICC, not the courts, the dominant government agency regulating railroads. Debates prior to passage of this act emphasized the administrative character of the commission and its duties. Its mix of executive, legislative, and judicial powers was to give it positive, maximum rate-making power. Congress also hoped to restrict the negative powers of the courts, which could abolish but not adjust. Despite the Hepburn Act's vagueness on judicial review and despite the hopes of conservatives and the fears of Progressives, the courts adopted a narrow-review policy. The Supreme Court pronounced that even if it believed administrative power had

18. Sharfman, *ICC*, 1:41–48, 4:68.

not been wisely exercised, it could not usurp administrative functions. "Power to make the order and not the mere expediency or wisdom of having made it," the Court declared, "is the question."[19]

Roosevelt continued his efforts to make the ICC effective. In 1905 before the Hepburn bill passed, he appointed Franklin K. Lane to the commission. Fearing that railroad policies would "lead to the wildest kind of a craze for government ownership of everything," Lane, an antirailroad California Democrat, hoped to teach corporations that they were "not the creators, the owners, and the rightful managers of the government." Charming and forceful, Lane remained a friend to shippers and an effective opponent of rate increases until he left the ICC in 1913 to become Woodrow Wilson's secretary of the interior. As the two additional commissioners allowed under the Hepburn Act, Roosevelt named James S. Harlan, son of Supreme Court Justice John Marshall Harlan, who was renowned for his dissent in the 1897 *Alabama Midland* case, and Edgar Erastus Clark, a leader of the growing railroad labor movement. After the Hepburn Act's passage, Roosevelt moved closer to La Follette's position that rates should be proportioned to the actual value of railroads and closer to the Supreme Court's 1898 dictum that railroads were entitled to a "fair return" on the "fair value" of their property. By 30 May 1907 Roosevelt demanded physical valuation of railroads, federal control of railroad securities, and federal, rather than state, incorporation of railroads. Finally, Roosevelt moved to stiffen the backbones of Interstate Commerce commissioners, whose timidity had been noted in administration circles. He urged Chairman Knapp and the ICC to adopt a positive administrative, rather than a passive judicial, approach to railroad regulation. "Your Commission should . . . lay greater stress upon the administrative side of its functions. . . . If your body becomes simply a court, then it had better be abolished. The only justification for [it is] its active

19. Interstate Commerce Commission v. Ill. Cent. R.R., 215 U.S. 452 (1910), ibid., 1:48, n. 46, 2:390–91.

exercise in constantly increasing measure of administrative supervision and control over the railroads."[20]

The Hepburn Act increased ICC activities, but whether the commission would imaginatively administrate or simply adjudicate remained to be seen. In 1905 it received only 65 formal and 503 informal complaints. Beginning with 1907—the first full year under the Hepburn Act—formal complaints rose to 415 and by 1909 had reached 1,097, or two and a half times all the formal complaints lodged with the commission during its first nineteen years. Informal complaints from 1907 to 1909 averaged roughly 4,500 annually.[21] The ICC was no longer ignored. No longer did it need to beg for power. The commission's new problem was to rise above the minutiae and harness its power to develop an adequate national transportation system —a system that would reflect the needs of railroads, shippers, and consumers.

The commission did not adjust its case-by-case approach to develop broad administrative principles for the nation's railroads. Enveloped by the details of individual rate cases and unconcerned that the entire rate system was discriminatory, the ICC used its newly acquired, enormous power merely to tinker with the status quo. Aiming "not to impose a new rate structure, but rather to mitigate, with a minimum of disturbance, the improprieties of the existing structure" and not possessing information necessary for detecting price discrimination, the ICC "legalized, legitimatized, and systematized" the existing discriminatory rate system. Finding value-of-service pricing (higher shipping rates for expensive manufactured items than for cheap farm products and raw materials) practiced by railroads to

20. Lane to Edward B. Whitney, 13 November 1905, in Franklin K. Lane, *The Letters of Franklin K. Lane, Personal and Political*, ed. Anne Wintermute Lane and Louise Herrick Wall (Boston, 1922), pp. 51–52; Martin, *Enterprise Denied*, pp. 175–80; Mowry, *Era of Theodore Roosevelt*, p. 206; Kolko, *Railroads and Regulation*, p. 157; Miller, *Interstate Commerce Commissioners*, pp. 53–62; Smyth v. Ames, 169 U.S. 466 (1898), in Sharfman, *ICC*, 1:74–76, 3A:124–32.

21. Sharfman, *ICC*, 1:41, n. 40.

maximize use of tracks and rolling stock, the ICC hallowed and extended this discriminatory practice as a policy to develop areas producing raw materials, to promote desirable industries, to help weak railroads, and to secure lower rates for necessities, such as soap, flour, salt, and fertilizer. Because railroads enjoyed a transportation monopoly until the 1920s, value-of-service pricing increased their profits, but it built the nation's economy on false and wasteful premises, causing manufacturers to locate factories away from raw materials and affecting the price of nearly all commodities, while unfairly transferring income from one group of consumers to another.[22]

To right these wrongs that had become precedents, the ICC would have had to disturb many powerful elements in the economy and to hurt some of the very groups that had clamored most for regulation. If cost-of-service pricing were instituted, favored shippers, including the many farmers and industrialists who enjoyed cheap bulk commodity rates, would no longer receive income rightfully belonging to consumers of manufactured goods. Most Progressives, like most politicians, were not interested in righting wrongs that helped their constituents. Blinded to the waste caused by value-of-service rates, Progressive congressmen attacked discriminatory rebates and short-haul rates but agitated for discriminatory cheap freight rates on farm products and necessities. Equally shortsighted, the ICC did not consider adopting cost-of-service pricing, which would allocate transportation facilities rationally and benefit consumers enormously. Such a sweeping reform would have aroused the opposition of farmers and others enjoying low rates, manufacturers who would have to relocate closer to raw materials, railroads whose ton-miles would shrink, and politicians more sensitive to the needs of these groups than to the needs of the transportation system and the country as a whole.

22. Ibid., 3B:414–16, 667; John R. Meyer et al., *The Economics of Competition in the Transportation Industries* (Cambridge, Mass., 1959), pp. 178–88.

In addition to not challenging the discriminatory basis of railroad rates, the ICC did not question the level of those rates. In effect its administration of the Hepburn Act in a rapidly expanding, inflationary economy froze rail rates at 1906 levels, which were only slightly higher than low 1899 rates. Primarily interested in eliminating rebates, railroad officials initially did not worry. Since 1897, railroads had enjoyed a decade of unparalleled prosperity and were America's prime growth industry. Indeed, they appeared so prosperous that their net new investments in the banner year 1907 were $1.5 billion as compared to $859 million in 1906 and $232 million in 1898. But the relatively minor 1907 financial panic started the railroad investment curve downward. To be sure, new investments continued—roughly $750 million annually from 1908 to 1911—but disaster struck in 1912 when new investments plummeted to approximately $100 million. Carrying 10 percent more traffic in 1910 than in 1907, railroads continued to appear prosperous; but 1910 earnings failed to equal 1907 earnings. Even though railroads retained considerably less of their earnings for capital needs (in 1911 less than any year since 1898, and in 1912 still less), they had to cut dividends in 1911 and 1912. While gross income rose in 1911, net earnings fell. The operating ratio, or the percent of operating revenue consumed by operating expenses, which railroad lore dictated should not go above 66 percent to maintain adequate profits, was at that figure in 1910 and had jumped to 72.2 percent by 1914.[23]

What caused railroads to earn less profits and attract less capital? Apparently the Hepburn Act, the *Northern Securities* decision, the hostility of state legislatures, the growth of labor organizations, and railroad mismanagement, when combined, raised operating costs, kept down freight rates, and caused would-be investors to turn to more promising ventures. Albro Martin blames zealous regulators and aggressive laborers for

23. Martin, *Enterprise Denied*, pp. 129–36, 374–75; *Historical Statistics*, pp. 430–31, 434.

railroads' financial problems but ignores the unscrupulous rail-road managers, who had damaged the reputation of all rail-roads. Indeed, J. W. Midgley, a railroad official, remarked in 1905 that "no commission, Federal or State, has ever done the railroads the harm that several adventurers or schemers in the profession have repeatedly worked." Speaking for investors, James Speyer on 1 April 1907 blamed "the recent violent de-cline of railroad shares (panic) on the New York Stock Ex-change" on higher wages and operating costs, on public hostility to further mergers, on tightening international money markets, aggravated by the capital needs of American railroads, on the lack of confidence in all railroad managers because some had paid exceptionally large dividends and had watered their stock, and on existing and anticipated federal and state legislation.[24]

Whatever the cause of their difficulties, railroad officials recognized the need to raise rates, but in 1908 both Roosevelt and the ICC frustrated their attempts. Hearing of proposed in-creases and eager to aid William Howard Taft's election, Roosevelt warned J. P. Morgan's man George W. Perkins that a rate increase would help Democrats. Politics triumphed, and Perkins reluctantly abandoned his rate hike. Roosevelt both cautioned the ICC to investigate any general-increase applica-tion and warned Attorney General Charles Bonaparte and New York Central Vice-President William C. Brown that railroads should not agitate for an increase until after the election. When a group of roads in August 1908 raised Texas rates (Bonaparte labeled the increases just, but the concerted action a con-spiracy), the ICC investigated and, though it ultimately ap-proved the commodity-rate increases, it denied virtually all the class-rate increases. The commission also ordered the Rock Is-land and Burlington lines to reduce rates in the Missouri River and Denver rate cases. When in 1910 the Supreme Court up-

24. Martin, *Enterprise Denied*, p. 132; Midgley to John C. Spooner, 27 November 1905, Spooner Papers; Memorandum by Speyer, 1 April 1907, enclosed in Speyer to Theodore Roosevelt, 1 April 1907, George B. Cortelyou Papers, Library of Congress.

held these reductions, it dispelled lingering doubts about the ICC's power over rates, and railroad stocks broke violently.[25] The Hepburn Act, coupled with Roosevelt's prodding, had transformed the ICC from an ineffectual peripheral body to an agency central to railroad interests. The ICC, however, used its considerable strength to preserve the status quo.

Not only did the ICC have power over rates, but its chairman began playing an important role in labor-management relations. Under the 1898 Erdman Act, he and the commissioner of labor could mediate railroad-labor disputes upon the request of one of the parties and could recommend arbitration if mediation failed. When the law was first invoked in 1899 by Pittsburgh district conductors and trainmen, railroad managers refused to mediate and the law remained a dead letter until 1906. Between that date and 1913, when the tougher Newlands Act replaced the Erdman Act, 61 requests were made and 28 were mediated, four arbitrated, eight decided by a combination of mediation and arbitration, and 21 by outside agreement either after mediation failed or one party refused to mediate. Reflecting the ICC's new-found power was the 10 percent raise and more significant 10-hour day with no pay loss (in effect a 20 percent raise) for those who had been on a 12-hour day, which Chairman Martin A. Knapp, mediating under the Erdman Act, secured in 1907 for western conductors and trainmen. Following Knapp's breakthrough award, railroad unions in the South and East had by 1910 secured substantial pay increases. Rising with the railway workers' standard of living was the cost of labor and with it railroad operating expenses.[26]

25. Martin, *Enterprise Denied*, pp. 132, 144–45, 187; Kolko, *Railroads and Regulation*, pp. 174–76; Railroad Commission of Texas v. Atchison, T. & S.F. Ry. Co. et al., 20 ICC 463 (1911); Interstate Commerce Commission v. Chi., R.I. & Pac. Ry. Co. et al., 218 U.S. 88 (1910), in *24th Annual Report*, 1910, p. 18; Interstate Commerce Commission v. Chi., B. & Q. R.R. Co., 218 U.S. 113 (1910); Sharfman, *ICC*, 2:390–92.

26. Gerald G. Eggert, *Railroad Labor Disputes: The Beginings of Federal Strike Policy* (Ann Arbor, 1967), pp. 224–25; Martin, *Enterprise Denied*, pp. 127–28.

Rejecting a General Rate Increase

Until 1910 railroads attempted individual rather than general rate increases. In late April 1910 the Western Traffic Association, representing twenty-four railroads west of the Mississippi River, filed with the ICC increased rates on 200 commodities. This move involved several hundred thousand individual rates and amounted to a general rate increase. A few days later the big eastern roads in Official Classification territory (north of the Ohio and east of the Mississippi) filed similar general increases. Since both commodity and class rates were to be increased, traffic volume would determine percentage increases, estimated from a conservative 3.7 percent (by eastern roads) to a more plausible 10 to 15 percent. Railroads filed these increases against a background of public hostility to carriers and rate increases and while Congress deliberated legislation to strengthen further the ICC. The injunction that Taft's Attorney General George W. Wickersham secured against the proposed western advances and the threat of an injunction against the eastern proposals postponed rate increases until the ICC could determine under new legislation whether they were merited.[27]

The new legislation—the Mann-Elkins Act of 18 June 1910 —originated in 1908 Republican campaign promises to increase railroad regulation. Wickersham constructed a bill enabling the ICC to supervise railroad securities and to suspend rate advances pending investigation, but also providing, at Taft's behest, for a commerce court to review ICC decisions and the legalization of traffic or pooling agreements between competitors. The last provision was especially objectionable to insurgent Progressives, particularly Senator Albert B. Cummins. Failing to please insurgents, Democrats, and even Elkins (who had introduced it), Wickersham's bill perished in the Senate Interstate Commerce Committee after Cummins had tacked on

27. Martin, *Enterprise Denied*, pp. 140–42; Sharfman, *ICC*, 3B:33– 34.

100-odd amendments. When Elkins and Cummins produced a new bill, the insurgents—younger and more vigorous than conservative champions Elkins and Aldrich—rallied around Cummins, who became the bill's chief architect. Unhappy with Taft's proposals, railroad officials inadvertently strengthened congressional insurgents by trying for a general rate increase in the last days of the debate. This rate-hike blunder outraged public opinion, hampered conservatives, and produced both an injunction and a more stringent act.

In the end the Mann-Elkins Act (named for its sponsors who were the heads of the appropriate House and Senate committees) offered something for everyone and passed the Senate by a 50-to-12 vote. Though not mentioning legalized pooling, the act allowed carriers to continue to set rates by concerted action, but as a check empowered the ICC on its own initiative to suspend rate changes up to ten months pending an investigation, and made railroads responsible for proving the reasonableness of both proposed increases and original rates. In addition, the act revitalized the long-short-haul clause by dropping the qualifying phrase "under substantially similar circumstances and conditions" and by providing that exceptions to section 4 be made only by the ICC, and it extended commission jurisdiction over telegraph, telephone, and cable lines. Though Cummins "crowed lustily," insurgents had not won everything. Despite Taft's wishes the act merely called for investigation rather than federal supervision of railroad finances and because of Taft's wishes established the Commerce Court, which Cummins predicted would quickly perish. While debate on the Hepburn bill had stressed the commission's administrative character, debate on the Mann-Elkins bill emphasized that the ICC was neither a court nor an executive branch but a committee or arm of Congress exercising "administrative legislative functions."[28]

28. Sharfman, *ICC*, 1:52–70; Winthrop M. Daniels, *American Railroads: Four Phases of Their History* (Princeton, 1932), p. 82; Martin, *Enterprise Denied*, pp. 183–93; Kolko, *Railroads and Regulation*, pp. 188–

Strengthened by the new law, the commission throughout
the fall of 1910 held hearings and took ten volumes of testimony on proposed freight-rate advances. First in New York and
later in Washington, the eastern railroads presented their case,
while western roads argued for advances in Chicago. Despite
the importance of the case, no commissioner went to New York
—special examiner George Brown presided—but Commissioners Franklin K. Lane, Judson C. Clements, and Edgar E. Clark
journeyed to Chicago for the western hearings. In both of these
proceedings, railroads were in trouble. Congress had insisted in
the Mann-Elkins Act that railroads justify rate increases. Fearing a conspiracy label, railroads in the New York hearings presented their cases separately and poorly with their officials
(usually vice-presidents) examined by their counsel, then cross-
examined by shippers' representatives. Railroad testimony that
the rising cost of wages, materials, and capital rendered the
proposed increases modest was unconvincing without comprehensive statistics and even failed to prove that some existing
rates were reasonable. Far more impressive were the "people's
lawyer" Louis D. Brandeis, representing the Traffic Committee
of the Commercial Associations of the Atlantic Seaboard, and
Clifford Thorne, representing several midwestern state-regulatory commissions and farm-marketing organizations. "So far as
the rates you do make are concerned," Brandeis rhetorically
questioned Charles F. Daly, vice-president of the New York
Central, "all you know about it is that inner feeling that comes
in the experienced man as to what is high enough and what is
not?" As Brandeis perceived, the gut reaction of railroad executive would not convince the ICC of a rate's reasonableness.[29] Railroads knew their overall operating costs and reve-

95; Cushman, *Independent Regulatory Commissions*, pp. 99–102. The
idea of a commerce court had been suggested as early as 1893, Commissioner Prouty had urged it in 1902, and the idea was kept alive primarily
by William Randolph Hearst. Ibid., pp. 84–85, 92.

29. For discussions of Advances in Rates—Eastern Case, 20 ICC
243 (1911), and Advances in Rates—Western Case, 20 ICC 307 (1911),
see Sharfman, *ICC*, 3B:33–48, and Martin, *Enterprise Denied*, pp. 194–
230.

nues, but had difficulty justifying specific rates; value-of-service ratemaking combined with the primitive state of cost accounting meant that a rate had little or no relationship to its cost, which at best was imagined.

With western roads as ill-coordinated as eastern roads, the Chicago hearings also went badly for railroads. When trying to prove western rates reasonable, Edward P. Ripley, the president of the Sante Fe, asserted that railroads based rates on "what the traffic will bear." His attempts to clarify his pungent, accurate, and unwise description of value-of-service pricing only intensified his blunder. "That does not mean all the traffic will bear," he explained, "it does not mean all that can be extorted or squeezed out of it, but what the traffic will bear having regard to the freest possible movement of commodities, the least possible burden on the producer and on the consumer. The Middleman," Ripley added in a hearingroom full of hostile middlemen, "can take care of himself." H. C. Lust of the Illinois Manufacturers Association proved him correct. Claiming that railroads had failed to substantiate their case, he urged the permanent suspension of rate advances. Nor were commissioners a comfort to railroad officials. Obviously unsure of what the Mann-Elkins Act meant, Commissioner Clark asked Lust how the ICC should proceed if railroads failed to justify the increases. Lane, the dominant commissioner at the Chicago proceedings, made his feelings clear when he asked, "Is it not true that deep down in the mind of the traffic manager he knows that even the present rate is too high?"[30]

When the eastern hearings reassembled in Washington, Chairman Knapp presided, but Louis Brandeis continued to dominate. He examined railroad Presidents James McCrea of the Pennsylvania, William C. Brown of the New York Central, and Daniel Willard of the Baltimore & Ohio to demonstrate that each of their railroads was "so large that no human being is capable adequately to supervise it." To prove that railroads could be more efficiently run, Brandeis produced scientific man-

30. Martin, *Enterprise Denied*, pp. 200–5.

agers, including Harrington Emerson, who maintained that railroads could annually save $300 million in labor costs. Emerson assumed railroads annually paid wages of $6 billion when in fact they paid $1.1 billion. To save $300 million, railroads would have had to fire nearly a third of their employees. Although both organized labor (which regarded scientific management as nothing more than a speedup) and railroad managers knew the $300 million figure was absurd, no effective response was made to Brandeis's accusations. Railroads in the future, however, would make more coherent, effective presentations. In late 1910 they established the Bureau of Railway Economics, equipped with a reference library and staffed by economists and statisticians.[31]

Before the ICC decided these rate-advance cases, important changes occurred in its personnel that indicated further trouble for railroads. Chairman Knapp, who appreciated the accomplishments and problems of railroads more than other commissioners, resigned in December 1910 to head the ill-fated Commerce Court. As a result of friction between the strong-willed Knapp and his colleagues, the commission seriously jeopardized its future effectiveness by rotating the chairmanship annually after Knapp's departure. Ironically Knapp—who left the ICC to become a judge—was the best-equipped commissioner to formulate a national railroad policy, while the remaining commissioners conceived of themselves as judges rather than as policy makers. To replace Knapp and to fill a second vacancy, Taft appointed the chairmen of the Kentucky and Wisconsin railroad commissions, Charles C. McChord and Balthasar H. Meyer respectively. McChord wrote the Kentucky railroad rate law, while Meyer, a nondoctrinaire, independent scholar of the railroad problem, favored cooperation rather than competition among railroads, coupled with rate regulation by a strong central body. Despite his dim view of the *Northern*

31. Ibid., pp. 206–19, 256–59; Samuel Haber, *Efficiency and Uplift: Scientific Management and the Progressive Era, 1890–1920* (Chicago, 1964), pp. 51–57.

Securities decision and his occasional prorailroad rulings as a state commissioner, Meyer as an ICC member consistently opposed rate increases and gave Senator La Follette (from his home state) no cause to oppose his reappointment to the commission.[32]

With the help of its new members, the ICC decisively vetoed freight increases. Dominant commissioners in February 1911, however, were Franklin K. Lane, who wrote the decision in the western case and privately argued that "the fixing of a rate is a matter of politics," and Charles A. Prouty, who spoke for the commission in the eastern case. After reducing the railroad's justification for an increase to "We need the money," Lane denied that money was needed. Relying heavily on statistics for 1910 (the best railroad year since 1907) and comparing them with those of 1900 or 1909, Lane concluded that "from the standpoint of net revenue and of dividends upon stocks the railroads of the United States as a whole have never before prospered . . . as they did in 1910." Lane taunted railroad officials for their propaganda that "railway regulation . . . is injurious to the American railroad" while seeking from the ICC rates which they could not reach or maintain without regulation. He blamed whatever problems railroads had on the questionable skill of railroad operators and the dubious ethics of railroad financiers, rather than on ICC regulation. Lane suggested that "under skillful management an additional tonnage may be handled under a higher wage schedule without increasing the cost of the service given," and that any lack of confidence in "railroad securities has come, we are convinced, rather from the too reckless policy of stock manipulators parading under the title of financiers than from any course of governmental policy on the part of the American people." Concluding that the carriers sought an increase not because they needed it, but "to discover the mind of the Commission with respect to the policy which the carriers might in future pursue and to secure if possible some commit-

32. Martin, *Enterprise Denied*, pp. 180–81, 238–39, 357–58; Miller, *Interstate Commerce Commissioners*, pp. 63–70.

ment on our part as to a nationwide policy which would give the carriers loose rein," Lane rejected "the effort of railroad counsel to establish this Commission *in loco parentis* toward the railroads."[33]

Though less hard-hitting than Lane, Prouty concluded that eastern railroads also had failed to justify an increase. Like Lane, he lectured railroad officials on scientific management and claimed that government regulation of railroad securities would improve, not harm, railroad credit. In addition, Prouty stressed the Progressive doctrine that reasonable rates could not be determined until profits were compared to actual railroad value and asked Congress to authorize the ICC to valuate railroad property. Prouty also warned railroads not to charge shippers for the "extravagant compensation" of their laborers and reproved railroad officials for their failure to handle increasing traffic adequately, particularly in 1907. Prouty insisted that investors should pay for improvements—even those not adding to earning power. "The stockholder," he said, "should not obtain both an adequate dividend upon his stock and an addition to the value of his property." Lane's and Prouty's decisions disappointed railroad managers and labor leaders, elated Progressives, pleased shippers, and convinced the nation that "the public gains and the railroads don't lose." Clearly in 1911 the ICC was not the captive of railroads; indeed it was hostile to them and friendly to shippers. And in these attitudes it reflected the Progressive views of Presidents Roosevelt and Taft and Senators La Follette and Cummins.[34]

The Commerce Court Threat and the Express System Triumph

Flying high after its popular rate decisions, the commission resented having its wings clipped by the new Commerce Court, headed by former ICC Chairman Martin A. Knapp. Keenly

33. Martin, *Enterprise Denied*, pp. 179, 224–25, 227; Sharfman, *ICC*, 3B:34–47.
34. Martin, *Enterprise Denied*, pp. 227–29, 231–34; Sharfman, *ICC*, 3B:34–47.

aware of conflicting economic interests and numerous regulatory bodies, Knapp hoped to rationalize their differences. He
clearly stated the problem:

> I see constant dangers in the present condition. Congress is con-
> stantly agitated. So are the legislatures of all the states. Forty state
> commissions are wrestling with the subject. There is the menace of
> stubborn conflict between the railroads and their two million or-
> ganized employees. Finally there is the menace of political influence.
> . . . The shipper is not always the underdog. Too often it happens
> that he is dishonest and that the carrier is wronged. The selfishness
> of human nature is apparent in all of these trials.

Under Knapp the Commerce Court tended to become, in the
words of Emory R. Johnson, "a second and superior" ICC. The
court enabled Knapp—who in his last years as head of the ICC
failed to dominate the commission—to reverse his former colleagues. And reverse them he did. By December 1911 the new
court had ruled on twenty-seven cases and in twenty had issued
either preliminary injunctions or final decisions favoring railroads. The Commerce Court sustained the ICC in only three of
these early cases in which the ICC and shippers were aligned
against a carrier. The Supreme Court, however, rescued the ICC
by reversing the Commerce Court in four of its first five decisions appealed to the higher court.[35]

The new court could ill afford to challenge the ICC in the
last years of the unpopular Taft administration. "The Commerce Court," Senator William E. Borah exclaimed, "was created under the lash." It owed its existence to Taft alone; the
public had not demanded it and Congress had not wanted it. It
could not afford what Felix Frankfurter called its courageous
"indifference to popular sentiment." The advantages of quickly
resolving disputed ICC decisions (six to eight months, rather
than nine to thirty months) were outweighed by the Commerce
Court's apparently prorailroad rulings in an era when the shipper, no matter how powerful, was still considered the underdog.

35. Martin, *Enterprise Denied*, p. 238; Emory R. Johnson, *Government Regulation of Transportation* (New York, 1938), p. 230; Sharfman,
ICC, 1:64–65, n. 71.

Congressmen and the public rallied to support the ICC when the Commerce Court seemed bent on pushing the commission back to its pre-Hepburn Act status. The Commerce Court sustained mortal wounds in July 1912 when the House impeached one of its members, Judge Robert W. Archbald, for securing contracts from litigants before the court and in January 1913 when the Senate convicted him of corrupt conduct. Congress killed the Commerce Court in October 1913 and with it the dream that it would create a "harmonious, consistent, and justly proportioned system of laws, rules, and regulations, governing interstate commerce in all its branches and phases."[36]

Congress strengthened the ICC not only by killing the Commerce Court but also by enlarging the commission's duties. The Locomotive Boiler Inspection Act (17 February 1911) increased the ICC's power to administer safety requrements and the Panama Canal Act (24 August 1912) required the ICC to prevent railroads from owning coastwise ships which used the canal. More important, Congress in March 1913 authorized the ICC to physically value railroad property. Prouty in 1914 resigned from the ICC to direct the new Bureau of Valuation, whose staff and expenditures became greater than those of all the rest of the ICC. The Bureau of Valuation's final report, issued after a twenty-year study costing the public and the railroads hundreds of millions of dollars, disproved assumptions by Progressives that railroads were overcapitalized, that dividends on watered stock masked excessive profits, and that railroads were making fabulous returns on their true investment. By the time the Progressive era arrived, water had been squeezed from

36. Sharfman, *ICC*, 1:60–70; Cushman, *Independent Regulatory Commissions*, pp. 89, 103. The Commerce Court rendered 43 decisions out of 94 docketed cases, and out of 22 that were appealed the Supreme Court reversed 13, modified 2, and affirmed only 7. Sharfman, *ICC*, 1:65, n. 71. Supporters of the Commerce Court argued, however, that these reversals were inevitable while its jurisdiction was being determined and were not relatively larger in number than reversals of circuit courts. Cushman, *Independent Regulatory Commissions*, pp. 103–4.

railroad stock by the reorganizations that followed railroad bankruptcies—particularly in the 1890s—and by the natural growth of value reflecting national development.[37]

While Congress could enlarge the ICC's authority, the extent to which the commission exercised its power depended on the energy and capacity of its members. The ICC could have rationalized the transportation system. The impact of the commission, particularly Franklin K. Lane, on rates and service of express companies illustrates what the ICC did accomplish in an important area and what determination by the commission could achieve for the transportation system. In 1912 the archaic, disorganized practices of the nation's thirteen express companies rendered their service unfailingly inefficient, consistently discriminatory, and frequently dishonest. Complex and confusing rates and classifications, universally misunderstood and misapplied, resulted in serious discrimination. In addition, unreasonable rates, frequent double charging, round-about routing, and difficulties in recovering damages and even COD collections compounded express company shortcomings. Wisely rejecting the case-by-case approach to the innumerable complaints against express companies, the ICC made all thirteen companies party to one proceeding.

The breadth and depth of the investigation and the two ensuing reports (1912, 1913) resulted largely from the tireless work of Commissioner Lane. "The express job is the biggest one yet," he reported as he threw his energy into working out a simple system for figuring express rates. Lane allowed only two classifications—general merchandise and foods and beverages —and divided the nation into 950 blocks bounded by each degree of latitude and longitude. For local rates, these blocks were subdivided 16 times. With rates no longer set from point

37. Sharfman, *ICC*, 1:105–11, 117–32, 271–72; Kolko, *Railroads and Regulation*, p. 173; Martin, *Enterprise Denied*, pp. 117, 228. For an extensive discussion of the valuation project, see Sharfman, *ICC*, 3A:95–319.

to point but from block to block, the possible number of rates was reduced from over 600 million to less than 345 thousand. The ICC also entered "into the minutiae of the billing, routing, and other details" and in all worked "a revolution and renovation in the methods and rates of express companies." Impressed by Lane's system, the post office adopted it when on 1 January 1913 it launched parcel post. With pardonable pride and a startling awareness of its potential, the ICC boasted: "This is probably the most important single piece of work ever done by the Commission, and is an illustration of the kind of constructive work by which this body can be of most assistance, both to the shipping public and to the carriers."[38]

Division and Confusion

Despite having overhauled express rates, the ICC soon neglected another opportunity to rewrite (on the basis of cost, not value-of-service) the more complex, more discriminatory, and the more significant freight-rate schedules. Though predicting in 1911 as he wrapped up the eastern case that future rate increases would be unnecessary, Commissioner Prouty had conceded that his forecast could be wrong and that "there might be ground for asking a further consideration of this subject." Eastern railroads, arguing in May 1913 that the ICC had misjudged the future, asked that the case be reopened. Citing "increases in capital charges, in wages, in the cost of fuel and ties, and in taxes, and because of the heavy additional burdens imposed by hours of service statutes, extra crew laws, employers' liability acts, elimination of grade crossings, and the installation of various safety devices and appliances," the carriers insisted that existing rates were unreasonable and unjust. "The plight of the railroads," labor economist W. Jett Lauck observed in January 1914, was that operating expenses per train-mile were 42 percent higher than in 1901 while revenues per train-mile had

38. In re Express Rates, Practices, Accounts, and Revenues, 24 ICC 380 (1912), 28 ICC 131 (1913), in Sharfman, *ICC*, 2:69–78; *Letters of Lane*, pp. 100–2.

increased only 33 percent. Increases in productivity—more powerful locomotives, bigger freight cars, longer and faster trains—could not compensate for rising operational costs.[39]

The ICC held hearings lasting from 24 November 1913 until 1 May 1914 on rates east of the Mississippi and north of the Ohio and piled up 19,000 typed pages of evidence. The railroad argument that operating costs were outrunning revenue elicited sympathy in unexpected quarters. "All rates on railroads should be increased, and at once," declared one of the nation's largest meat packers, J. Ogden Armour, even before the hearings began, and the Illinois Manufacturers Association —so effective in frustrating railroads in 1910—offered no opposition. While Daniel Willard of the Baltimore & Ohio led expert railroad witnesses, the ICC retained Louis Brandeis as special counsel to represent those opposed to a general rate increase. Although the *New York Times*—sympathetic to the railroad's cause—complained, "If Mr. Brandeis pleads in his former successful manner it will show to the country that the Commission is prosecutor rather than judge," Brandeis conceded that railroads needed relief. He estimated that they were underpaid $15 million for carrying the mail and that passenger rates and net earnings in Central Classification territory (Pittsburgh and Buffalo west to the Mississippi) were too low. He argued, however, that by eliminating switching and spotting freight cars on private sidings, carriers could save $50 million annually. Representing the regulatory commissions of eight western states, Clifford Thorne denied that railroads needed relief, claimed that their books were doctored and their stock watered, and insisted that a reasonable investment return could not be determined until the completion of the scarcely begun valuation program. Railroad managers accused Thorne of juggling data to argue his views and when pressed he admitted

39. Sharfman, *ICC*, 3B:47–48; Martin, *Enterprise Denied*, p. 248. On the Five Per Cent Case, 31 ICC 351 (1914), see Sharfman, *ICC*, 3B:48–66, and Martin, *Enterprise Denied*, pp. 267–94.

misunderstanding data, but blamed his blunders on confusing ICC reports.[40]

Both the personnel of the commission and the world situation changed during the fourteen months the ICC took to reach and publish its rate decision. Congress had enacted much of Wilson's domestic New Freedom program and a month-old crisis, starting with the assassination of Austria's Archduke Francis Ferdinand, culminated, the day before the ICC announced its decision, with Europe's plunge into World War I. Although Wilson did not intervene directly in what he conceived to be the judicial process of the ICC, his annual message in January 1914 observed that the prosperity of the railroads and the nation were inseparable, that railroad managers had "spoken very plainly and very earnestly" of their needs, and that "we ought to be quick to accept" their purpose. Both Franklin K. Lane and Charles A. Prouty, respective authors of the 1911 western and eastern rate decisions, had left the commission, as had Lane's promising young successor John H. Marble. Lane had become Wilson's secretary of the interior in March 1913; Marble, who as secretary of the ICC had become an expert on railroads and their problems, had died suddenly in November; and Prouty in February 1914 had become head of the railroad valuation program. Henry C. Hall, a Democratic lawyer from Colorado, and Winthrop M. Daniels were the commission's new members. Daniels had been Wilson's colleague and friend at Princeton, had served on the New Jersey Public Utilities Commission, and was the ICC's first economist, despite the fact that, as Lane perceived, it was "not . . . law but economics" that the commission dealt with.[41]

Bereft of Prouty's experience and Lane's force, the commission agreed neither on its role nor its new decision. The ICC ignored both the elaborate publicity campaign mounted by rail-

40. Martin, *Enterprise Denied*, pp. 271–85; Miller, *Interstate Commerce Commissioners*, pp. 71–76.

41. Martin, *Enterprise Denied*, pp. 267-70, 287–88; *Letters of Lane*, p. 71.

roads and Wilson's suggestions. Echoing the judgment of Brandeis, a divided commission granted a 5 percent increase—(with some significant exceptions—in Central Classification territory, denied any rate advance in Trunk Line (Pittsburgh and Buffalo east to the seaboard) or New England territories, and urged railroad officials to become more efficient. The commission had tinkered with but not questioned value-of-service ratemaking. McChord and Daniels dissented because they thought railroads deserved a 5 percent increase throughout Official Classification territory. The ICC also argued that it was responsible neither for general economic prosperity nor for keeping a particular railroad solvent. "We have no authority," the majority declared, "to approve rate increases with a view to stimulating business." While insisting that the poor fiscal condition of a railroad was no justification for upping rates, the majority reasoned that the poor financial condition of railroads in a given region did justify an increase. With a better grasp of the economic situation than his fellow commissioners, Daniels estimated the inflation rate since 1906 to be between 30 and 50 percent. He recognized that shrinking profits discouraged railroad investment, that higher rates were warranted throughout Official Classification territory, and that "such a solution of the present case would have done no less than justice to the carriers and would have promoted the welfare of the community they serve."[42]

Prompted by World War I and by disturbing statistics for the fiscal year ending in June 1914, the ICC agreed by mid-September to reconsider rate advances in Official Classification territory. While gross revenue in that year fell only 3.4 percent, net revenue shrank by 17.7 percent, with the war initially accentuating the pronounced traffic decline. When hearings were held in October, Thorne and Willard made their familiar arguments, but Brandeis attacked the inconsistent and unequal rate

42. Sharfman, *ICC*, 3B:63–66. Martin, *Enterprise Denied*, pp. 288–89, confuses the vote on this July decision with the December 1914 *Five Per Cent* decision.

system and stressed that mere need did not make rates just and reasonable. Less delicate about influencing the ICC than earlier, Wilson wrote Commissioner Daniels on October 29 of his "deep and serious anxiety. I believe," he said, "that a concession to the railroads is absolutely necessary to steady and relieve the present extraordinary difficulties of the financial situation." The ICC moved quickly; on 16 December 1914, by a five-to-two vote it extended the earlier 5 percent increase to Trunk Line territory. Once again the commission divided, but this time Clark, Meyer, and Hall agreed with McChord and Daniels while Harlan and Clements voted against the new increase. Agreeing with Brandeis, Harlan insisted it was "morally wrong" to raise standard rates before eliminating "inconsistencies, discriminations, and wrongful practices" that deplete carrier revenues in the rate structure itself. Harlan noted how New England carriers, shippers, and state commissions by revising and rationalizing rates had recently increased net revenue more than it would have been increased by a 5 percent rate hike. Clements, on the other hand, thought the financial condition of railroads irrelevant in deciding just-and-reasonable rates.[43]

Clearly there was an enormous range from Clements's narrow judicial view of the ICC's role to Daniels's broader administrative concern for the welfare of the carriers and the health of the economy. Based, as it was, on the financial needs of the railroads, the award marked, as Clements perceived, "a new and radical departure." Neither the ICC nor the courts had held previously that a carrier's need justified a rate increase.[44] Had the commission been swayed by Harlan's attack on the rate structure and exercised the same vision and power to reform rail rates that it had previously utilized to revolutionize express rates, it would have made a far more radical departure—one of incalculable value to the carriers and the nation. The 5 percent

43. Five Per Cent Case, 32 ICC 325 (1914), in Sharfman, *ICC*, 3B:66–71; Martin, *Enterprise Denied*, pp. 295–304; Kolko, *Railroads and Regulation*, p. 214.
44. Sharfman, *ICC*, 3B:71.

rate increase established a principle and a precedent, but besides accentuating inequities it was a mere token, offering railroads little relief.

The ICC promptly ignored its new precedent in the rate advance cases of 1915. Having carefully studied the eastern *Five Percent* case, leaders of western railroads based their proposed increases on need for adequate revenue. Rather than an across-the-board 2 percent rate hike, they requested increases (on ten heavily shipped commodities with unduly low rates) that would result in an overall 2 percent increase in freight revenue. The proposed passenger fare increased the previous 2 cents per mile to from 2.5 to 3 cents. The ICC hearings began in early March and lasted through late June. Railroad leaders argued their need to pay 7 percent dividends and to lay up a surplus to attract investors, while shipping interests—led by Clifford Thorne—claimed the roads exaggerated their operating ratio, watered their stock, and should wait for the physical valuation program's results (the equivalent of indefinite postponement).

The ICC's decision, rendered in August 1915, agreed that the western railroad-operating ratio had increased from 69 percent in 1901 to 79 percent in 1914, that labor costs were up, that returns on recently invested capital were down, that the market for railroad stock had declined, and concluded that the "increase in expenditures [was] not offset by an increase in receipts." After sympathetically discussing carrier finances the ICC largely ignored revenue needs in determining minuscule increases. The award raised freight revenue one-fourth of 1 percent and increased passenger fares from two cents per mile to 2.4 to 2.6 cents per mile. Reverting to the Clements position, the ICC made its previous *Five Percent* decision an aberration rather than a precedent.[45]

Again, the commission divided with Harlan and Daniels

45. Western Rate Advance Case, 35 ICC 497 (1915), and Western Passenger Fares, 37 ICC 1 (1915), in Sharfman, *ICC*, 3B:71–79; Martin, *Enterprise Denied*, pp. 306–9.

dissenting. Since railroads needed revenue and the proposed increases reflected the cost of service on specific commodities, Harlan did not object to their request. Daniels argued that western roads were needier than eastern roads, which had received 5 percent relief, and also suggested that the western decision—justified partly by the financial mismanagement of the Rock Island, the Frisco, and the Alton railroads—punished the "proprietors of a railway conducted with integrity and honesty" as well as the "luckless shareholders of a looted road." Arguing that the ICC should have a constant policy to which railroads could adjust, Daniels insisted that the commission choose either to deny rate increases despite rising costs—except in "individual instances of gross injustice"—or to permit reasonable increases to yield "earnings sufficient to provide a service commensurate with public needs."[46] Daniels, Clements, and Harlan had notions of the commission's role; confusion engulfed other commissioners and pervaded the ICC.

War, Chaos, and Another Rate-increase Rejection

Despite Daniels's warning, the ICC did not define its mission. It continued to hesitate, failed to enunciate a policy, and refused an administrative role. The commission remained blind to the signs impelling it to rationalize the national transportation system. With war raging in Europe and war preparations increasing in the United States, an efficient rail system was crucial. The Supreme Court had recently in the *Minnesota Rate* cases (1913) and in the *Shreveport* cases (1914) upheld ICC power to regulate intrastate rates that discriminated against interstate commerce. Pointing the way to federal supremacy in railroad regulation, the Court had elevated the ICC over state legislatures and commissions with their conflicting laws and regulations. Furthermore, when Congress destroyed the Commerce Court it in effect increased ICC responsibility for ra-

46. Sharfman, *ICC*, 3B:79–83; Martin, *Enterprise Denied*, pp. 309–10.

tionalizing regulations into a national transportation policy.[47]

More portentous were signs flashed by Wilson. His close advisers on railroad matters were Commissioner Daniels, former Commissioner Lane, and Senator Francis G. Newlands, chairman of the Senate Committee on Interstate Commerce; none of whom was pleased with the ICC. Wilson's December 1915 message proposed a "commission of inquiry" to investigate the entire transportation problem. After some additional prodding, Congress responded with a joint subcommittee chaired by Senator Newlands. Trying in the summer of 1916 to avert a nationwide rail strike during both his preparedness and presidential campaigns, Wilson urged railroads to concede labor the eight-hour day, while he promised to press the ICC to raise freight rates. Indeed his message to Congress on the eight-hour day called for two additional ICC members (who presumably would vote with Daniels and Harlan to raise rates), but the resulting Adamson Act (3 September 1916), which in five days passed both houses of Congress and received the president's signature, fixed the eight-hour day but failed to alter ICC composition. When Wilson renominated Daniels for a full seven-year ICC term, his appointment was confirmed despite strenuous opposition from Republican Progressives. By supporting Daniels in the face of this blistering attack, both Wilson and the Senate affirmed that they thought Daniels's viewpoint valuable for the ICC.[48]

Signs signaling the need for rationalizing the national rail system soon escalated into a demand for action. The severe winter of 1916 and 1917 was characterized by more freight—thanks to Allied war demands—rather than the usual post-harvest traffic decline. By February unrestricted submarine warfare made loaded ships loath to leave port and empty vessels scarce. With nowhere to unload, burgeoning freight cars glutted

47. Minnesota Rate Cases, 230 U.S. 352 (1913), Shreveport Cases 234 U.S. 342 (1914), in Sharfman, *ICC*, 1:84–86; Kolko, *Railroads and Regulation*, pp. 217–18.
48. Martin, *Enterprise Denied*, pp. 313–18; Cushman, *Independent Regulatory Commissions*, pp. 106–7.

eastern seaports while western centers needed empty cars. Railroad officials tried to alleviate traffic snarls caused by extra freight but were hampered by the ICA's antipooling clause. What was needed, exclaimed A. H. Smith of the New York Central, was a "super-commission."[49]

With freight entanglement increasing, the Newlands committee—including Congressman John J. Esch and Senator Cummins—began hearings in November 1916 and met sporadically throughout 1917. Congress had asked the committee to determine whether the ICC was overworked and to establish whether reorganization of the commission with increased membership or geographical decentralization was necessary. The committee was also to decide whether the ICC could approve blanket rate adjustments, whether railroads were or would be in need of capital, and whether the federal government should incorporate railroads engaging in interstate commerce and should regulate wages and hours as well as rates. Hoping to eliminate much state regulation and taxation, railroad officials pressed the committee for federal incorporation of railroads but were opposed by William Jennings Bryan and state commissioners. Julius Kruttschnitt, chairman of the Southern Pacific, argued that in real dollars (adjusted to inflation) freight rates had declined since 1899, that inflation had cost the roads $8 billion in revenue, and furthermore that higher wages (imposed by state legislatures and Washington) had absorbed savings achieved through increased freight-train tonnage. After April 1917, however, American participation in World War I preoccupied the Newlands committee and postponed its impact until Congress considered the 1920 Transportation Act.[50]

The war united carriers. After the Wilson administration urged railroads to cooperate, they formed on 11 April 1917 the Special Committee on National Defense of the American Railway Association (War Board). This ICC-supported effort to

49. Martin, *Enterprise Denied*, pp. 335–40.
50. Ibid., pp. 340–45; Cushman, *Independent Regulatory Commissions*, p. 116.

coordinate railroad operations broadened the scope of contemporary efficiency thinking, shattered old antitrust views, but proved unequal to the situation. Threatened with major rail strikes, the War Board tried unsuccessfully throughout 1917 to cope with car shortages and traffic congestion.[51]

The war emergency also led all railroads in March and April 1917 to request a 15 percent freight-rate increase. The ICC proceeded with unusual dispatch. It held hearings for a month and took 6,000 pages of testimony. As usual, the parade of witnesses included railroad officials rehearsing their litany of empty treasuries, rising costs, and high interest rates. Volume of traffic, however, had made 1916 a good year. After E. P. Ripley of the Santa Fe admitted under cross-examination that he hoped his road would earn a 15 or 16 percent profit in 1917, Clifford Thorne embellished his familiar litany with the taunt that if railroad presidents "were really patriotic they would withdraw these tariffs, say the emergency they anticipated has not transpired, and announce they were going to do their bit." Although many shippers, including agricultural interests and oil companies without pipeline access, agreed with Thorne, many others, among them industrialists, particularly from Illinois, were willing to pay more for better service. The shipper argument that an across-the-board percentage increase would upset competitive relationships impressed the ICC. The freight increase for western pine, for example, would be double that for southern pine in competing for the eastern market.[52]

By late June the ICC decided to reject again the railroads' pleas. Compared to their coveted, all-commodities 15 percent increase, they received little. Western carriers received a 15 percent increase merely on soft coal and coke; southern carriers received a 15 percent increase on soft coal, coke, and iron ore; and eastern carriers—having already received the soft coal,

51. K. Austin Kerr, *American Railroad Politics, 1914–1920: Rates, Wages, and Efficiency* (Pittsburgh, 1968), pp. 43–48, 54.
52. Kerr, *American Railroad Politics*, pp. 49–52; Martin, *Enterprise Denied*, pp. 348–49.

coke, and iron ore increase—were allowed a class-rate increase. The ICC estimated revenues would be increased by $100 million, which would offset the expenses incurred by the Adamson Act. The commission conceded that railroad revenue had dropped in February because of the severe winter, congestion, and increased labor, fuel, and supply costs but argued that the crisis was temporary. Confidently predicting that 1917 operating revenues would exceed those of previous years, the ICC insisted that improvements had occurred while the hearings were underway. Though many shippers did not protest the proposed 15 percent increase, the ICC would not disrupt rate relationships "between competitive localities, commodities, and territories" by granting a percentage increase on all commodities.[53] Carriers suffered the consequences of their elaborate complex of differentials among regions. These differentials reflected not the differing costs of providing transportation but what the traffic could afford to pay.

Though supported by four commissioners, the decision merely reflected the views of Clark and Hall. Objecting to the class-rate increase for eastern roads, Meyer and McChord dissented. Meyer argued that eastern roads had failed to prove a real emergency, and McChord reasoned that unsettled conditions made it unwise to advance rates and suggested that the ICC report the essential facts to Congress. If Congress should decide the prices railroads paid for fuel and supplies were reasonable, then the ICC should approve rate advances. At the other extreme, having hoped for more, both Daniels and Harlan supported the meager awards. Daniels said nothing, but Harlan exclaimed that the ICC's "month-to-month and purely statistical view" was neither adequate nor safe. All agreed, he pointed out, that to meet both war exigencies and peacetime needs the country must have "much larger terminals, more tracks, more cars, and more locomotives," yet, while population and commerce had increased since 1910, expansion of rail facilities had

53. Fifteen Per Cent Case, 45 ICC 303 (1917), in Sharfman, *ICC*, 3B:83–89; Kerr, *American Railroad Politics*, pp. 52–53.

decreased. Harlan was in agreement with large-scale shippers who equated increased rates with improved service and argued that the 15 percent increase would advance the public interest by increasing transportation facilities. Agreeing with Harlan, I. L. Sharfman, the sympathetic historian of the ICC, views the 1915 and 1917 rate-advance decisions as "strikingly hesitant and meager" responses to the railroads' plea of financial need.[54]

ICC Reorganization, Final Rate-increase Rejection, and Federal Control

The war also witnessed the reorganization of the ICC. Burdened with its workload, the commission both in 1915 and 1916 had asked Congress for two more members. In December 1916 Wilson had again asked that Congress enlarge and reorganize the ICC to enable it to deal promptly and thoroughly with its "many great and various duties." More commissioners and a commission reorganization were badly needed because of duties heaped on the ICC by the Hepburn Act (1906), the Mann-Elkins Act (1910), and particularly the Valuation Act (1913), which more than doubled the ICC staff. Additional duties were imposed by the Locomotive Boiler Inspection Act (1911), the Panama Canal Act (1912), and the Clayton Antitrust Act (1914), which compelled the ICC to enforce antitrust provisions upon carriers under ICC jurisdiction. The Clayton Act specified that certain types of railroad combinations restrained trade, and it forbade stock acquisitions between corporations engaged in commerce if the result lessened competition. Finally, with the Esch Car Service Act (29 May 1917), urged by the ICC on Congress to alleviate the wartime freight-car shortage, the commission's duties were again increased. This act required the ICC to establish reasonable car-service rules and to deal with service emergencies.

The national emergency coupled with renewed presidential and ICC prodding for more commision members brought action. On 9 August 1917 Congress increased the ICC to nine

54. Sharfman, *ICC*, 3B:89–97.

members and authorized it to form divisions of at least three members with power to act subject to review by the entire commission. In its October 1917 general administrative reorganization, the ICC formed three rotating divisions to hear and decide cases. Division 1 specialized in valuation matters, Division 2 in rate-increase applications and long-short-haul complaints, and Divison 3 in formal cases not orally argued. The commission also changed into bureaus its offices, previously called divisions. In 1917 there were bureaus of Correspondence and Claims, Tariffs, Safety, Locomotive Inspection, Car Service, Valuation, Carrier Accounts, Statistics, Inquiry, and Law. Neither the secretary's office—charged with administrative details—nor the special examiner's office—empowered by the Hepburn Act to administer oaths, examine witnesses, and take evidence in formal proceedings—was organized into bureaus. The shift in decision making from commissioners to examiners, which had begun with the creation of special examiners in 1906, was accentuated in 1917 when special examiners began preparing proposed reports (to which contending parties could object and argue against before a division or the full ICC).[55] By combining intelligence, energy, and will, a commissioner could still decide issues, but when presented with a proposed report weaker commissioners tended to ratify the examiner's views. The Progressive ICC boasted some independent commissioners, such as Knapp, Prouty, Clements, Lane, Daniels, and Harlan, who made up their own minds; later commissioners tended to rubberstamp their staff.

Besides reorganizing its administrative machinery in October 1917, the ICC also responded to railroad prodding and reopened the *Fifteen Percent* case. The hearings began the next month against a background of severe traffic congestion. Freight-car shortages that autumn closed coal mines for weeks, curtailed steel production, and alarmed shippers and government officials. Although the War Board tried to meet traffic snarls by

55. Ibid., 4:49–53; 70–86; Cushman, *Independent Regulatory Commissions*, pp. 106–7; *31st Annual Report*, 1917, pp. 59–61.

embargoing congested areas and by pooling eastern trunk-line facilities, confidence in the War Board ebbed sharply. Railroads warned the ICC that the war effort would be crippled and they would go bankrupt unless relief were granted. If the ICC refused the 15 percent raise, the alternatives were either a federal subsidy or federal ownership. Representing agricultural shippers, Clifford Thorne reasoned that since the Pennsylvania Railroad had a good credit rating and since freight receipts were high, there was no need to increase rates. Conceding that railroads had difficulty in obtaining capital and arguing that the government could command credit at low interest rates, unify the rail system, and prevent rate increases, Thorne proposed that the government operate the railroads. By 5 December the ICC once again refused the 15 percent raise, but to meet the war emergency it suggested unified railroad operation by either the carriers or the government. If carriers unified the rail system, antitrust laws and the ICA's antipooling clause would have to be suspended (though the War Board already was pooling eastern trunk-line facilities) and the government would have to provide capital and regulate railroad security issues. If, on the other hand, the president would operate the railroads as a unit, carriers would have to be insured a fair return, roads would have to be properly maintained, and the government would have to be repaid for its capital investment. Convinced that carriers were unable to unify the system and that only the government's strong arm could radically improve the transportation situation, McChord dissented. Growing chaos as another rigorous winter set in strengthened his view, and on 26 December 1917 Woodrow Wilson proclaimed presidential control of all rail and combined rail and water transportation systems (beginning 28 December 1917). Public control replaced private enterprise; compulsory unification replaced voluntary cooperation; and aggressive presidental administration replaced negative ICC regulation.[56]

56. Kerr, *American Railroad Politics*, pp. 54–71; Sharfman, *ICC*, 1:150–53; Martin, *Enterprise Denied*, pp. 349–51.

3

Power to Plan: World War I and the Twenties

~~~~~~

WORLD WAR I had enormous impact on the ICC. Although during the Progressive era the commission's objectives had been progressive, its tactics had been conservative. In effect, it was a standpat body that ignored inflation and refused rate increases, that accepted existing value-of-service rates, bearing little or no resemblance to the cost of service. It is impossible to say how long the ICC would have continued its negative, judicial stance if war had not exacerbated the growing transportation problem. To cope with wartime needs, the Wilson administration bypassed the ICC. For two years, while individual commissioners had influence and the commission itself performed assigned tasks, the ICC was subordinated; Wilson judged that independent regulatory commission unequal to the crisis. When the crisis passed, Congress—having learned some lessons and misunderstood others—restored a newly revised and updated ICC.

The Railroad Administration

By December 1917 virtually everyone backed federal control. Shippers thought unified federal control would manage railroads scientifically and produce savings, labor thought federal control would implement the eight-hour day and secure wage increases, and wartime administrators thought federal control would benefit the entire economy while expediting traffic. Even those whom federal control deprived of power agreed to the experiment. The ICC thought railroads' unification imperative, and railroad management—having been guaranteed income—thought Wilson's decision understandable. Universal acquiescence, however, should not obscure the fact that federal control was, in Commissioner Clyde B. Aitchison's words, a "mild revolution in transportation"—a revolution more acceptable in theory than in practice. Shippers soon discovered that efficient, unified scientific wartime control aimed to move traffic, not to keep down costs. In bypassing the ICC, federal control deprived shippers of their power over rates and ended the shipper-dominated Progressive phase of railroad regulation.[1]

As director general of the railroads, Wilson picked his secretary of the treasury and son-in-law. William Gibbs McAdoo was hard-working, pragmatic, able, and forceful, but besides running the railroads and the Treasury Department, he was chairman of the Federal Reserve Board, the Federal Farm Loan Board, and the War Finance Corporation. His chief task was financing the war, not directing railroads; but McAdoo nevertheless moved with dispatch. His general order number one (29 December 1917) outlined his policies. All railroads would be operated as a national transportation system, all equipment and facilities would be pooled, shippers could not designate routes for their consignments, and, to improve service, traffic agreements could be ignored and new routes established.[2]

1. K. Austin Kerr, "Decision for Federal Control: Wilson, McAdoo, and the Railroads, 1917," *Journal of American History* 54 (1967):556–60; K. Austin Kerr, *American Railroad Politics, 1914–1920: Rates, Wages, and Efficiency* (Pittsburgh, 1968), pp. 63–71. On federal control in general, see Walker D. Hines, *War History of American Railroads* (New Haven, 1928).

2. *Dictionary of American Biography*, Supplement Three, s.v. "McAdoo, William Gibbs" (hereafter cited as *DAB*); John J. Broesamle, *William Gibbs McAdoo: Passion for Change, 1863–1917* (Port Washington, N.Y., 1973), passim; I. L. Sharfman, *The Interstate Commerce Commission: A Study in Administrative Law and Procedure*, 5 vols. (New York, 1931–37), 1:155 (hereafter cited as Sharfman, *ICC*).

In both his proclamation of 26 December 1917 and his 4 January 1918 address to Congress, Wilson explained that the railroad's War Board lacked the authority to unify the nation's railroads; there are, he observed, "some things which the government can do and private management cannot." The financial condition of railroads concerned him, as did expediting the movement of men and matériel. Wilson maintained that it was necessary to protect railroad securities and that "all great financial operations should be stabilized and coordinated with the financial operations of the government. No borrowing should run athwart the borrowings of the federal treasury, and no fundamental industrial values should anywhere be unnecessarily impaired." To ensure a fair return, Wilson suggested railroads be compensated the average annual net operating income for the three years ending 30 June 1917.[3]

Congress ratified Wilson's actions and proposals on 21 March 1918. The Federal Control Act extended government operation no longer than 21 months after ratification of peace (not armistice) and appropriated $500 million for a revolving fund to finance federal operation. It detailed the payment of carrier compensation, authorized the president to initiate rates, allowed the ICC to review those rate changes on complaint but not to suspend them before its final decision, and admonished the ICC to remember that a unified, rather than a competitive, system was in operation and to take seriously a presidential decision to increase rates. Despite the general conditions specified by the act, contract agreements between the Railroad Administration and railroads were reached only after protracted negotiations. Sticking points usually concerned apportioning maintenance and improvement costs.[4]

In a variety of ways—many never contemplated by the ICC—the Railroad Administration profoundly affected rail

3. Sharfman, *ICC*, 1:144, 153–54.
4. Ibid., pp. 154–55, n. 31; Robert E. Cushman, *The Independent Regulatory Commissions* (New York, 1941), p. 108.

operation and wage and rate structure. To move men and war matériel more efficiently, the Railroad Administration required railroads to share cars and locomotives and to repair them at the closest facility; to share yards, depots, engine houses; to move freight by permit to prevent congestion; to speed loading and unloading by upping the penalty for detaining box cars; to consolidate small shipments into carloads; to ship basic commodities by trainload; to end cross-hauling soft coal; to reduce passenger service; to consolidate ticket offices; to curtail advertising; to centralize purchasing; to standardize new equipment; to simplify interroad accounting; and to assemble and analyze statistics.[5]

Before federal control, neither the ICC nor any government agency regulated railroad wages. Anxious to avoid strikes, the Railroad Administration created a Railroad Wage Commission —with former Interstate Commerce Commissioner Franklin K. Lane at its head—to investigate railroad wages. That commission reported on 30 April 1918 that wages were low in relation to living costs, and on 25 May 1918 the Railroad Administration ordered wage increases retroactive to 1 January 1918. To study inequities and to formulate labor policies, this celebrated general order 27 set up a Board of Railroad Wages and Working Conditions, which awarded several supplementary wage raises. These substantial war-cycle raises, upping hourly rates 100 percent and costing $965 million, reflected rising living costs. The Railroad Administration accepted collective bargaining and allowed labor and management equal representation on the Board of Railroad Wages and Working Conditions and its three subordinate adjustment boards (designed to settle grievances and disputes). Thanks to the Railroad Administration and to strengthened unions, railroad labor made greater gains during the 26-month period of federal control than in all previous years.[6]

5. Sharfman, *ICC*, 1:155–57.
6. Ibid., pp. 158–60, n. 36.

Under wartime federal control, rate regulation yielded vastly different results. For years the ICC had refused significant general rate increases; but within five months (again on 25 May 1918) the Railroad Administration bowed to the rising price level and ordered an 18 percent passenger and a 28 percent freight raise. Charged with managing railroads, the Railroad Administration looked on rates with a manager's eye, while the ICC, charged with maintaining just-and-reasonable rates, looked on rates with a shipper's eye. Even with higher rates and increased war traffic, the Railroad Administration lost $200 million in 1918; with peace and a business slump, the deficit multiplied in 1919 and reached $1.2 billion for the 26 months of government operation. Most of that loss represented war-cycle raises.[7] Unified, scientific government-operation achieved enough efficiency to win the war but could not hold down rates, operating expenses, and deficits. The Railroad Administration experience frustrated shippers and bolstered prewar railroad arguments for more revenue.

During the 26 months of federal control, the Railroad Administration sidetracked the ICC but made frequent use of individual commissioners and staff members. Balthasar H. Meyer, Edgar E. Clark, Henry C. Hall, and George W. Anderson, for example, helped draft the standard contract agreement between the Railroad Administration and the roads; Robert W. Woolley worked on economizing locomotive fuel; Aitchison strove to eliminate soft coal cross-hauling; James S. Harlan mediated local disputes; and Charles C. McChord served on Lane's Railroad Wage Commission. Perhaps more significant, the ICC's Bureaus of Safety Inspectors, Carriers' Accounts, and Statistics "helped launch the Railroad Administration" and functioned throughout federal control. The commission made a significant contribution when it investigated and recommended that the director general institute uniform rules and descriptions throughout the Official, Southern, and Western freight classification territories. The administration, however, ignored the com-

7. Ibid., pp. 157–58, n. 35.

mission's advice to mollify shippers by holding hearings before changing rates. Fearing a delay of two to three years, Wilson bypassed the ICC and raised rates administratively. The Railroad Administration consulted ICC rate experts but not the commission, except to gain informal approval for a scheme already agreed upon. The ICC could not suspend wartime rate increases, and it chose not to exercise its power to review them. With its workload cut in half, the ICC continued hearing "in a half-hearted sort of way" rate cases begun before federal control.[8]

Angered by rate increases, shippers and their state-regulatory-commission allies sought and received Republican congressional support to curtail the Railroad Administration and revive ICC power. McAdoo countered with three regional and thirty local traffic committees charged with modifying rate changes and settling disputes. Although at first railroad managers dominated these committees, Walker D. Hines, who early in 1919 succeeded McAdoo as director general, increased shipper representation and resisted pressure to raise rates. Still resentful despite these conciliatory actions, shippers backed a Federal Control Act amendment restoring ICC power to suspend proposed rate increases and granting state commissions authority over intrastate rates. With the ICC remaining discreetly neutral, the measure—formulated in part by Clifford Thorne and sponsored by Senator Albert B. Cummins—passed the Republican-dominated Congress in November 1919 despite concerted opposition from the Railroad Administration, railroad managers, labor, and investors. Unified federal control was in danger even though Hines and the Railroad Administration convinced Wilson to veto the bill, which divided responsibility between the Railroad Administration and the ICC and gave state commissions veto power over a federal agency.[9]

8. Kerr, *American Railroad Politics*, pp. 110–14; Sharfman, *ICC*, 1:166, n. 42; Hines, *War History of American Railroads*, pp. 192–94.
9. Kerr, *American Railroad Politics*, pp. 116–27; Sharfman, *ICC*, 1:163–64, n. 40; Hines, *War History of American Railroads*, pp. 86–87, 199–200.

Scientific Management

The Railroad Administration had functioned credibly in difficult times, but its enemies refused to acknowledge that fact. Before the armistice, it successfully provided transportation necessary to win the war; after the armistice, it provided adequate transportation at wartime rates but failed to expand facilities, to sustain employee morale, and to halt mounting deficits. There is no reason to believe that private management, which failed in the early war months, could have weathered better the 1919 postwar recession, spiraling costs, and disastrous coal strike. While acquiescing to wartime control, private management after the armistice became eager to resume command, and the public became less willing to continue federal railroad control as a scientific experiment.[10]

Most people, however, gave lip service to scientific management, and many were convinced it could be achieved through continued federal control. On 11 December 1918, a month after the armistice, Director General McAdoo asked Congress to extend unified control until 1 January 1924, approximately five years. Extension, McAdoo argued, would "Take the railroad question out of politics for a reasonable period," would "give composure" to railroad management and employees, would "increase the efficiency of the transportation machine" through better roads and terminal facilities, would ease the financing of improvements, and would help "indicate the permanent solution of the railroad problem." Hines agreed that federal control in the difficult reconstruction period would both stabilize railroads and help solve their problems.[11]

It was natural for McAdoo and Hines to protect their agency, but even the ICC warned against a "precipitate" end to federal control while arguing for a "broadened, extended, and

10. Sharfman, *ICC*, 1:166–70; Hines, *War History of American Railroads*, pp. 230–33.
11. Sharfman, *ICC*, 1:170–71, n. 49; Kerr, *American Railroad Politics*, pp. 136–43.

amplified governmental regulation" of private ownership and operation. Indeed, despite its diminution of ICC power, two commissioners wished to extend federal control. Stressing its success and its "promise of better things," Commissioner Woolley concluded that a five-year extension was necessary since no workable plan for restoring railroads to private management existed.[12]

The ICC's newest member, Joseph B. Eastman, had the highest hopes for federal control. Destined to become the most distinguished commissioner between the wars, Eastman as a progressive protégé of Louis D. Brandeis had been identified with shipper concerns and had served on the Massachusetts Public Service Commission before joining the ICC in early 1919. Objective and independent, Eastman had neither party, church, nor wife, and favored neither shippers, management, nor labor. He not only backed extension but thought that permanent national control would solve the railroad problem by ensuring necessary low-cost capital, by avoiding "unduly high rates," by solving the weak-road problem, by obtaining "operating advantages . . . from unification," and by promoting good labor relations. Despite the pleas of McAdoo and Hines and the advice of Woolley and Eastman, congressmen—swayed by public dissatisfaction with the Railroad Administration—refused to extend federal control. "More deliberate lies were told," Eastman later wrote, "in regard to what happened during federal control than there have been upon almost any subject that I am acquainted with."[13]

In the name of scientific management, the railroad labor

12. Sharfman, *ICC*, 1:171, n. 49; U.S., Congress, Senate, Committee on Interstate Commerce, *Extension of Tenure of Government Control of Railroads*, 3 vols., 65th Cong., 3d sess., 1919, 1:232–39, 271. Woolley had earlier served under McAdoo as director of the mint. Broesamle, *McAdoo*, p. 80.

13. *DAB*, Supplement Three, s.v. "Eastman, Joseph Bartlett"; Sharfman, *ICC*, 1:171, n. 49; Kerr, *American Railroad Politics*, p. 142; Clarence Atha Miller, *The Lives of the Interstate Commerce Commissioners and the Commission's Secretaries* (Washington, 1946), pp. 87–95.

unions proposed the only serious plan for nationalization. It was originated by Glenn E. Plumb—general counsel of the Railroad Brotherhoods—who blamed the "low degree of managerial skill" among railroad officials on the manipulations of Wall Street financiers. The Plumb plan proposed that the federal government purchase the railroads by selling $18 billion in bonds (roughly the physical value of railroads); that the government lease the roads to a corporation run by fifteen presidentially appointed directors equally representing the public, the operating officials, and the operating employees; that the corporation pay a rental fee; that the government halve surplus revenue with operating officials and employees; that the government's surplus revenue-share be used either to finance additions and improvements or to amortize bonds and that the railroad's half be distributed among officers, who would receive a double dividend, and employees; and that the ICC regain control over rates and lower them when the government's profits exceeded 5 percent of its investment. Attracting enthusiastic support from the Railroad Brotherhoods and some intellectuals, the Plumb plan got lukewarm support from the American Federation of Labor and encountered hostility from farmers and shippers, fearing rate hikes; the general public, fearing Reds and nationalization; the ICC; and railroad investors and management. By the fall of 1919, it was obvious, even to the Railroad Brotherhoods, that Congress would neither enact the Plumb plan nor extend federal control.[14]

With the war over, the Republican-dominated Congress reasserted both its and the ICC's authority. Long a Progressive foe of railroads and a friend of farmer-shippers, Senator Albert B. Cummins, who was open to new ideas, had quietly communicated with Director General Hines and had learned from the Railroad Administration experience. Cummins became convinced that the railroad problem was rooted in weak-road-strong-road competition, making it impossible to regulate rates

14. Sharfman, *ICC*, 1:171, n. 50; Kerr, *American Railroad Politics,* pp. 161–74.

equitably without impoverishing weak roads or enriching strong ones. To preserve private ownership and the operational advantages of federal control or public ownership, Cummins proposed that a new transportation board consolidate, by force if necessary, profitable and unprofitable railroads into regional systems. He further suggested that the transportation board admininister railroad corporation finances and security issues, that the ICC set rates to insure invested capital a fair return, that the government guarantee minimum earnings, that excess earnings be recaptured and placed in a fund jointly administered by the transportation board and industry, and that money from this fund be redistributed both for capital improvements and as a cushion against depression. Cummins's proposal also mandated that labor disputes be arbitrated (by the transportation board, if necessary) and that railroad strikes be outlawed. The ICC would continue its ratesetting, accounting, and valuation functions, while the transportation board would concern itself with consolidating, financing, and operating railroads—even directing their traffic when necessary.[15]

Though less revolutionary than the Plumb plan, the Cummins bill also proposed to manage railroads scientifically and differed sharply from Progressive-era regulatory practice. Shippers feared and labor loathed this bill, which sought to eliminate competition, guarantee earnings, prescribe a ratesetting rule, and eliminate strikes. Although railroad management liked guaranteed earnings and a rate formula, strong roads disliked compulsory consolidation and most roads opposed the redistribution clause. On the other hand, Daniel Willard of the Baltimore & Ohio, whom Cummins had consulted, recognized that Congress could not guarantee a weak road's earnings while permitting a competing strong road exorbitant profits. Willard supported the Cummins bill's financial sections, as did railroad investors.[16]

In place of the Cummins bill's mandatory consolidation by

15. Kerr, *American Railroad Politics*, pp. 143–49.
16. Ibid., pp. 149–59.

a transportation board, the ICC favored permissive consolidation under its supervision. By eliminating many competing railroads, consolidation would reduce and simplify rate cases. Indeed if consolidation could not be achieved, the ICC urged that railroad pools—banned since 1887—be legalized and regulated to reduce competition. In defending its record and its preserve, the commission aligned itself with shippers who were disenchanted with the Railroad Administration, who feared mandatory consolidation, and who wished to restore the Progressive-era ICC. Implying that regulation had failed, the Cummins bill gnawed at the commission's self-esteem. In addition to supervising consolidations, the ICC suggested—and shippers agreed—that with the return of normalcy the commission should regulate minimum as well as maximum rates, control new issues of railroad securities and capital expenditures, and plan for national railroad coordination in emergencies. "The Commission," *Traffic World* confidently announced, "is the friend of the shipper."[17]

The Transportation Act of 1920

To formulate a plan was simpler than getting it through Congress. While seriously considering neither the extension of federal control nor the Plumb plan, Congress did grapple with both the Cummins bill and the ICC's proposals as summarized in the Esch bill. Chairman of the House Committee on Interstate and Foreign Commerce, John J. Esch was the lower house's counterpart of Cummins. Probably written mainly by Commissioner Clark, the Esch bill formed the substance of the 1920 Transportation Act. It guaranteed railroad earnings for only a six-month period between public and private control and empowered the ICC to regulate union terminals, car service and other facilities, extension or abandonment of lines, issuance of new railroad securities, and the creation of consolidations and pools. The bill did not provide a separate agency to supervise railroad operation but trusted ICC wisdom and initiative, did

17. Ibid., pp. 146, 179–80, 198–203.

not draw guidelines on consolidation and pooling, and did not lay down a ratemaking rule, which the commission had requested. Unchanged except for the addition of a Railway Labor Board to mediate wage disputes, the Esch bill passed the Republican-dominated House by a 204-to-161 partisan vote on 17 November 1919. The Senate altered the Cummins bill by replacing guaranteed minimum railroad earnings with instructions to the ICC to set rates for a five-year period to provide a 5.5 percent return on the fair value of railroad property. Despite general opposition by La Follette, who warned in a speech ("practically prepared" in Commissioner Woolley's office) that the bill would "mortgage the people of this country to the railroads," and opposition to the antistrike provision by prolabor senators, the Cummins bill passed the Senate on 20 December by a 46-to-30 bipartisan vote.[18]

Neither house, however, would agree to the other's bill, and a conference committee, meeting from late December to mid-February, wrote the Esch-Cummins bill. The committee's stormy sessions reflected the concerns of shippers pressing for the Esch bill's competition and ICC regulation, of railroad management and investors agitating for the Cummins bill's financial arrangements, and of labor insisting on the right to strike. In the end, Cummins made more concessions than Esch, railroads gained less than shippers, and unified scientific management was left to ICC discretion. Compulsory consolidation, the transportation board, and the antistrike clause were swept away, but Cummins salvaged most of his bill's financial sections. The compromise transportation bill passed by comfortable majorities on 21 February 1920. After hesitating because of labor opposition, Wilson signed the bill into law on 28 February. He had been assured by Commissioner Winthrop M. Daniels that, though cumbersome, the bill was desirable. The new act ended federal control on 1 March 1920, guaranteed railroad earnings for a transitional six-month period, created a

18. Ibid., pp. 204–11; Cushman, *Independent Regulatory Commissions*, p. 117.

Railroad Labor Board to settle disputes, and increased both the
membership of the ICC (from nine to eleven) and its power
over railroad rates, finances, and service. The act also empowered the commission to protect weak roads from destructive
competition by setting minimum and even exact rates, departed
from the old just-and-reasonable rule, but stopped short of
guaranteeing income in prescribing that for the next two years
rates should yield well-run roads a 5.5 to 6 percent return on
their physical value, stipulated that the ICC recapture half the
earnings of a road exceeding 6 percent of its physical value for
a contingent fund—from which weak roads could borrow at 6
percent interest—and instructed the ICC to favor weak roads in
dividing joint-haul rates. The act further allowed carriers to
pool and combine if the ICC judged service would be improved
and competition would not be "unduly" restrained, required the
ICC to prepare a consolidation plan dividing railroads into a
limited number of systems which would preserve competition
"as fully as possible," allowed the ICC to regulate intrastate
rates that discriminated against interstate rates, and made into
law the commission's long-short-haul policies. The new law also
required that railroads obtain ICC permission to issue new railroad securities, regulated—through the commission—car distribution, called for automatic train control and other safety
devices, required ICC permission for building new lines and
abandoning old ones, empowered the ICC to insist on an adequate transportation service even if it would mean extending
existing lines, and in emergencies empowered the commission to
unify the nation's railroads.[19]

Reflecting shipper desires more than railroad interests and
ignoring the aspirations of labor, the Esch-Cummins Transportation Act left the hard and crucial decisions to the Railway
Labor Board and the ICC. The act endorsed but failed to im-

19. Kerr, *American Railroad Politics*, pp. 211–21; U.S., Interstate
Commerce Commission, *Interstate Commerce Commission Activities,
1887–1937*, 1937, pp. 44–45; Clair Wilcox, *Public Policies Toward Business*, 4th ed. (Homewood, Ill., 1971), pp. 376–77; Sharfman, *ICC*, 1:177–
244.

plement or adequately define principles of scientific management, competition, and consolidation. Its answers to the questions of guaranteed earnings for railroads, of a ratemaking rule, of the right to strike also were limited, tentative, or ambiguous. If its public and railroad members agreed, the Labor Board could force labor agreements and prevent strikes. The ICC could plan but not force consolidations, could approve but not mandate pools, could foster or hinder competition, could guarantee or deny railroad earnings through its ratesetting powers, and could determine for a community the quantity, quality, or existence of rail service. By giving enormous authority to the ICC, the Transportation Act seemed to revive Progressive-style regulation, but the commission's task of keeping rates down and competition up was replaced by the broader, more positive challenge of planning for the needs of both the shipping public and the carriers. The war experience had forced railroad officials, congressmen, and the general public to make the "most thoroughgoing and intelligent examination of the railroad problem . . . that had ever taken place" and to accept changes that under ordinary circumstances would not have come for decades.[20]

Enforcing the New Rule of Ratemaking

Congress had protected the shipper and, thanks to wartime transportation experience, also had empowered the ICC to fashion "a more rationally conceived, stable, and profitable railroad industry." The Supreme Court in upholding the constitutionality of the 1920 Transportation Act emphasized that it introduced a new railroad policy. Congress had previously instructed the ICC to prevent abuses—particularly rate discrimination—but the 1920 act, Justice Brandeis remarked, "sought to ensure, also,

20. Kerr, *American Railroad Politics*, pp. 222–31; Cushman, *Independent Regulatory Commissions*, pp. 105, 116. We are indebted to Kerr for sorting out the views of railroad management, investors, shippers, and labor. Although he recognizes the innovations in the Esch-Cummins Act, Kerr emphasizes more than we have that it restored the Progressive era system of private operation and ICC regulation, that it "involved no fundamental changes in the regulatory system."

adequate transportation service." Speaking for a unanimous
Court, Chief Justice William Howard Taft declared that the
"new act seeks affirmatively to build up a system of railways,"
that it "aims to give the owners of the railways an opportunity
to earn enough to maintain their properties and equipment,"
and that to "achieve this great purpose, it puts the railroad
systems of the country more completely than ever under the
fostering guardianship and control of the commission."[21] Far
from hampering the ICC as it had in the 1890s, the Supreme
Court of the 1920s agreed that the commission was responsible
for a rail system adequate to handle interstate traffic; that it
would have to solve transportation problems; that it would have
to lead; that, despite Franklin K. Lane's earlier denial, Congress
had established the ICC in loco parentis toward the railroads.
The ICC's Progressive stance of simply negating rate-increase
requests no longer sufficed.

New tasks led the ICC in 1920 to reorganize further along
lines drawn in 1917. Eleven commissioners formed five divisions (with some commissioners serving on more than one division). The new Division 4 handled the commission's recently
acquired financial powers and Division 5 its authority over service. In addition, Division 4 soon entered into rotation with the
first three divisions in hearing cases. Continuing its reorganization, the ICC (with a staff of approximately two thousand appointed under Civil Service Commission rules) thoroughly
overhauled its bureaus. It created a Bureau of Administration
with the ICC secretary at its head and a Bureau of Finance. It
also converted the Bureau of Correspondence and Claims into
the Bureau of Informal Cases, the chief examiner's office into
the Bureau of Formal Claims, the Bureau of Tariffs into the
Bureau of Traffic, the Bureau of Car Service into the Bureau of
Service, and the Bureau of Carrier Accounts into the Bureau of
Accounts. The ICC left intact the existing Bureaus of Safety,

21. Kerr, *American Railroad Politics*, pp. 222–23; New England Divisions Case, 261 U.S. 184, 189 (1923), and Dayton-Goose Creek Ry. v.
U.S., 263 U.S. 456, 478 (1924), in Sharfman, *ICC*, 1:178–79.

Locomotive Inspection, Valuation, Statistics, Inquiry, and Law.[22]

Although commissioners increased their capacity by dividing their responsibilities, they were still unable to keep up with their burgeoning workload in the 1920s. In the fiscal year 1928, for example, Division 4 decided 469 rate cases and 548 finance cases, or approximately four cases each working day. The overwhelming press of work required the staff of the ICC to originate all and to make most of its decisions. Former Commissioner Thomas F. Woodlock recalled in 1930 that each formally docketed case came to the commissioner as a staff report summarizing "the pleadings, the testimony and the contentions of the parties" and providing the division or the commission with a decision for adoption. To apply the law to the facts in the case, Woodlock noted, the commissioner must be certain of them and "for this surety he must rely largely upon his staff, and the staff of the commission."[23] Furthermore, overwork, fragmentation, and specialization made long-range, overall planning difficult. With commissioners working in separate divisions and involved in different cases, it became even harder for the commission to formulate the broad principles that would seek "affirmatively to build up a system of railways."

Rate regulation remained the commission's central activity. The ICC could set minimum as well as maximum rates, could prescribe rates that would provide efficient carriers a fair-investment return, and could recapture a portion of excess earnings. These powers, coupled with control over railroad finance and organization, gave the ICC the capacity to regulate rates constructively. Unfortunately, a farsighted rate policy was neither formulated nor implemented. Beginning with a postwar inflation, the decade experienced in 1921 a sharp recession which was followed by general prosperity until the 1929 crash. But throughout the twenties agriculture and coal, both important to rail freight, remained depressed. Competition from the new

22. Sharfman, *ICC*, 4:53–54, 70–86.
23. Ibid., pp. 292–96.

trucking industry kept railroads from petitioning frequently for rate increases and caused them occasionally to seek permission to lower their rates in accordance with the ICC's new minimum-rate power. Aware that increased rates did not always produce increased revenue, railroads relied more on increased efficiency. Despite ICC power over rates, railroads did not earn the prescribed fair-return on their investment. The 1929 crash and the ensuing depression accentuated railroads' financial problems.[24]

There were thousands of specific rate cases in the 1920s but only three general ones: *Increased Rates* (1920), *Reduced Rates* (1922), and *Revenues in Western District* (1926, argued in 1925). By the summer of 1920, mounting rail deficits made increases necessary. Consonant with the new ratemaking rule, the ICC suggested that all railroads ask for increases to enable a 6 percent investment return. The suggestion pointed up the controversy over railroad worth. Although railroads claimed to be worth more than the aggregate book value of eastern roads ($9 billion), southern ($2.2 billion), and western ($8.8 billion), the commission disagreed. "Without the slightest analysis of the pertinent evidence," Sharfman notes, "and without the slightest reference to guiding principles" (the Valuation Bureau had not completed its findings), the commission arbitrarily valued the eastern group at $8.8 billion, the Southern at $2 billion, and the western at $8.1 billion. These "precise" figures, based on impressionistic use of fragmentary data, were not only utilized in the 1920 rate decision (the first time valuation figures were used to compute rates), but were revised, updated, and used in subsequent decisions.

Computing a fair return from either set of figures revealed a low net operating income. By early 1920 eastern railroads, with an operating ratio of 97.68, were showing a deficit. This high ratio demonstrated that operating expenses, which excluded fixed charges, virtually wiped out operating revenue. While southern and western railroads were better off, their net operating incomes were a mere fraction of 6 percent of either their

24. Ibid., 3B:98–102.

book value or the scaled-down ICC figure. The financial situation became more serious in July 1920 when the Railroad Labor Board increased wages $618 million, a figure exceeding railroad net operating income. Relief was needed and, with valuation figures, the amount could be calculated. A unanimous ICC upped passenger rates 20 percent (during the war they had been raised to three cents a mile). Freight rates were increased 40 percent for eastern roads, 25 percent for southern, 35 percent for western, 25 percent for mountain-Pacific roads, and $33\frac{1}{3}$ percent for intergroup freight. The urgent situation impelled the commission to grant railroads enormous percentage increases, which it realized would destroy existing differentials and relationships.

Only three years earlier the ICC had refused a 15 percent rate increase. During the intervening years, however, America had participated in World War I and had experienced federal railroad operation, increased inflation, an enormous rate increase (1918), shifting congressional attitudes, and passage of the Transportation Act. The congressional shift from just-and-reasonable rates to fair-investment-return rates changed the ICC's vantage point from that of the shipper to that of the railroad and changed the commission's almost automatic refusal to disturb rates to its almost mechanical formula computation of new rates.[25]

In 1921 a business depression shrank railroad traffic and revenues. The commission realized that rates must be reasonable for shippers as well as profitable for railroads and that higher rates could reduce revenue, while lower rates could yield larger returns. After considering rates anew in late 1921, the commission in 1922 ordered general decreases and reduced the fair-return rate to $5\frac{3}{4}$ percent. Although the actual 1921 return rate was only $3\frac{1}{3}$ percent, by early 1922 traffic volume was up and operating expenses down. The commission predicted that net railroad income would exceed $5\frac{3}{4}$ percent of railroad value. Agreeing with shippers that "freight rates . . . must come down,"

25. Increased Rates, 1920, 58 ICC 220 (1920), ibid., pp. 102–15.

the ICC cut the 1920 advances from 40 to 26 percent for eastern railroads, from 25 to 12½ percent for southern and mountain-Pacific roads, from 35 to 21½ percent for western roads, and from 33⅓ to 20 percent for interterritorial traffic. The ICC initiated an investigation, unhesitatingly forecast the future, reduced rates to increase volume and revenue, and harmonized shipper and railroad interests. Shucking its usual passive, negative, judicial stance, the commission in 1922 displayed imagination, flexibility, forcefulness, and dispatch.[26]

After 1922 the commission maintained status-quo rates. Neither agricultural groups suffering from depressed conditions nor western roads arguing inadequate income—resulting from the agricultural depression—were able to lower or raise rates. The ICC generally rejected reduced-rate petitions because railroad returns—already below the 5¾ percent level—were inadequate. Clamoring for relief, farmers induced Congress to pass the Hoch-Smith Resolution (30 January 1925) directing the ICC to consider adjusting freight rates to aid depressed industries in general and agriculture in particular. Realizing that railroads based their rates on the value, not the cost of service, Congress asked the ICC to adjust rates to what the depressed agricultural traffic could bear. When the ICC accordingly created Division 6 and investigated freight-rate charges for agricultural products, western railroads seized the initiative and petitioned for a general 5 percent rate increase (plus 15 percent for northwestern carriers). Changing emphasis, the resulting ICC hearings focused more on the proposed advances than on adjusting the rate structure of agricultural products. Though western railroad's 4.12 percent 1925 return seemed inadequate, the commission, refusing to accentuate the agricultural depression with higher rates, authorized no change. Shippers could not afford higher rates nor could railroads afford lower ones. Had

26. Reduced Rates, 1922, 68 ICC 676 (1922), ibid., pp. 115–34. Sharfman regards this ICC investigation and decision as its high-water mark in rate regulation.

rates been based on the cost of service, the ICC's task would have been relatively simple, but the rate system was an elaborate network of discriminations balancing discriminations, which the ICC was loath to disturb. From time to time, the commission made specific rate adjustments but only when circumstances were particularly distressing.[27]

Adjusting rates to alleviate distressing circumstances plunged the ICC into its greatest controversy of the 1920s. Besides illustrating how value-of-service ratemaking arbitrarily discriminates between regions, the lake-cargo-coal controversy showed how difficult it was to implement the Hoch-Smith Resolution, how Congress applied pressure on the ICC, and how control over minimum rates enhanced ICC power. In 1925 the commission refused to reduce coal rates from the depressed Pennsylvania and Ohio fields to Lake Erie ports, but the ICC reversed itself in 1927 and gave those fields, despite their high production costs, an advantage over nonunionized, competing southern fields. When railroads serving southern coal fields in West Virginia and Kentucky wiped out that advantage by cutting rates to maintain the previous, narrow 25 cents differential between the northern and southern fields, the ICC in 1928 refused that reduction. The amount of the differential determined whether the northern or the southern fields would control the Lake Erie coal markets, whether one region would prosper while the other languished. The Federal District Court, however, reversed the ICC's attempt to maintain the broad 45 cents differential with Judge John J. Parker accusing the commission of regulating "industrial conditions under the guise of regulating rates." The ICC carried its struggle to the Supreme Court, but the carriers involved in the controversy worked out a compromise differential, the ICC did not interfere, the issue became moot, and the Supreme Court made no determination. After getting its bearings in 1927, the ICC maintained that although it

27. Revenues in Western District, 113 ICC 3 (1926), ibid., pp. 134–61.

considered the Hoch-Smith Resolution in rate deliberations the commission's primary aim was relatively reasonable rates. But in the two-year span the commission had reversed itself regarding relatively reasonable rates, and the resulting fierce sectional controversy had generated enormous political pressure. Wholly or in part because of that controversy, the Senate, stressing with unusual vigor regional representation on the ICC, in 1928 rejected the reappointment of Commissioner John J. Esch—the prestigious former congressman who had shaped the 1920 Transportation Act—because he had reversed himself in the lake-cargo-coal controversy, voting with the majority both times. The Senate was aware that the ICC with its complete power over rates could not only make or break communities but—far exceeding traditional railroad power—could make or break sections.[28]

The recapture of half a railroad's earnings above 6 percent was the 1920 Transportation Act's most novel feature. Although the Supreme Court found these recapture clauses constitutional ("the key provision" of the new rate policy), they proved impossible to administer. There was a fundamental controversy over property value (which determined excess income), and to avoid having their earnings recaptured railroads attempted to hide their net income by artificially linking strong-road earnings with weak-road earnings and by excessive payments to affiliates or officers. Attempts to recapture earnings provoked bitter and prolonged litigation and yielded little income for the little-used railroad contingent fund. The recapture clauses failed to average good and bad years, often penalized weak roads and favored strong ones by using property values to

28. Lake Cargo Coal Rates, 1925, 101 ICC 513 (1925), 126 ICC 309 (1927), Lake Cargo Coal 139 ICC 367 (1928), Anchor Coal Co. v. U.S. 25 Fed. (2d) 462 (1928), United States v. Anchor Coal Co., 279 U.S. 812 (1929), ibid., pp. 651–56, 661–67. See also ibid., 2:461–64. The Senate in 1930 rejected Parker's appointment to the Supreme Court not because of the lake-cargo-coal controversy but because of his conservative, antilabor, anti-Negro, partisan Republican reputation. Richard L. Watson, Jr., "The Defeat of Judge Parker: A Study in Pressure Groups and Politics," *Mississippi Valley Historical Review* 50 (1963):213–34.

determine excess income, and failed to help troubled roads through the contingent fund by requiring too much security and interest. Although the commission estimated that between 1920 and 1930 recapturable excess income amounted to over $300 million, railroads from 1920 to 1931 merely reported $23.5 million, half of which was subject to recapture. By November 1932 payments to the fund totaled only $9.9 million, most of which was subject to litigation and unavailable for loans. Beset with administrative problems, the commission suggested amendment of these clauses and then called for repeal. In 1933 Congress ended the experiment, and the contingent fund was returned to contributing carriers.[29]

Planning Railroad Consolidations

The ICC's greatest opportunity for constructive leadership was in planning consolidations and in permitting traffic revenue pools. Originally created to foster railroad competition, the ICC was told in 1920 to foster railroad combinations. Consolidation became the panacea competition had been in the decades surrounding the turn of the century. The antipooling clause of the 1887 Interstate Commerce Act, the 1890 Sherman Antitrust Act, and the Supreme Court's 1904 *Northern Securities* case had all emphasized competition, while the 1920 act, though attempting to preserve competition, put its faith in consolidation. Consolidation would provide better service and more economy, would eliminate excess profits by solving the weak-road-strong-road problem, and would facilitate the implementation of the new ratemaking rule and the recapture of excess earnings. Of all these, service was the most important. As Sharfman remarks, the financial as well as the consolidation provisions of the 1920 act reflect "the new emphasis upon service, conceived in terms of national need rather than of corporate advantage."[30]

The congressional theory of consolidation seemed perfect,

29. Sharfman, *ICC*, 3B:221–55.
30. Ibid., 1:187, n. 24.

but the ICC's half-hearted attempts to achieve it yielded less than perfect results. In May 1920 the ICC began work on consolidation and in August 1921 the commission announced its tentative plan consolidating railroads into nineteen competitive systems. The ICC plan modified—by eliminating two systems— the plan prepared for the commission by William Z. Ripley, professor of economics at Harvard University and one of the nation's leading transportation experts. Although the ICC did not elaborate on its plan, it published Ripley's maps and explanations. Over the next two years, while transportation conditions improved, the commission held extensive hearings and discovered not only hostility to specific groupings in its plan, but strong feeling that consolidations were neither necessary nor desirable. Above all, railroads, particularly strong ones, wished to plan their own consolidations. These essentially negative hearings left the ICC divided and intimidated. Initially the commission had jealously guarded its "complete control over . . . this constructive policy" of consolidation, but by 1923, with Commissioners Eastman, Esch, and Hall dissenting, the ICC narrowly construed the 1920 act to permit consolidations under state law without the commission considering their effect upon the overall consolidation plan. "It is an ill-considered and unsound finding," Eastman exclaimed, that "will gravely impair, if it does not destroy, our power to administer successfully what the authors of the transportation act, 1920, deemed to be one of its most constructive and important provisions. . . . I am wholly unable to accept a construction of the law which reduces the plan of consolidation to a state of helpless futility."[31]

Overwhelmed by conflicting proposals and a mountain of

31. Henry J. Friendly, *The Federal Administrative Agencies: The Need for Better Definition of Standards* (Cambridge, Mass., 1962), p. 159; Securities Application of Pittsburgh & West Virginia Ry., 70 ICC 682 (1921), in Sharfman, *ICC*, 2:253; Acquisition and Stock Issue by N.Y.C. & St.L. R.R., 79 ICC 581 (1923), ibid., p. 256, n. 137; Robert B. Carson, *Main Line to Oblivion: The Disintegration of New York Railroads in the Twentieth Century* (Port Washington, N.Y., 1971), pp. 74–79.

contradictory evidence, the commission failed to agree on a final consolidation plan. After a year, on 4 February 1925, the ICC informed the Senate Committee on Interstate Commerce that a majority of the commission would prefer merely to guide consolidations that develop "in a more normal way." Unaccustomed to planning and unable to break habits of more than three decades, the ICC tried to relinquish its responsibility to plan consolidations. In 1926, 1927, and 1928 the commission repeated its plea to be relieved of this obligation. When Congress took no action, the commission in 1929 reluctantly adopted a plan (similar to its earlier tentative effort) that would consolidate railroads into nineteen systems plus two Canadian ones.[32]

That the commission had little sympathy for its plan soon became obvious. The four major eastern systems—New York Central, Pennsylvania, Baltimore & Ohio (B&O), and Chesapeake & Ohio (C&O)—objected to the fifth eastern system (Wabash-Seaboard) proposed by the ICC but could not decide how that system's properties should be divided. On 30 December 1930, however, President Herbert Hoover, having prodded the four major railroads into negotiations, announced with obvious approval that they agreed on a four-system consolidation plan. By publicizing his prejudgment of the plan, Hoover applied pressure on the ICC and, given his power to appoint, threatened its independence. On the other hand, the commission, even without presidential encouragement and apart from whatever virtues the new plan possessed (practicality for one) preferred to follow rather than lead railroads into consolidation. After extensive hearings, it adopted as its own the four-system plan (which involved no actual consolidations but was simply a blueprint).

The commission's failure to shape consolidations galled

32. Consolidation of Railroads, 159 ICC 522 (1929), in Sharfman, *ICC*, 1:189–90, n. 27; 3A:474–88; U.S., Congress, Senate, Committee on Commerce, *National Transportation Policy*, 87th Cong., 1st sess., 26 June 1961, S. Rept. 445, pp. 237–39, 262–63; Carson, *Main Line to Oblivion*, pp. 79–86.

Eastman. Congress, he growled in his dissent, should "have asked a few of the larger railroads to agree upon a plan for the distribution of the lesser railroads among them. . . . In fact, the [four-system] plan has in large part already been accomplished. This has been done at great cost and mostly without our approval. We have found that to a very considerable extent it was done illegally." Specifically, Eastman cited the Pennsylvania, which for years had controlled the Norfolk & Western, which had violated the Clayton Act and paid extravagant prices to control the Wabash and the Lehigh Valley, and which through its Pennroad Corporation (a holding company) had controlled the Pittsburgh & West Virginia and had a substantial interest in the Seaboard Air Line. The B&O also violated the Clayton Act by controlling the Western Maryland, as did the Nickel Plate (controlled by the C&O) when it acquired control of the Wheeling & Lake Erie. "Thus," Eastman concluded, "were the essential parts of the proposed system No. 7 [Wabash-Seaboard] seized, shackled, and kept out of mischief." Thus also did the ICC supinely ratify the seizure.[33]

In addition to consolidation planning, the 1920 Transportation Act granted the ICC authority over railroad combinations —power to regulate interlocking directorates, pools, leases, and stock purchases. By prescribing terms and conditions for its permission, the commission could determine cooperation among carriers and "mold in full detail" a national transportation policy. Unless the ICC approved, the new act forbade officers or directors from serving more than one railroad. This provision empowered the ICC to allow communities of interest congruent with its consolidation plan while preventing combinations among competitors. To prevent "patent and flagrant abuses," the ICC generally kept an individual from sitting on competing

33. Consolidation of Railroads, 185 ICC 721 (1932), in Sharfman, *ICC*, 2:457–58, 3A:488–93; Carson, *Main Line to Oblivion*, pp. 87–91. Sharfman, however, thinks that the modification "on the basis of realistic considerations, appears to merit approval." Sharfman, *ICC*, 3A:492.

railroad boards but allowed multiple directorships within a system and where there was no conflict of interest. But the commission was flexible and encouraged the twenties' "unbridled speculative temper" by occasionally approving temporarily interlocking directorates of competing carriers if one had acquired a controlling interest in the other. From 1922 to 1933, out of 4,920 applications involving 10,827 persons wishing to serve on more than one board, the ICC denied only 17. By not prohibiting interlocking directorates outside of its proposed systems, the ICC failed to mold a national rail system.[34]

Though railroads had demanded legalized pooling since 1887, by the time the 1920 Transportation Act permitted it (subject to ICC approval), railroads preferred to combine through the more effective options of lease-control and stock-purchase (also subject to ICC approval). Throughout the 1920s carriers proposed only two freight and two passenger pools, which the ICC unhesitatingly approved. The ICC could request but not force railroads to pool, and its efforts to foster that policy were not successful.[35]

While vacillating over its consolidation plan, the commission acquiesced to at least 298 combinations, involving 51,000 track miles, and facilitated piecemeal consolidation "at the expense of the comprehensive and orderly reorganization of the railroad systems of the country." Indeed despite dissenters—particularly Eastman—the ICC, by complaisantly authorizing newly consolidated companies to issue stock, allowed consolidations which had taken place under state laws without ICC approval. Furthermore the commission claimed no jurisdiction when a holding company acquired all the stock of two carriers "inasmuch as the holding company is not a carrier" and the 1920 Transportation Act referred only to acquisitions by carriers. While preferring proposals that conformed with its tentative consolidation plan, the ICC doomed that plan and failed to

34. Sharfman, *ICC*, 3A:25–27, 385–404, 430.
35. Ibid., pp. 404–22.

direct railroad consolidation by authorizing contrary acquisitions of control.[36]

The 1920 Transportation Act with its emphasis on service also gave the commission sweeping power over extensions and abandonments. Railroads usually sought to abandon unprofitable lines, and these applications were opposed by the communities served. The ICC had to determine public dependence and whether it justified forcing a railroad to absorb operating deficits. "Guided primarily by financial considerations," the commission generally approved abandonments, particularly when alternative transportation was available. The new act also required the commission to approve and even compel extensions. Proposed extensions into another road's territory proved most controversial. In addition to determining the self-sufficiency of the proposed line, the ICC had to estimate the competition it would engender and the traffic it would divert. In the 1920s the results of such crystal-ball gazing were mixed: the commission both denied applications to construct "needless, costly, and wasteful duplication of existing facilities" and approved applications to construct competing lines to stimulate "efficient operation" because "competition, within reason, rather than monopoly, is in the public interest." Striving to avoid interference with carrier initiative, the ICC tended, in Sharfman's words, "to subordinate the long-time interests of the railroad system . . . to the immediate advantages of the parties directly concerned." Solving the emerging problem of excess carrying capacity required not only a liberal policy on abandonments—which the ICC had—but also a stringent policy on extensions.[37]

Responding to the desires of railroad management, the ICC was reluctant to prevent and loath to compel railroad extensions. It initiated no demand; either shippers or communities

36. Ibid., pp. 430–74, particularly 436–40, 451.
37. Construction by Piedmont & Northern Ry., 138 ICC 363 (1928), Construction of Lines in Eastern Oregon, 111 ICC 3 (1926), ibid., pp. 356–59. See also ibid., pp. 327–67.

provoked the few involuntary-extension proceedings. In these cases the ICC largely determined public need by estimating the proposed line's self-sufficiency. Since financial considerations dominated its thinking, the ICC attempted to enforce but one involuntary extension. In this lone case, decided by the ICC in 1929, the prosperous Union Pacific balked at being forced to construct a 185-mile line in eastern Oregon, and in 1933 the Supreme Court concurred. Although three Interstate Commerce commissioners (Ezra Brainerd, Patrick J. Farrell, and Thomas F. Woodlock) agreed to curtail their power, three Supreme Court justices (Benjamin N. Cardozo, Louis D. Brandeis, and Harlan Fiske Stone) vigorously dissented. Justice Cardozo maintained that Congress intended the Transportation Act of 1920 to make the commission "an effective instrument for the development of railroad transportation."[38]

While the ICC traditionally preferred inaction, its lethargy in the 1920s reflected the drift of the federal government away from progressivism. Specifically, the controversy surrounding Woodlock's appointment to the ICC revealed a formidable but declining Progressive influence, a more formidable and ascending big-business influence, and an underlying concern for sectional representation heightened by the lake-cargo-coal-rate controversy. Initially a combination of southern and Progressive senators twice blocked the confirmation of Woodlock—financial editor of the New York *Sun* and a board member of the Pere Marquette and Frisco railroads. Undaunted, President Calvin Coolidge in March 1925 with the Senate in recess appointed Woodlock (who had resigned his railroad offices) and gained his subsequent confirmation by also appointing Richard Taylor of Mobile and promising Senator David A. Reed of Pennsylvania that he could name the next ICC commissioner (in December 1926 Reed named Cyrus E. Woods, and while

38. Public Service Commission of Oregon v. Central Pac., Ry. Co., 159 ICC 630 (1929), Interstate Commerce Commission v. Oregon-Washington R. Co., 288 U.S. 14 (1933), ibid., pp. 377–85. See also ibid., pp. 367–73.

Coolidge agreed the Senate did not concur). Robert M. La Follette—the recently defeated Progressive presidential candidate—predicted on the evidence of Woodlock's appointment to the ICC that for four years big business would govern the nation.[39]

Supervising Railroad Finances

Planning the consolidation of carriers into a national rail system and controlling the organization of those carriers were opportunities the Transportation Act gave the ICC to lead; supervision of railroad finances provided the commission a further opportunity to shape the railroad industry. Since financial abuses destroyed profits and credit, upped rates, and cut service, the ICC had long desired to supervise railroad securities. Supervision, the ICC hoped, would protect investors from fraud and would rehabilitate railroad credit, which in turn would enable railroads to maintain reasonable rates and adequate service. Furthermore by approving new security issues and new financial obligations through leases and other arrangements, the ICC had further control over railroad combinations.[40] Once again, however, the ICC failed to use its new power.

Maintaining that railroads policed themselves and reluctant to interfere with their management, the ICC administered the Transportation Act's financial sections permissively and approved most applications for security issues. Although few twentieth-century railroads watered their stock, the prime reason Congress gave the ICC authority over securities was the persistent fear of overcapitalization. The commission's modest attempts to prevent overcapitalization caused railroads little hardship. Indeed the ICC permitted overcapitalized roads new issues of stock, provided the new stock itself did not represent

39. Ibid., 4:26–27, n. 80; *New York Times*, 1925 and 1926, passim, particularly 25 and 29 January, 26 and 27 March, 2 and 17 April, 13 September, 2 October, 22 and 23 December 1925, 3, 4, and 10 January, 24, 25, and 27 March, 18 November, 20, 21, and 24 December 1926.
40. Sharfman, *ICC*, 1:189–93.

overcapitalization. In general, the commission sought to keep capitalization below a carrier's road and equipment assets, but since valuation-project results were not available until 1933, the ICC simply relied on the carrier-reported book value and judged each case on its apparent merit.[41]

The commission's tendency, however, to authorize the distribution of surpluses as stock dividends met with strong dissent. Eastman opposed this practice, arguing that since surplus earnings were derived from the public they should be held in trust for public benefit and were not owned absolutely by the carriers. Besides violating the implied trust doctrine, capitalization of surpluses impaired a road's credit by increasing fixed charges, while surplus reserves strengthened a road. The main objective of stock dividends, Eastman pointed out, was to disguise actual profits by increasing stockholder dividends without increasing dividend rates. Although railroads did not become overcapitalized in the 1920s, the ICC's "undue readiness" to approve stock dividends weakened railroads' ability to cope with the Great Depression.[42]

The commission in 1920 also gained power over the types of securities issued, but once again it failed to lead forcefully. During the twenties the ICC in the "vast majority of instances . . . accepted without question" proposed new security issues, which assumed many forms of stocks and bonds. The types and proportions of stocks and bonds issued by a railroad frequently spelled the difference between a sound or a weak financial condition, between control by relatively small investors or large investors. Generally speaking, railroads secured more capital from long-term, interest-bearing bonds than from dividend-paying stock and made little effort to replace maturing bonds with new stock issues. The greater a railroad's bonded indebtedness the heavier were its fixed charges and the more vulnerable its finances, particularly during a depression, because bondholders could foreclose if a railroad defaulted. Although

41. Ibid., 3A:506–13.
42. Ibid., pp. 513–26.

sound railroad and public policy demanded that railroads reduce their bonded debt by issuing more stock, the ICC sought
simply to prevent increased debt. The commission, once again,
did not initiate policy but reacted—usually favorably—to railroad proposals which throughout the 1920s maintained, with
minor fluctuations, a 56 percent ratio of debt to capitalization.
In the late twenties railroads did issue relatively more stock
(from 5 percent of railroad securities issued in 1925 to almost
35 percent in 1930), but, despite the demand for their stock,
railroads failed to reduce their bonded indebtedness by increasing stock issues further. Finding railroads unprepared for its
onslaughts, the depression devastated their traffic receipts and
pushed their stock issues back to their 1925 level. Though the
commission usually rejected schemes to issue nonvoting preferred stock which would provide new capital for an enterprise
without unseating its management, it routinely accepted proposals to issue no-par stock without critically examining its
effect on the ICC's valuation project. Encouraging but not forcing railroads to issue sound types of securities, the commission
steered a course that avoided both the laissez faire attitude of
Woodlock and the watchdog attitude of Eastman. The ICC refused proposals it deemed unworthy but did not "impose any
far-reaching reforms upon prevailing financial practice."[43]

The ICC was reluctant to shift from passive railroad regulating to active railroad administration. Despite the fact that the
terms on which a railroad sells its securities can affect its financial strength and endanger the public interest, the commission
was hesitant to substitute its judgment for that of railroad managers. Even though selling securities below par value and allowing excessive discounts, fees, and commissions can result in
overcapitalization and exorbitant dividends and interest rates,
the ICC refused to prevent this practice and, after judging individual circumstances, sometimes permitted weak roads to sell at
less than par value. In addition, against its better judgment the
commission in 1929 allowed the Chesapeake & Ohio to issue

43. Ibid., pp. 527–53.

300,000 new shares at par value rather than insisting that it follow the ICC's suggestion to issue 200,000 new shares at $150, which was close to market value. "We are not greatly impressed," the ICC noted, "with the advantages" of the new proposal. In disapproving of a policy that might reduce the common-stock dividend rate, the ICC observed that stockholders who sold their rights under the new proposal would "more than double the amount which would follow from an issue at $150 per share." Having stated its misgivings, the commission eschewed positive leadership by concluding, "We realize, however, the latitude in action which must be preserved to private management."[44]

The cost of floating bond issues occupied the ICC more than the price of stock. Bankers and underwriters secured their fees and commissions by buying securities low and selling them high. For example, in 1920 the New York Central sold noncompetitively $25 million worth of 7 percent collateral-trust bonds at a 3.4741 percent discount to J. P. Morgan & Company, which sold the bonds at a 3 percent discount to its own syndicate, which in turn sold them at par to the public. Though the public oversubscribed the issue, the whole transaction cost the road $868,525 and J. P. Morgan & Company received $118,525 for organizing the syndicate which grossed $750,000 of which $274,870 was net profit. Though it questioned the noncompetitive liberal commission, the ICC approved the terms because the postwar securities market was unsettled. In the 1920s, however, by scrutinizing proposed issues and frequently insisting that banks pay railroads a higher price, the commission narrowed the gap between what bankers and the public paid for railroad bonds. The 1920 Transportation Act may have contributed further to this scaling down of bank profits by prohibiting investment bankers from serving as railroad officers and directors. Yet the ICC was content to influence rather than to

44. Control of Erie R.R. and Pere Marquette Ry., 138 ICC 517 (1928), Proposed Control of Erie R. and Pere M. Ry. Cos., 150 ICC 751 (1929), ibid., pp. 556–60.

command and exercised its control of railroad finances with marked restraint. After some delay, it required in 1926 competitive bids for equipment-trust certificates (a safe, stable security) and the spread between what bankers and the public paid shrank from $1.80 per $100 in 1925 to $.64 in 1928. In contrast, the spread in noncompetitive bond sales during the same period merely dropped from $2.95 to $2.33. Despite obvious advantages to carriers, the ICC in 1930 rejected competitive bidding except for guaranteed terminal bonds.[45]

Control over securities issued enabled the ICC to influence the reorganization of bankrupt railroads. Since courts supervised the complex negotiations for reorganizing a bankrupt road, the ICC was loath to reject court-approved arrangements even when it doubted the road's capacity to meet fixed charges. Most commissioners were willing to approve an admittedly defective reorganization plan for the Chicago, Milwaukee & St. Paul, or any other road, if the new plan improved previous conditions, while Eastman and his supporters insisted that the reorganized St. Paul be financially "prepared to face periods of business depression as well as periods of prosperity" without increasing its bonded indebtedness. Eastman's positive and constructive policy would have forced reorganization managers to structure finances both to avoid future bankruptcy and attract new capital. In part the commission remained aloof because it did not wish to determine the losses suffered by the various classes of security holders. For example, the St. Paul reorganization (under the auspices of Kuhn, Loeb, and the National City Bank) involved great sacrifice on the part of the bondholders and scant loss by stockholders—who had plunged the road into bankruptcy. While Eastman labeled the plan unfair, the majority of the commission, citing agreement by coerced and unorganized bondholders, accepted the plan. The ICC struck a positive note in the St. Paul and other late-1920s cases when it regulated the compensation of reorganization managers, but the

45. Bonds of New York Central R.R., 65 ICC 172 (1920), ibid., pp. 560–62. See also ibid., pp. 562–77.

Supreme Court in 1931, with Justices Stone, Oliver Wendell Holmes, and Brandeis dissenting, would not allow the ICC to alter the amount stockholders agreed to pay the St. Paul reorganization managers. Further castigating the "arbitrary and irresponsible" way in which the St. Paul was reorganized, Eastman suggested that in the future bankers and lawyers not dominate proceedings but simply provide technical advice, that various groups of security holders be represented, that reorganization managers not be affiliated with interested bankers or security holders, that the plan be ICC-approved before submission to security holders, and that the confusing dual railroad bankruptcy jurisdiction of the ICC and the courts be ended. These recommendations, needed in 1928, became imperative with the Great Depression and helped shape section 77 of the 3 March 1933 Bankruptcy Act. While jurisdiction remained divided, that act assigned the commission "an intimate and perhaps dominant rôle" in reorganizing bankrupt railroads.[46]

Clearly the results of the 1920 Transportation Act were disappointing. Prior to that act, the ICC primarily regulated rates and practices, but thanks to the war experience the ICC had power not simply to check abuses but to control and shape the nation's rail system. The commission, however, chose not to lead and shied away from interfering with private management's decisions concerning railroad organization and finance. Having originally programed the ICC to reflect congressional bidding, Congress gave the commission authority to determine policy, but the ICC was unwilling to innovate bold plans or to generate power to support its policies. To solve the railroad problem and provide a rational transportation system, the ICC needed to plan, shape, innovate, and act, but it continued merely to reflect power and respond to pressure from other sources. By the mid-1920s Congress was more concerned with local and sectional interests and with laissez faire than with scientific management,

46. Ibid., pp. 577–617. See in particular Chicago, Milwaukee & St. Paul Reorganization, 131 ICC 673 (1928), and United States v. Chicago etc., R. Co., 282 U.S. 311 (1931), ibid., pp. 587–611.

and the commission reflected this change. Rather than act upon the nation's transportation problem, the ICC reacted to it.

In the 1920s the ICC was usually content to accept management's inclinations to abandon old or build new facilities, and its passive regulation of railroad securities deferred to private management's wishes even against the dictates of the commission's better judgment. Furthermore, the commission's reluctance to formulate a consolidation plan and its willingness to approve combinations with scant reference to its tentative plan negated the ICC's capacity to organize a consolidated rail system. The ICC did not, Sharfman observed, "free the railroad industry, by drastic and painful action, of the accumulated burden of past ills," nor did it "establish principles and practices for this regulated industry beyond and above those recognized in the general competitive field." Although railroads during the twenties both grew in strength and improved in service, they later failed to recover from the Great Depression because the ICC had not pressed them during the prosperous twenties to reduce their bonded indebtedness and to consolidate, as Congress desired, into a few strong competing rail systems.[47]

47. Ibid., pp. 617–27. Carson, *Main Line to Oblivion*, pp. 91–97, stresses that the ICC "subordinated itself to the policies of the railroads."

4

Powerless to Cope:
The Great Depression
and World War II

THE GREAT DEPRESSION began with the 1929 stock market crash. The *New York Times* list of industrials gradually declined from its highpoint of 449 on 31 August, plummeted disastrously in late October, and slid sickeningly to 58 on 8 July 1932. President Herbert Hoover's and business leaders' assurances that the economy was fundamentally sound proved wrong. With income maldistributed (5 percent of the people received a third of the personal income), with corporate structure emphasizing dividends rather than adequate production investment, with strong banks unable to help weak ones, and with high tariffs curtailing not only imports but also exports, since the former paid for the latter, the economy was too weak to sustain the stock market crash. Railroads, with their enormous fixed charges, were particularly vulnerable and could only be saved by drastic federal action.[1]

Struggling with the Depression

For American railroads the depression brought disaster. Tonnage and revenues were halved from 1929 to 1932. In 1929

1. John Kenneth Galbraith, *The Great Crash, 1929* (Boston, 1954), passim. See in particular pp. 173–99.

railroads carried 1,419 million tons of freight for $4,899 million; in 1932 they carried 679 million tons for $2,485 million. Passenger revenue declined even more rapidly than did freight receipts—from $1,305 million in 1920 to $876 million in 1929, to $378 million in 1932, to $330 million in 1933. Even though from 1929 to 1932 railroads countered by nearly halving their operating expenses and reducing their dividends by almost three-quarters, their taxes fell less than a third and their interest on bonds rose from $581 million to $591 million. American railroads' $977 million net income in 1929 had dropped by 1932 to a $122 million loss, and during these years their miles in receivership rose from 5,703 to 22,545. Only once—during the war year 1942—did net income surpass the 1929 figure, and, despite generous government aid during the 1930s, bankruptcies multiplied until in 1939 receivers operated over 77,013 railroad miles.[2]

By 1929 railroads had lost their virtual monopoly on freight and passenger service. While railroads languished during the Great Depression, the federal government liberally subsidized their motor-driven competitors with massive spending on roads, bridges, and airports. Since railroads had already encountered a decade of increasing competition, their problems were compounded. With competition decimating passenger receipts, railroads became increasingly dependent on freight revenue and allowed passenger equipment and service to erode. Rail-passenger revenue approximated a third of rail-freight revenue before 1920, was down to a fourth in the early twenties, a fifth in the late twenties, an eighth in the thirties, and a ninth in 1941. Peaking at 57,451 in 1924, railroad passenger cars in service dropped by 1941 to 38,334. Partly responsible for railroad decline and profiting from it, trucks increased their registrations, which were less than 100,000 in 1914, to over 1.1 million in 1920, over 3.5 million in 1929, and 5.2 million in 1941. Cut-

2. U.S., Bureau of the Census, *Historical Statistics of the United States, Colonial Times to 1957* (Washington, 1960), pp. 430–31, 434–35 (hereafter cited as *Historical Statistics*).

ting into railroad profits, buses increased their registrations from 34,000 in 1929 to 120,000 in 1941, while automobile registrations grew from 1.2 million in 1913 to 8.1 million in 1920, to 23.1 million in 1929, and to 29.6 million in 1941. Although 1929 was the first year airline passengers topped 100,000, they reached 476,041 in 1932 and almost 3.5 million in 1941. These statistics indicate that the depression accentuated problems already confronting the rail industry.[3]

The ICC provided little help. Having failed to shape the national rail system into nineteen strong links and neglecting to force stronger financial structures on the existing systems, the ICC's story was one of lost opportunities. Having acted indecisively in the past, the ICC could do little to save railroads after the crash. With their income declining more rapidly than their operating expenses, railroads received in 1930 a 3.54 percent return on their property and projected for 1931 only a 2.25 percent return. In addition, falling revenue impaired their credit; railroad securities' market value shrank; and large investors, such as banks, trust companies, insurance companies, and endowed institutions, lost heavily. Large-scale railroad security holders agreed with carriers that a rate increase was needed to maintain essential railroad credit. Aiming for a modest 4 percent return, carriers asked for a 15 percent increase but failed to demonstrate either that their proposed rates would be reasonable or would increase revenue. Probably aware of their slim chances for a 15 percent increase, railroads most likely seized the offensive to prevent rate decreases and to strengthen their positions in wage negotiations.

Shippers protested the proposed increases. They, too, were hit by the depression, and while the prices they charged fell, freight rates remained constant. Finding constant freight rates increasingly onerous, shippers were ready to abandon trains for trucks if transportation costs were increased. Embracing shipper arguments, the commission reasoned that a 15 percent advance

3. Ibid., pp. 430–31, 462, 467.

would divert freight to water routes, motor carriers, and pipe lines and would force industrial decentralization to eliminate long hauls. A depression advance would also engender hostility toward railroads and would "disturb business conditions and an already shell-shocked industry."[4]

Recognizing the plight of railroads and wishing to soften its adverse decision, the commission called railroads "the backbone and most of the other vital bones of the transportation system," predicted that industrial prosperity would restore their earnings and credit, and insisted that they were not "doomed . . . to go the way of the stage coach and canal." To aid railroads, the commission proposed that the recapture clauses be repealed, that the fair-return rate be computed by averaging lean and fat years, and that motor and water carriers be regulated. To meet competition, the ICC suggested that railroads drastically overhaul passenger service—which, with its staggering deficits, was primarily responsible for impaired credit—that railroads make freight rates and services competitive, and that they cooperate among themselves (as contemplated by the 1920 Transportation Act's consolidation provisions) to eliminate waste and duplication and to achieve stability.

More concretely, to help needy roads meet interest payments and stave off bankruptcy, the ICC allowed some small increases to create an aid-granting contingency fund. Objecting on legal grounds to this "pooling plan," strong railroads suggested instead a carrier-administered lending plan. Over the vigorous dissent of Joseph B. Eastman (with Frank McManamy, Claude R. Porter, and Charles D. Mahaffie concurring), the commission approved the increases without tying them to its aid fund. Angry with carriers for not cooperating with the ICC's plan to save needy roads and annoyed with the ICC majority for bowing to the obstructionist tactics of strong roads, Eastman

4. Fifteen Per Cent Case, 1931, 178 ICC 539 (1931), in I. L. Sharfman, *The Interstate Commerce Commission: A Study in Administrative Law and Procedure*, 5 vols. (New York, 1931–37), 3B:161–79, 191 (hereafter cited as Sharfman, *ICC*).

attacked the railroad lending plan because the lending agency would be unregulated, because that agency had unquestioned discretion over what constituted need and proper security, and because loans would give only temporary relief and would increase the debts of already overburdened roads. Called the Railroad Credit Corporation, the loan program amassed $75.4 million in emergency rates throughout 1932 and during the first quarter of 1933, and prevented numerous defaults by lending $73.7 million to needy railroads at 2½ to 3 percent interest. Although the ICC extended the emergency rates six months beyond 31 March 1933 and asked railroads to continue the lending plan, they abandoned it while retaining the surcharges collected after 31 March.[5]

The Reconstruction Finance Corporation (RFC; created by Congress January 1932), enabled railroads to abandon their lending plan without serious consequences. Despite standards more rigid than the Railroad Credit Corporation, the RFC quickly became a major source of emergency aid. Lending only to railroads that had been refused funding by banks and the public, the RFC insisted that either the railroad or its receiver provide security and that the ICC approve the loan. By 1 November 1934 (in slightly less than three years) the ICC approved loans totaling $512.5 million to 81 carriers. By rescuing these railroads, the federal government also saved many banks and insurance and trust companies deeply involved with railroads.[6]

Despite the RFC, institutions with heavy railroad investments (particularly insurance companies and universities, such as Columbia, Harvard, Chicago, and Yale) grew jittery and formed in 1932 a National Transportation Committee to study regulation in hopes of saving their investments. That committee, chaired by former President Calvin Coolidge until his death in January 1933, boasted as members Alfred E. Smith, a recent presidential nominee; Bernard Baruch, former War Industries

5. Ibid., pp. 179–91.
6. Ibid., p. 191, n. 409.

Board head; Clark Howell, editor of the *Atlanta Constitution*; and Alexander Legge, president of International Harvester Company. Basing its February 1933 report on an analysis by Harold G. Moulton and his Brookings Institution associates (*The American Transportation Problem,* 1933), the committee suggested changes which illustrate creditor disappointment in both railroad management and the ICC. The report proposed that railroads be forced if necessary to consolidate regionally into a national system, that railroads be permitted to own competing transportation forms, that the government cease subsidizing rail competitors, and that the ICC regulate all transportation and reorganize into separate executive, legislative, and judicial divisions. Blaming the ICC's judicial organization for its "somewhat passive attitude toward acknowledged evils," the committee hoped reorganization would give the commission "incentive or authority . . . to plan and to act affirmatively." Despairing of this hope and refusing to sign the committee report, Al Smith wished to abolish the ICC and to establish a separate department of transportation or a bureau in the Department of Commerce to enforce regulatory laws.[7]

Two weeks later Congress permitted a change in the ICC, but the innovation was far from the reorganization contemplated by the Coolidge committee. Pleased by the way its division structure multiplied its capacity to handle cases, the commission beginning in 1928 asked, and Congress on 28 February 1933 authorized, that the ICC could assign cases (subject to review by a division or the full ICC) to individual commissioners or to a board of one or more of its employees.[8] Re-

7. Earl Latham, *The Politics of Railroad Coordination, 1933–1936* (Cambridge, Mass., 1959), pp. 11–15; Robert E. Cushman, *The Independent Regulatory Commissions* (New York, 1941), pp. 144–45; Marver H. Bernstein, *Regulating Business by Independent Commission* (Princeton, 1955), pp. 58–60; Emory R. Johnson, *Government Regulation of Transportation* (New York, 1938), pp. 337–38; Sharfman, *ICC,* 4:314–15.

8. Sharfman, *ICC,* 4:58–64.

sponding to the demands of minutiae, the ICC further fragmented itself and increased its dependence upon its staff, but the commission could not rise above its numerous determinations and orders to plan a national transportation system.

The Emergency Railroad Transportation Act

Within a month of the Coolidge committee report, the banking system collapsed, the nation plunged to the depths of its worst depression, and Franklin Roosevelt became president. Having already promised a new deal, Roosevelt assured the nation that it would "endure . . . revive and . . . prosper" and told Americans that all they had to "fear is fear itself."[9] As time progressed, the Roosevelt administration—whose energy was matched by its inconsistency—gave the ICC and the transportation industry several new deals.

The first was the Emergency Railroad Transportation Act (16 June 1933). Roosevelt, Eastman, Secretary of Commerce Daniel C. Roper, and Sam Rayburn and Walter M. W. Splawn, chairman and special counsel, respectively, of the House Committee on Interstate and Foreign Commerce, all influenced the bill, as did an assortment of government officials, bankers, congressmen, security holders, railroad managers, presidential braintrusters, shippers, labor leaders, and volunteer advisers. Shaped by many hands, the act pleased no one. Unions objected that it aimed to cut labor costs; shippers feared service would go down and rates up; and Eastman lamented that the "employees of the privately owned railroads" had influenced Congress more "than the employees of the Government." Yet this makeshift legislation with its temporary emergency provisions and its permanent amendments to the ICA had merit.[10]

With Eastman in mind, Congress created a temporary co-

9. James MacGregor Burns, *Roosevelt: The Lion and the Fox* (New York, 1956), p. 163.
10. Latham, *Politics of Railroad Coordination*, pp. 9–11, 36, 57, 63, 75, 92; Johnson, *Government Regulation*, pp. 330–31.

ordinator of transportation, whom the president could designate from the ICC or appoint with the advice and consent of the Senate. The coordinator was to divide railroads into eastern, southern, and western groups, and coordinating committees— selected by roads within each group—were to eliminate duplication and promote joint use of tracks and terminals; encourage financial carrier reorganization to cut fixed charges; and study ways to improve transportation. Congress intended that the committee coordinate voluntary carrier action to eliminate waste and achieve economy. If, however, a carrier failed to cooperate, the coordinator could, upon committee recommendation, order action; and should the committee prove recalcitrant, he could order it to act. For disobedience, the new act prescribed prosecution and heavy fines.

Despite the fears of labor, economies were not to be achieved at its expense. The coordinator and the regional committees were required to consult with the appropriate labor committee before taking action affecting labor. With unemployment rife, the act specified that neither the number of employees nor their salaries could be reduced from the level of May 1933, except for a maximum of 5 percent for resignation, retirement, and death. Labor-management controversies were to be adjusted by regional boards established by the coordinator.

The coordinator, however, was not supreme; the ICC and the courts could reverse or revise his orders. To achieve the cooperation demanded by it, the Emergency Act exempted carriers from the antitrust laws while they were obeying the coordinator's directives. The act showed the effect of many authors; retrenchment was difficult with labor costs inviolate and was also contrary to New Deal efforts to increase consumer purchasing power. Before his appointment as transportation coordinator, Eastman thought the act's results were problematical, but he held hope because its possibilities were impressive. With trucks and buses adding to the "strife, confusion, and instability" of the transportation industry, he planned to help each mode find its proper place and to coordinate and weld diverse modes "into a well-knit whole, into a transportation system operating much more nearly as a unit, without cross purposes and all manner of lost motion."[11]

Other sections of the act directly affected the ICC. Two provisions simplified the work of the Valuation Bureau. The act both repealed the 1920 act's recapture clauses and no longer required the commission to revise all valuations. It was to continue storing valuation information, however, so periodic revisions could be made if deemed necessary. The Emergency Act also changed the 1920 act's ratemaking rule that called for a fair property-value return. Under the new rule, the ICC would determine just-and-reasonable rates by their effect on traffic, by the shipper's need for low-cost, adequate, and efficient service, and by the carrier's revenue needs. Finally, the 1933 act eliminated loopholes by giving the ICC authority over all railroad combinations (regardless of the technical device used to acquire control) including holding companies, and, since the commission had ample control, it eliminated a rigid capitalization requirement for consolidations, which depended on frequently unavailable valuation figures.[12]

Federal Coordinator Eastman

Eastman's apprehensions about the Emergency Railroad Transportation Act proved more accurate than his hopes. Despite his efforts and railroads' need to save millions, no significant coordination of facilities occurred. Coordination failed primarily because railroads, which controlled regional coordinating committees, did not wish to coordinate. Perhaps railroad managers lacked vigor and espoused unprogressive service, pricing, and operational policies because they were products of a rigid seniority system, in which they reached the top five years later and served at that level fewer years than executives of other corporations. During his first two years as coordinator, Eastman refrained, except in a few minor instances, from order-

11. Sharfman, *ICC*, 3A:424–29.
12. Ibid., pp. 310–11, 494–99.

ing railroad coordination. The following year, Eastman wielded more authority but succeeded only in coordinating opposition to him and his office. He shrewdly analyzed those opposing cooperation as management, unable to break old habits of thought; railroad officials and laborers, afraid to lose their jobs; communities, apprehensive about service; supply companies, worried about collective railroad scientific research and purchases; and large shippers, anxious to play railroads against each other.[13]

Eastman based his hopes on studies that would discover ways to integrate the carriers into a system. His duty, he thought, was to convince, not to order; his role was that of a teacher, not a czar. The coordinator, Eastman remarked, "should . . . be primarily a means of concentrating and bringing to focus the best thought of the industry rather than a means of supplying or imposing thought from without." Eastman and his staff focused that best thought in reports to regional coordinating committees relating to freight and passenger traffic, purchasing, research, car-pooling, fiscal operations, grain elevators, and labor and in four legislative reports submitted to Congress through the ICC. If heeded, these bold and imaginative reports would have improved services and achieved economies, but railroads either damned or ignored them. The merchandise traffic report of 22 March 1934 pointed out that slow, uncertain, unsafe, and incomplete delivery, high and complex charges, and rigorous packing requirements had lost the bulk of merchandise traffic to trucks and suggested that railroads establish two competing nationwide agencies (similar to the Railway Express Agency) to handle merchandise traffic, that it be moved in shockproof equipment faster than 20 miles per hour, that packing requirements be reduced, that classifications be simplified, and that charges be revised. The carriers, however, rejected these ideas and in October 1934, largely to frustrate federal

13. Latham, *Politics of Railroad Coordination*, pp. 3, 35, 139; Marshall E. Dimock and Howard K. Hyde, "Executive Appointment in Private and Public Bureaucracies," in *Reader in Bureaucracy*, ed. Robert K. Merton et al. (New York, 1952), pp. 321–24.

coordination, established the Association of American Railroads (AAR) to coordinate themselves. The AAR succeeded in scuttling Eastman's reports but failed to coordinate facilities. By the early 1940s Senators Burton K. Wheeler and Harry S. Truman discovered that over a three-year period the AAR coordinated facilities in only 24 small projects. "Railroad executives testified . . . that not only has nothing been achieved, but that it is futile to expect any results from this railroad association because it is dominated by a few powerful roads which are only working for their own interests."[14]

The federal coordinator's legislative reports fared somewhat better. His first report (January 1934), which both presented railroad nationalization favorably and advised against immediate implementation, angered opponents and annoyed proponents of public ownership. Eastman, who saw little public support for railroad nationalization and feared a move by security holders to unload their holdings on the government, told Felix Frankfurter that he had no desire "to rush the country either into public ownership and operation or into a great compulsory consolidation plan." Two months later Eastman released his second report, which advocated ICC regulation of motor and water carriers. His third report (January 1935) again concluded the time unripe for nationalizing railroads, again called for ICC regulation of motor and water carriers, and advocated a sweeping ICC reorganization. The fourth report (January 1936) argued anew for water carrier regulation and ICC reorganization.[15]

Congress utilized a bill Eastman proposed for the base of the 1935 Motor Carrier Act, and in 1940 empowered the ICC to regulate inland water carriers but failed to reorganize the commission and allowed the coordinator's office to die in June 1936. Eastman had proposed that the ICC be enlarged from

14. Latham, *Politics of Railroad Coordination*, pp. 119, 191, 196–201; Claude Moore Fuess, *Joseph B. Eastman: Servant of the People* (New York, 1952), pp. 216–20.

15. Latham, *Politics of Railroad Coordination*, pp. 90–96, 225–37, 240–43.

eleven to sixteen members with a permanent chairman; that it be subdivided into railroad, water and pipe, motor and air, and finance divisions; that the heads of these four divisions and the chairman form a control board to determine policy; and that the federal coordinator be a permanent part of the commission organization. The ICC was hostile to these proposals, which would transform equal commissioners into two more powerful, four powerful, and ten weaker ones. Indeed the ICC—possibly jealous of Eastman's power—did not want the coordinator a permanent part of the commission. Lining up with the AAR, the ICC insinuated that the coordinator's only function was research and planning, which perhaps "should be left primarily to the transportation industries."[16]

Eastman's greatest accomplishment as federal coordinator was the 1935 Motor Carrier Act, which a fellow commissioner called "the most important change in the scope" of the ICC since the 1906 Hepburn Act.[17] By 1935 anarchy prevailed in the trucking industry. Cutthroat competition among truckers, who were either common carriers, contract carriers, or private operators, was complicated by their small-scale operations, making it easy for new operators—many lacking training, finances, and scruples—to break into the industry. The depression accentuated the problem by making cheap labor, trucks, tires, and fuel available for new ventures. To the benefit of shippers, these circumstances demoralized rates. Eastman, through ICC regulation, wished to coordinate trucking and rail service with each "concentrating on the work it can do best with a minimum of overlapping." Basically, Eastman proposed extensive regulation of common carriers, some regulation of contract carriers, and no regulation of private carriers. Railroads, the ICC, motor common carriers, big truckers, buses, and later

16. Ibid., pp. 240–43; Sharfman, *ICC*, 4:317–41.
17. Sharfman, *ICC*, 4:101. In June 1934 Congress widened the ICC's range to include regulating air mail rates, but a few days later transferred the regulation of telephone, telegraph, and cable companies to the Federal Communications Commission. Ibid., pp. 3, 87–98, 286.

organized labor favored regulation of truckers; while smaller truckers, truck manufacturers, farmers, and shippers were opposed. Amendments exempting the hauling of livestock, unprocessed agricultural products, and newspapers helped placate the American National Livestock Association, the National Grange, and the American Newspaper Publishers Association, and the Eastman bill became the 1935 Motor Carrier Act.

The new act gave the commission power to prescribe employee qualifications, the maximum hours they could work, and motor carrier equipment standards. It authorized the ICC to issue certificates of public convenience and necessity, with a grandfather clause assuring certificates for common carriers in operation on 1 June 1935; gave the ICC broad powers over maximum and minimum rates, service, accounting, finances, organization, and management of common carriers; and allowed it to issue permits to contract carriers, with a grandfather clause again protecting operators. The Motor Carrier Act, however, regulated only minimum rates and accounting procedures of contract carriers and, apart from hours and safety regulations that applied to all truckers, did not regulate private carriers.[18]

Going into effect on 1 October 1935, the act increased enormously the workload of the ICC. The commission reorganized into five divisions: Division 1 dealt with valuation, Division 2 with rates and charges, Division 3 with service and safety, Division 4 with organization and finance, and Division 5, with Eastman at its head, handled motor carriers. John L. Rodgers, who had assisted Eastman when he was federal coordinator, directed the new Bureau of Motor Carriers, which was subdivided into sections—on certificates and insurance, traffic, accounts, research, statistics, complaints, finance, safety, and law and enforcement—and had field offices in sixteen districts. In addition, the Motor Carrier Act further decentralized administration by utilizing joint boards of representatives

18. Latham, *Politics of Railroad Coordination*, pp. 225–33; Sharfman, *ICC*, 4:99–121.

from state commissions for solving problems including certificates and permits, consolidations, violations, and complaints about rates, fares, and charges.

Inadequate appropriations, insufficient personnel, and an incredible work volume hampered the Bureau of Motor Carriers. By filibustering, Senator Huey Long delayed appropriations, and the Civil Service Commission waited until May 1936 to hold an examination geared to the new bureau's personnel needs. By 1 November 1936 there were 85,636 certificate and permit applications (80,000 under the grandfather clause), half of which were protested by railroads, other truckers, or state commissions. By that same date, 52,979 tariff publications, 16,897 schedules, and 1,867 contracts were filed with the ICC and indexed on 500,000 cards by the traffic section. With 110 employees, that section prepared 953 rate memoranda for the commission, received 47,666 letters, and wrote 54,864. The Bureau of Motor Carriers' task was complicated by numerous small operators and their inexperience with record keeping and the filing of tariffs and schedules. With many truckers ignoring the act, the swamped ICC could only prosecute them gradually. Since rates were depressed and shippers had few complaints, there were few rate cases initially, and the commission fostered this trend by encouraging motor carriers to stabilize rates through their own efforts. Recognizing in 1936 that ultimately it would have to decide differences between rail and motor carrier rates, the ICC hoped to improve rail-truck relations and to promote their coordination. Aware that Congress did not want trucks threatening the value-of-service rate structure, the commission reduced competition between the two modes by tying truck rates to rail rates. This ICC action, raising certain minimum rates of common and contract motor carriers, gratified railroads but further ingrained the traditional discriminatory value-of-service rate structure on the American transportation system. More interested in short-term benefits than far-reaching precedents, railroads determined their own destruction by accepting parity rates which assured competition with trucks on a service basis, where trains would have difficulty competing, rather than a cost basis, where they had a clear advantage.[19]

The Transportation Act of 1940

In 1935 President Roosevelt supported the Motor Carrier Act, which increased ICC authority, but in 1936 he appointed the Louis Brownlow committee which attempted to diminish that power. The Brownlow committee—the President's Committee on Administrative Management—anticipated suggestions of the subsequent Hoover commission, but Roosevelt's Court-packing plan, issued almost simultaneously with the Brownlow committee report in 1937, hogged attention. After observing that quasi-judicial commissions such as the ICC "have been the result of legislative groping rather than the pursuit of a consistent policy," the Brownlow committee suggested that the ICC be lodged in either the Department of Commerce or in a new department of transportation, that its administrative and judicial functions be divided, that the administrative section be directed by the appropriate secretary and the president, and that the judicial section—except for administrative housekeeping, such as budget, personnel administration, and supplies—be independent of the department and the president. Predictably Roosevelt embraced these suggestions enhancing his power and commissioners fought this threat to their independence. Even Eastman, who was usually receptive to administrative innovations, rejected the Brownlow scheme. His distrust of what he perceived to be autocratic management, whether in business or in government, reinforced his belief that the ICC must be autonomous. The Brownlow committee's link in the public mind with the unpopular Court fight made the committee report appear to be a grab for more presidential power and helped the independent regulatory commissions and their supporters keep

19. Latham, *Politics of Railroad Coordination*, p. 233; Sharfman, *ICC*, 4:55–58, 122–41; Ann F. Friedlaender, *The Dilemma of Freight Transport Regulation* (Washington, 1969), pp. 21–22; James C. Nelson, *Railroad Transportation and Public Policy* (Washington, 1959), pp. 115–17.

this proposal out of the Administrative Reorganization bill that finally passed in 1939.[20]

Regulation of motor carriers and proposals to overhaul the ICC did little to help railroads; by early 1938 they appeared doomed. In mid-March Roosevelt called a White House conference of members of the ICC, Securities and Exchange Commission, and Reconstruction Finance Corporation, officials from the Treasury, Agriculture, and Commerce departments, and representatives of management, labor, and investors to consider ways to relieve and improve the "serious situation of the railroads." To summarize the conference conclusions, Roosevelt selected a Committee of Three (called the Splawn committee and comprised of Commissioners Walter M. W. Splawn, Eastman, and Mahaffie), whose report urged immediate railroad relief by a $3 million equipment advance; by RFC loans to meet fixed charges, which would not require the usual ICC approval; by the federal government paying full rates, despite its land-grant reduction; and by congressional revision of the Bankruptcy Act. The Splawn committee's suggestions for a long-term program revived the federal coordinator in the guise of a relatively powerless federal transportation authority to plan consolidations and to recommend that Congress give the ICC power to unify roads when unification is sought by at least one carrier.[21]

The Splawn committee report pleased virtually no one. Roosevelt forwarded it to Congress with the observation that it

20. Cushman, *Independent Regulatory Commissions*, pp. 709–11; Latham, *Politics of Railroad Coordination*, p. 243; Fuess, *Eastman*, pp. 253–56; Paul P. Van Riper, *History of the United States Civil Service* (Evanston, 1958), pp. 336–37, 560; U.S., Interstate Commerce Commission, *Exercises Commemorating the Fifty Years' Service of the Interstate Commerce Commission*, 1 April 1937, p. 112; Richard Polenberg, *Reorganizing Roosevelt's Government: The Controversy over Executive Reorganization, 1936–1939* (Cambridge, Mass., 1966), pp. 21, 25–26, 42, 44–45, 85–86, 88, 91–92.

21. Fuess, *Eastman*, pp. 259–61; U.S., Congress, Senate, Committee on Commerce, *National Transportation Policy*, 87th Cong., 1st sess., 26 June 1961, S. Rept. 445, p. 241 (hereafter cited as *Doyle Report*); Charles L. Dearing and Wilfred Owen, *National Transportation Policy* (Washington, 1949), pp. 441–42.

was "common sense to place all executive functions relating to all transportation in one Federal Department" and that "all quasi-judicial and quasi-legislative matters relating to all transportation could properly be placed under an independent commission,—a reorganized Interstate Commerce Commission." Secretary of the Treasury Henry Morgenthau enlarged on the president's theme and suggested that the Splawn committee was overcautious and that Congress should create a department of transportation to "move vigorously to properly coordinate our national transportation facilities." On the other hand, organized labor feared that contemplated coordinations and consolidations would eliminate 200,000 jobs.[22]

In September Roosevelt appointed a Committee of Six (three representing railroad management and three railroad labor), whose December 1938 report was concerned with relieving the symptoms rather than curing the malady. The Committee of Six report emphatically rejected compulsory consolidation, asked that railroads be relieved from the limitations and restrictions of the consolidation plan, and predicted that the "best results will be achieved by leaving all initiative in the matter to the railroads themselves." It also called for a new independent federal agency to study the transportation problem and ultimately to promote and regulate all transportation modes. Throughout 1939 and well into 1940, despite extensive hearings and the advice of the Committee of Three, the Committee of Six, the ICC, and the AAR (or because of the conflicting views expressed), neither the Senate nor the House could agree on legislation. The ICC, however, on 1 July 1939, modifying an Eastman idea, abandoned the annual rotation of the chairmanship for a three-year term, and appropriately named Eastman as the first and, as it turned out, only three-year chairman.[23]

22. Fuess, *Eastman*, pp. 261–62.
23. Ibid., pp. 262–63; Dearing and Owen, *National Transportation Policy*, pp. 339–40, 385, 442–43; *Doyle Report*, p. 241; Cushman, *Independent Regulatory Commissions*, p. 141; U.S., Interstate Commerce

Roosevelt signed the 1940 Transportation Act in August, after Congress had passed it with few dissenting votes. Congress prefaced the act by defining the national transportation policy as the "fair and impartial regulation of all modes of transportation . . . to recognize and preserve the inherent advantages of each," to promote adequate and efficient service, to maintain reasonable charges, to cooperate with state agencies, to encourage fair wages and equitable working conditions, "all to the end of developing, coordinating, and preserving a national transportation system by water, highway, and rail, as well as other means." Significantly, however, Congress rejected an amendment that would permit each type of carrier to reduce rates to no less than the fully distributed service-cost. This action preserved value-of-service ratemaking with its inequities, rejected cost-of-service ratemaking and a rule for minimum rates, and ensured that minimum-rate policy would be the most important question facing the ICC. Specifically, the act agreed with the Committee of Six, rather than the Committee of Three, and relieved the ICC of the duty imposed in 1920 to promulgate a consolidation plan. Having failed to lead in twenty years, the ICC was shorn of its responsibility to lead railroads into efficient consolidations.[24]

The 1940 act also gave the ICC jurisdiction over coastwise, intercoastal, inland, and Great Lakes common and contract water-carriers in interstate and foreign commerce. Congress, however, exempted bulk commodities from regulation, and bulk shipments (defined as no more than three commodities to a tow) made up most inland-waterway traffic. Apart from air transportation—regulated by the Civil Aeronautics Authority after 1938—the ICC after 1940 regulated all significant modes

Commission, *53d Annual Report*, 1939, pp. 1–5. At the expiration of Eastman's three-year term as chairman, the ICC returned to annually rotating its chairmanship.

24. Henry J. Friendly, *The Federal Administrative Agencies: The Need for Better Definition of Standards* (Cambridge, Mass., 1962), pp. 113–14, n. 23; Friedlaender, *Dilemma of Freight Transport Regulation*, pp. 22–23; *Doyle Report*, pp. 241–42.

of interstate commerce. Indeed, the Omnibus bill of 1938—the earliest version of the 1940 Transportation Act—had proposed to extend the ICC's authority over air transportation. The suggestion by the Committee of Three and the Committee of Six that a transportation authority be appointed survived in the act as a three-member Transportation Investigation and Research Board charged with determining the relative place of rail, motor, and water carriers in a national transportation system and with anything else that would implement the new transportation policy. The board was presidentially appointed, had a two-year tenure renewable for another two years, and had no ICC connection. Perhaps because of World War II, most of the board's reports discussing carrier taxation and advocating new agencies to research, plan, and promote solutions of the transportation problem had little impact, but its work on interterritorial freight rates was important.[25]

Ironically, considering its later effect, the congressional statement of national transportation policy pleased the railroads. It did not, however, clarify the ICC's task. The statement itself had problems and inconsistencies, and these were complicated by the fact that all transportation statutes were, in effect, national transportation policy. Defining the inherent advantages of the three modes of transportation, for example, would be difficult. Were lower rates resulting from government promotion or assistance an inherent advantage? Should rates be judged compensatory if they covered only out-of-pocket expenses or should they cover the carrier's fixed charges as well? How could one mode's inherent service advantage be compared to another's inherent cost advantage? Again the ICC was admonished both to prevent destructive competition and to encourage

25. *Doyle Report*, pp. 130–32; Dearing and Owen, *National Transportation Policy*, pp. 443–45; Cushman, *Independent Regulatory Commissions*, pp. 415–16, 738–39. The 1936 Merchant Marine Act created the Maritime Commission and gave it the little existing authority over domestic and foreign water commerce. The 1940 act extended regulations similar to those in rail and motor transportation to interstate water commerce and transferred its administration to the ICC. Ibid., pp. 142–43.

competition. When, if at all, should a mode with an inherent advantage be allowed to eliminate another mode? Should constructive competition be considered destructive when it takes over 5 percent, 25 percent, 50 percent, or 100 percent of a rival's traffic? The ICC had to determine rates that would promote the free movement of commodities, cover the service cost, and protect the inherent advantages of each transportation mode. With so many factors to consider, the Doyle report concluded in 1961, "the Commission can decide almost any case just about as it pleases and, by leaning upon, first, one aspect, and in another case, upon another aspect of our transportation policy, successfully withstand almost any scrutiny of the courts."[26] Most of the confusion, however, awaited the postwar years.

Regional Discrimination and Political Pressure

Southern politicians used the Transportation Investigation and Research Board's report on interterritorial freight rates in their decade-long struggle against discriminatory freight rates. With five rate territories—Official or Eastern, Southern, Western Trunk Line, Southwestern, and Mountain-Pacific—and three classification zones—Official, Southern, and Western—an item could be classified differently from region to region and rates differed from section to section. In the early 1940s, first-class freight rates were 37 percent higher in Southern than in Official territory, 46 percent in Western Trunk Line, 61 percent in Southwestern, and 71 percent in Mountain-Pacific. The East's advantages with class rates, which usually applied to manufactured products, were offset in part by some lower commodity rates on bulk products in the South and West and by the fact that 95 percent of the freight moved on special rates for specific commodities and only 5 percent paid class rates. Never-

---

26. *Doyle Report*, pp. 120–24; Friendly, *Federal Administrative Agencies*, pp. 113–31; Robert B. Carson, *Main Line to Oblivion: The Disintegration of New York Railroads in the Twentieth Century* (Port Washington, N.Y., 1971), p. 119.

theless, southerners paid higher freight rates than easterners; a region with higher class rates generally paid higher commodity rates and had an overall higher freight bill.

Regional rate differentials reflected nineteeth-century geographic factors and sectional economic differences. The Ohio and Mississippi rivers had been barriers; compared to the East, the West and South had low-density population and produced more bulk commodities; and, with little through traffic, southern railroads relied heavily on local traffic. Higher nineteenth-century operating costs in the South and West had resulted in higher rates. The development of rate bureaus and of ICC-rate regulation in the twentieth century organized, institutionalized, and fixed these patterns into a rigid system.[27]

Until the Great Depression, southerners accepted regional differentials with reasonably good grace. Large-scale and bulk-traffic shippers usually did not complain because they often negotiated advantageous special commodity rates. During the depression, however, the South became notorious for its economic backwardness, and southern politicians defensively—and with some justification—blamed their region's plight on discriminatory freight rates. To destroy these regional differentials, the Southern Governors Conference was organized in 1937. "If we can beat these barriers down," one governor predicted, "you will see millions of dollars worth of southern products going into areas north of the Ohio River and west of the Mississippi." A Tennessee Valley Authority (TVA) study by J. Haden All-dredge strengthened the governors' cause by documenting discriminatory rates against the South. In litigation before the ICC, the governors first concentrated on commodity rates. Although ICC hearings in 1938 revealed evidence of discrimination in only

27. David M. Potter, "The Historical Development of Eastern-Southern Freight Rate Relationships," *Law and Contemporary Problems* 12 (1947), reprinted in Richard M. Abrams and Lawrence W. Levine, eds., *The Shaping of Twentieth-Century America: Interpretive Articles* (Boston, 1965), pp. 26–57; Robert A. Lively, "The South and Freight Rates: Political Settlement of an Economic Argument," *Journal of Southern History* 14 (1948):357–62.

fourteen groups of commodities, southern politicians continued to press what became known as the *Southern Governors* case. Fearful of losing advantages for their states, northern governors organized to oppose change in the rate structure, but it was obvious that the Roosevelt administration favored the South when Harry Hopkins, Works Progress Administration head, declared in 1938 that the "freight rate structure was planned to clinch the industrial supremacy of the North and East." Impatient with the slow-moving ICC, southern congressmen introduced bills in early 1939 to remove regional rate differentials.[28]

With Congress contemplating action, the ICC responded to political pressure. While shaping the 1940 Transportation Act, Congress in 1939 decided to direct the ICC to investigate rates within and between territories and to prevent rate discrimination between regions. Before the bill became law, the ICC initiated in July 1939 its historic class-rate investigation. By November it finally decided the commodities case in favor of the southern governors by a five-to-four sectional vote. The invasion of politics and sectionalism into ICC deliberations disturbed Eastman. He protested that the case "has in effect been decided, in advance and without regard to the record, by many men in public life, of high and low degree," and warned that the ICC must rule with "cold impartiality, for this Commission has an equal duty with respect to every part of the country, and nothing will speed its ruin more quickly than the disease of sectionalism."[29]

Eastman's pleas were ignored. While the ICC class-rate investigation slowly proceeded, southern politicians continued their fight against differentials. Many southern industrialists—particularly coal, iron, and steel men—who shipped commodities that enjoyed lower rates than those charged in Official territory feared that equity in class rates would destroy their

28. Potter, "Eastern-Southern Freight Rate Relationships," pp. 57–61; Lively, "South and Freight Rates," pp. 362–69.

29. Southern Governors Case, 235 ICC 255 (1939), in Lively, "South and Freight Rates," pp. 369–71.

advantages and preferred not to disturb the existing rate structure. They were in a minority, however, and were castigated by politicians for "seeking to profiteer from the South's freight-rate fight at the expense of other Southern businessmen." Political pressure mounted during the ICC's long class-rate investigation. Southern governors complained that the South did not get its share of war industries because of inequitable freight rates, southern senators refused to appropriate money for the Transportation Board of Investigation and Research unless it would investigate interterritorial rates, and Senator Kenneth McKellar of Tennessee told the board its report "would not be worth two bits" if it failed to discover discrimination. The board did find discrimination and by a sectional two-to-one vote recommended in March 1943 that Congress instruct the ICC to institute a uniform nationwide classification-and-rate system. Also in March 1943, while the ICC held class-rate hearings, the TVA issued a third study which argued that rate discrimination stunted southern and western growth.[30]

After a six-year investigation, the ICC ruled in May 1945 that the existing class-rate structure "reacts to the disadvantage of the South and West," and in May 1947 the Supreme Court agreed. Basing its ruling on findings by commission statisticians that lower population density in the South than in the East did not result in higher operating costs, the ICC ordered an immediate, uniform, nationwide classification system and ultimate uniform class rates. Six of the seven commissioners who fully supported the decision came from the South and West. The key commissioner, without whom, the southern governors' attorney said, they could not have secured the decision, was J. Haden Alldredge of Alabama, who wrote the first TVA report attacking regional discrimination. Intense political pressure, primarily from southern governors, not only forced the ICC to investigate regional rate differences but also changed the sectional composition of the commission and insured the victory of a more equit-

30. Ibid., pp. 372–77.

able system. In 1933 six out of eleven commissioners were from Official territory, but by 1945 seven commissioners were from the South and West. Since railroads in 1953 derived only 5 percent of their revenue from class rates, the economic impact of this political victory can be exaggerated, but the decision assured smaller southern shippers, particularly manufacturers, equitable treatment and encouraged the migration of industry south.[31]

World War II

When the 1940 Transportation Act passed, France had recently fallen, the air Battle of Britain was raging, and the 7 December 1941 attack on Pearl Harbor would soon plunge the nation into total war. Having already begun war preparations, the United States continued to step up defense measures. Railroading, which had been picking up after the disastrous year of 1938, quickened and boomed with the war; 1942, 1943, and 1944 broke previous tonnage and revenue records. In 1938 railroads moved 820 million freight tons for $2,901 million, but in 1942 they moved 1,498 million tons for $6,026 million, and in 1944 moved 1,565 million tons for $7,087 million. Wartime shipments traveled farther and were more profitable. In 1940 railroads hauled each ton an average of 351 miles; in 1944 the figure was up to 473 miles, and by 1946 down to 415 miles. Passenger revenue rose almost twice as rapidly as freight receipts, from $406 million in 1938 to $516 million in 1941, to $1,030 million in 1942, and to the all-time peak of $1,793 million in 1944. Rail passenger revenue, which in 1941 was only a ninth of rail-freight revenue, by 1944 equaled a quarter of freight receipts.[32]

World War II placed railroads in an advantageous position. Their surplus equipment from the 1930s was put to work and

31. Class Rate Decision, 262 ICC 447 (1945) and New York v. United States, 331 U.S. 284 (1947), ibid., pp. 380–84; Nelson, *Railroad Transportation and Public Policy*, p. 336, n. 11.
32. *Historical Statistics*, pp. 430–31.

their enormous hauling capacity was fully utilized. At the same time their competitors—motor and water carriers—were hampered by submarine sinkings of coastwise freighters and by severe fuel and equipment shortages. Not only tires and gasoline but trucks and truck engines were needed for the armed forces. Motor truck registrations declined from the 1941 figure of 5.2 million to 4.7 million in 1943 and 1944. Although bus registrations steadily rose during the war, automobile registrations dropped from 29.6 million in 1941 to 25.6 million in 1944. With railroads carrying 97 percent of troops and 90 percent of army and navy supplies moved within the United States, the locomotive was still king, and victory again rode the rails.[33]

To coordinate war transportation, Roosevelt did not resort to federal control. In May 1940 even before the nation went to war, he appointed Ralph Budd, president of the Chicago, Burlington & Quincy, transportation commissioner of the Advisory Commission to the Council of National Defense, and in January 1941 Budd's office shifted to the Office of Emergency Management. Budd could only suggest, not compel, but railroads, anxious to avoid federal control, cooperated. Shortly after Pearl Harbor, Roosevelt established the Office of Defense Transportation (ODT) and named Eastman director. No one was more qualified than Eastman to coordinate wartime transportation. In contrast to his unsuccessful efforts as federal coordinator, Eastman was a rousing success as ODT director. The difference was not in Eastman but in the attitude of railroad officials. From 1933 to 1936 with railroads in the throes of the depression, their officials feared that cooperation with the federal coordinator might lead to unwanted consolidations and further loss of managerial independence; from 1941 to 1945, with railroads enjoying sudden prosperity, their officials realized that failure to cooperate with the ODT director would lead to federal control and loss of managerial independence. So railroads through the AAR and its Car Service Division and shippers

33. Ibid., p. 462; John F. Stover, *American Railroads* (Chicago, 1961), p. 203.

through their regional Shippers Advisory Boards cooperated with Eastman and the ODT.[34]

Neither Roosevelt nor Wilson attempted to coordinate wartime transportation through the ICC. Apparently the commission impressed neither president with its capacity to coordinate and lead the transportation industry. While utilizing ICC staff and commissioners in these emergencies, both presidents set up offices divorced from the commission to coordinate or control wartime transportation. Indeed, the judicial calm of the ICC was so unruffled by World War II that the commission's rate-making actions conflicted with the stabilization policies of the Office of Price Administration (OPA). Over OPA protests, the ICC raised passenger fares 10 percent and increased some freight rates, but, since OPA regulations did not extend to prices regulated by other federal agencies, the courts upheld ICC actions. These conflicts pointed up the problem of coordinating the regulations of independent commissions with the programs of executive agencies.[35] When the war ended the ICC was neither coordinated with executive agencies nor closer to coordinating the transportation industry. Furthermore, the ICC emerged from the war rudderless. Having completed twenty-five years on the commission and having through the ODT obtained maximum railroad cooperation in the war effort, Eastman died in early 1944. Though often a dissenter, he made the commission aware of its larger purposes through the depth of his understanding and the breadth of his vision. No commissioner of comparable talents rose to take his place.

34. Latham, *Politics of Railroad Coordination*, pp. 274–75; Stover, *American Railroads*, pp. 201–2.
35. Bernstein, *Regulating Business by Independent Commission*, p. 68; Samuel P. Huntington, "The Marasmus of the ICC: The Commission, the Railroads, and the Public Interest," *Yale Law Journal* 61 (1952): 486–87; Charles S. Morgan, "A Critique of 'The Marasmus of the ICC: The Commission, the Railroads, and the Public Interest,'" ibid. 62 (1953):207.

5

Dissipated Power:
The Postwar Years

~~~~~~

THE LOCOMOTIVE may have been king during World War
II, but it was dethroned in the postwar years. As rail transportation declined—partly in consequence of commission policies—
so did the ICC. Two factors contributed to the commission's
debilitation in the postwar years: the proportion of nonregulated interstate traffic increased as rail service declined, and
weak appointments left the commission bereft of leadership and
dependent upon an entrenched staff following established procedures. With a serious transportation problem and a changing
transportation industry, the ICC needed heroic leaders and wise
decisions to stave off disaster.

Regulation and Railroad Decline

The war proved to be a prosperous interlude in the long,
relative decline of railroads. Their share of intercity freight fell
from 62.4 percent in 1939 to 41.6 percent in 1967. During the
same years, intercity freight ton-miles went up only 116 percent
for railroads—compared to 636 percent for motor carriers, 185
percent for water carriers, and 549 percent for pipelines. The
relative decline of railroads led to a decline of ICC-regulated
traffic. Again using the years 1939 to 1967, regulated carriers'
share of intercity freight fell from 74 to 67 percent. While unregulated freight grew 311 percent, regulated traffic grew only
194 percent. Barred from exploiting, through rate-competition,
their cost advantage over trucks for most shipments in excess of
200 miles, railroads were forced to compete in the service

sphere, where they had a decided disadvantage. Not only did they lose high-value goods to trucks, which in 1962 topped them in total freight revenue, but they lost bulk freight to pipe lines and water carriers.[1]

With passenger rail traffic resuming its absolute decline after the war, passengers dropped in number from 897 million to 413 million between 1945 and 1957, and the revenue they paid fell from $1.7 billion to $736 million. During the war, passenger revenue had equaled a fourth of freight revenue; by 1957 it equaled but a fourteenth. In these same years, rail passenger cars deteriorated and declined from 46,863 to 32,231. When the triumph of automobiles, buses, and airlines saddled railroads with horrendous losses, they sought permission to abandon unprofitable passenger trains. In 1958 jurisdiction over these passenger-train discontinuances was taken from state commissions and lodged with the ICC. In making these Solomon-like decisions, the commission sought to weigh passenger rail deficits against loud community demands for adequate service.[2]

While the transportation industry underwent a postwar transformation, both the jurisdiction and administration of the ICC changed. The Administrative Procedure Act of 1946 mixed the ideas of the bar, which advocated more traditional judicial procedures by the regulatory agencies, with the ideas of those who would retain and reform these agencies' administrative functions. The result insured fairer and more uniform administrative procedures, but the added emphasis on judicial procedures further delayed decisions. Unhappy with the Administrative Procedure Act because it contradicted the ICA and caused confusion, particularly for hearing examiners, the ICC

1. Ann F. Friedlaender, *The Dilemma of Freight Transport Regulation* (Washington, 1969), pp. 100–3; James C. Nelson, *Railroad Transportation and Public Policy* (Washington, 1959), pp. 7–66; *New York Times*, 15 April 1963.

2. U.S., Bureau of the Census, *Historical Statistics of the United States, Colonial Times to 1957* (Washington, 1960), pp. 430–31; George W. Hilton, *The Transportation Act of 1958: A Decade of Experience* (Bloomington, Ind., 1969), pp. 35–38.

lobbied unsuccessfully to be exempted from its provisions. In 1947 Congress created the Commission on Organization of the Executive Branch of the Government (called the Hoover commission from its chairman, former President Herbert Hoover). Noting in 1949 that the ICC's executive duties interfered with its regulatory work and sometimes were performed badly and that its great workload caused the ICC to neglect promotional and planning functions, the Hoover commission recommended that safety and car service responsibilities be transferred to the Department of Commerce and "that all administrative responsibility be vested in the Chairman of the commission." Comfortable with rotation and divided responsibility, the ICC opposed a powerful chairmanship and influenced Congress not to enact these Hoover commission recommendations. At the behest of the ICC, Congress passed, over President Harry Truman's veto, the 1948 Reed-Bulwinkle Act, which legalized existing railroad rate bureaus—that had been in apparent violation of the Sherman Antitrust Act—and subjected their collusive pricing agreements to ICC approval. Tending to inflate rates and to eliminate intramodal competition, rate bureaus were partly responsible for railroad freight and passenger losses. Striving for near unanimity, these bureaus were unable to respond quickly to competition from other transportation modes. Ironically, railroads set up and Congress approved private bureaucracies that surpassed the ICC in limiting rate action by individual railroads.[3]

3. James M. Landis, *Report on Regulatory Agencies to the President-Elect*, submitted by the chairman of the Subcommittee on Administrative Practice and Procedure to the Committee on the Judiciary of the United States Senate (Washington, 1960), p. 16 (hereafter cited as *Landis Report*); John R. Meyer et al., *The Economics of Competition in the Transportation Industries* (Cambridge, Mass., 1959), pp. 208–11; U.S., Interstate Commerce Commission, *60th Annual Report*, 1946, pp. 57–59, *63d Annual Report*, 1949, pp. 56–57 (hereafter cited as *Annual Report*); Charles L. Dearing and Wilfred Owen, *National Transportation Policy* (Washington, 1949), pp. 388–89; The Commission on Organization of the Executive Branch of the Government, *The Independent Regulatory Commissions: A Report to the Congress* . . . (March 1949), pp. 5–6, 12, 15–16; Hilton, *Transportation Act of 1958*, p. 9.

Faced with the challenge of regulating fairly all transportation modes while preserving their inherent advantages, the postwar ICC vacillated. Despite the enormous economic and military consequences of its actions, it failed to devise or stick to a formula allowing carriers to flourish where they had inherent advantages. In regulating competition between different transportation modes, the ICC's power to set minimum rates was crucial and would determine whether trucks or trains would be the nation's chief carriers.

Minimum-rate policy was complicated by value-of-service ratemaking—price discrimination based on precedents which charged some items more and others less than their actual transportation costs. With the ICC's blessing, these unfair rates dominated American transportation. In 1956 there were 75,000 railroad tariffs, ranging from those covering only 15 percent of fully distributed costs to those covering 566 percent. Twenty-two percent of all railroad freight in 1961 paid rates that covered less than out-of-pocket costs. As a rule, valuable manufactured goods paid high shipping rates while cheap bulk commodities paid low rates, and the farther a shipment traveled the less it paid per ton-mile. The system was inconsistent, unfair, and absurd. Railroads charged different rates to haul horses for slaughter and draft horses, sand for concrete and sand for glass, lime for agriculture and lime for industry. Wheat in 1961 paid railroads more revenue above out-of-pocket costs than any other commodity; while wine—a high-priced, nonbulk luxury—carried from West to East paid only 79 percent of out-of-pocket costs. Oranges could be shipped from California to New York as cheaply as from Florida.[4]

When combined with intermodal competition among rail, motor, and water carriers, value-of-service ratemaking accentu-

4. Friedlaender, *Dilemma of Freight Transport Regulation*, p. 24, n. 27; Merton J. Peck, "Competitive Policy for Transportation?" in *Perspectives on Antitrust Policy*, ed. Almarin Phillips (Princeton, 1965), p. 247: Robert C. Fellmeth, project director, *The Interstate Commerce Omission: The Public Interest and the ICC* (New York, 1970), pp. 156–57, 179–80.

ated the massive misallocation of transportation resources. Although in a monopoly situation value-of-service ratemaking maximized railroad profits, it encouraged excessive transportation and, when coupled with parity rates in the postwar years, enabled motor carriers to capture from railroads profitable high-tariff, less-than-40-ton shipments. Railroads were left primarily with low-tariff, bulk traffic. Through control of minimum rates, the ICC, Ernest W. Williams Jr. concluded in 1958, consistently deprived railroads of their cost advantage, which often prevented them from competing for traffic. The ICC determined whether railroads could reduce value-of-service rates to compete on a cost-of-service basis with other transportation modes and further determined whether the lowered rate should be based on long-run marginal (out-of-pocket) costs or must cover fully distributed costs, which include fixed charges. Most rates, however, were based on value-of-service, and both a railroad's profits and rates were proportionately higher where it had a monopoly, with rates from 50 to 400 percent higher where there was no water competition.[5]

Apparently, Congress in 1940 did not wish to prevent a transportation mode from charging a lower rate simply because it hurt a rival mode (assuming the fee more than covered cost of service). The Senate report accompanying the 1940 act declared, "If one or more forms of transportation cannot survive under equality of regulations, they are not entitled to survive." To the former ratemaking rule requiring the ICC to consider "the effect of rates on the movement of traffic," the 1940 act added the narrowing phrase "by the carrier or carriers for which the rates are prescribed," and the national transportation policy spoke of preserving inherent advantages of all modes.[6]

5. Fellmeth, *Interstate Commerce Omission*, pp. 157–58, 166, 181; Peck, "Competitive Policy for Transportation?" pp. 247–49; Friedlaender, *Dilemma of Freight Transport Regulation*, p. 103; Ernest W. Williams, Jr., *The Regulation of Rail-Motor Rate Competition* (New York, 1958), p. 212.

6. U.S., Congress, Senate, Committee on Commerce, *National Transportation Policy*, 87th Cong., 1st sess., 26 June 1961, S. Rept. 445, p. 396

The ICC, however, has been on all sides of the ratecutting question. In the 1939 *Petroleum* case, it refused to let railroads cut rates to a still compensatory level and required that they up their rates to match those of their river-truck competitors in the Pacific Northwest. Despite passage of the 1940 Transportation Act, the Supreme Court's *Scandrett* decision (1941) affirmed the ICC's *Petroleum* ruling. The commission, however, in *Seatrain* (1940)—its first major decision under the 1940 act—declared that "no carrier should be required to maintain rates which would be unreasonable, judged by other standards, for the purpose of protecting the traffic of a competitor." Five years later in *New Automobiles*, the ICC refused to raise rail rates, yielding something between out-of-pocket and fully distributed costs, to equal truck rates, since raising rail rates would have given trucks, with their service advantage, the interstate transportation of new automobiles. The ICC, however, soon abandoned its *New Automobiles* position for umbrella ratemaking (artificially high railroad rates protecting truckers and water carriers), upheld earlier in the *Scandrett* case. In several cases beginning in 1951, the ICC, stating that a rate should "not be lower than necessary" to secure a fair share of traffic, branded unfair remunerative rates that would have increased railroad freight.[7]

Congress in 1940 once again had challenged the ICC, and once again the ICC failed to meet the challenge. With its power over surface transportation, the ICC could have transformed the generalities of the national transportation policy into the reality of a system utilizing the advantages of rail, motor, and water

---

(hereafter cited as *Doyle Report*); Henry J. Friendly, *The Federal Administrative Agencies: The Need for Better Definition of Standards* (Cambridge, Mass., 1962), pp. 113–14.

7. Petroleum Between Wash., Ore., Idaho, Mont., 234 ICC 609 (1939), Scandrett v. United States, 312 U.S. 661 (1941), Seatrain Lines, Inc. v. Akron, Canton & Youngstown R.R., 243 ICC 199 (1940), New Automobiles in Interstate Commerce, 259 ICC 475 (1945), in Friendly, *Federal Administrative Agencies*, pp. 119–31; Hilton, *Transportation Act of 1958*, pp. 22–27.

facilities. Instead, the ICC was cautious, ambiguous, and inconsistent. Even the *New Automobiles* decision, which the commission considered a declaration of policy, insisted that reasonable minimum rates be determined individually. Unable or unwilling to enunciate a uniform policy, the commission continued its case-by-case approach. Determining individual cases on their facts led both to decisions ignoring the effect of rates on other modes and to decisions placing great weight on how rates would affect other modes. Efforts to define how low a rate is necessary and what is a fair share of the traffic led the ICC into further inconsistencies; at times the ICC insisted on rate parity between differing modes and at times it permitted rate differentials.[8]

The Transportation Act of 1958

The transportation industry's malaise and the desperate condition of railroads was obvious by the mid-1950s. The Eisenhower administration established the Presidential Advisory Committee on Transport Policy and Organization (headed by Secretary of Commerce Sinclair Weeks and called the Weeks committee), which in 1955 rejected the traditional panacea of more ICC regulation and indicated that the transportation industry was overregulated. The Weeks committee further proposed clarifying national transportation policy to permit common carriers more freedom in setting competitive rates and suggested that in these matters the ICC should "act as an adjudicator, not a business manager." Specifically, the Weeks committee suggested changing the ratemaking rule to prevent the commission from disapproving a compensatory rate —based on what the service cost the common carrier—merely because it fell below the rates of competitors or might hurt them. The Weeks committee also proposed eliminating state-public-service-commission control over discontinuing passenger trains by lodging complete control in the more sympathetic ICC. Apparently more interested in helping railroads than in

8. Friendly, *Federal Administrative Agencies*, pp. 127–31; *Doyle Report*, pp. 400–1.

simply promoting competition, the committee called for more
ICC regulation of contract and private carriers in motor and
water transportation.[9]

Suspect because it came out of Eisenhower's millionaire-
businessmen cabinet and was influenced by railroads, the Weeks
report needed reinforcement, which soon came from academic
scholars. James C. Nelson's study for the Brookings Institution,
Railroad Transportation and Public Policy (1959), blamed the
desperate plight of railroads on shortsighted policies of both
management and government. He suggested that management
utilize freight cars and labor more efficiently, abandon hope-
lessly unprofitable passenger trains but stimulate demand on the
salvageable routes with lower fares and better service, move
from value-of-service pricing to more competitive cost-of-service
pricing, and attract more capital investment for modernization.
Nelson further suggested that government be neutral in treating
rail, motor, water, and air carriers, that it charge transport agencies user fees for public facilities, and that it relax ICC regulation—minimum rates in particular—to promote competition
and economy in transportation.[10]

In *The Economics of Competition in the Transportation
Industries* (1959), written for the Harvard Economic Studies,
John R. Meyer, Merton J. Peck, John Stenason, and Charles
Zwick also evaluate the ICC's impact. Written in 1956 and
1957, their study concluded that the transportation industry had
grown and prospered less than other industries because it had
been overregulated. *The Economics of Competition* recommended that government controls be decreased and that competition be encouraged. The study suggested that value-of-service
ratemaking had "failed miserably as an allocator of transporta-

9. Friendly, *Federal Administrative Agencies*, pp. 131–32; Meyer
et al., *Economics of Competition*, p. 271; Hilton, *Transportation Act of
1958*, pp. 14–21; Nelson, *Railroad Transportation and Public Policy*, pp.
117–24, 193–230.
10. Nelson, *Railroad Transportation and Public Policy*, pp. 412–35.

tion resources," that average-cost pricing would allocate resources reasonably well, that truckers and airlines were sufficiently mature to do without government subsidies, that railroad passenger services were proliferated unnecessarily, that railroads charged totally uneconomic rates on small shipments, and that railroad management was unimaginative, complacent, and lethargic.

Bristling with specific suggestions, *The Economics of Competition* advocated that ICC restraints be relaxed and that railroad rate bureaus be abandoned so that rail rates, when justified by costs, could compete with truck rates. Other proposals were that piggyback services be available to all truckers including contract and private carriers (with maximum rates regulated to reflect service cost), that railroads abandon lines and services incapable of producing their long-run marginal cost or that could be provided more efficiently by a different mode. The study also suggested that mergers be used to improve efficiency and reduce overhead by meshing small roads into large systems rather than by joining large systems, which would save nothing since their costs would increase in proportion to their traffic. The Meyer study found that small truckers merged with large truckers not to reduce overhead, which is relatively low for all truckers, but to increase trucking industry stability, and suggested that railroads be allowed to operate rail-and-truck facilities. Arguing that completely integrated transportation companies were undesirable because they would eliminate competitive ratesetting between different modes, the study proposed that restrictions on entry into the trucking industry be relaxed for private and contract carriers, that motor and water common-carrier rates no longer be regulated, and that labor unions eliminate outmoded work rules that decrease productivity.

In short, Meyer et al. advocated virtually no regulation for motor, water, and air carriers; reduced regulation for railroads and pipelines; and relatively strict regulation only for certain

pipeline operations, bulk shipments, and piggyback operations
in which railroads had a monopoly. To bring about regulation
by competitive forces, they argued that "vigorous, imaginative,
and knowledgeable" transportation managers were more crucial
than new legislation. Regulatory practices rooted in the days of
enormous railroad power, the study noted, resulted in economic
absurdities. Those practices virtually ignored the development
of powerful industrial combinations of farmer and other producer organizations, and of competing transportation modes.[11]
The Economics of Competition confirmed and went beyond
most of the Weeks report's conclusions, but it was published too
late to influence the 1958 Transportation Act.

That act, which especially affected ratemaking and rail passenger service, evolved from the Weeks report. An earlier 1955
proposal included the "three-shall-nots" of minimum ratemaking: the ICC shall not consider the effect of proposed charges
on any other mode's traffic, the relation of proposed charges to
any other mode's charges, nor whether the proposed charges are
lower than necessary to meet competition from other modes.
Regarding the umbrella ratemaking controversy as trivial, the
ICC opposed both the three shall-nots and the requirement that
it set no maximum rate below the full service cost, denied that
the commission tried to manage the transportation business,
and demanded not less but more regulation. Facing additional
and even more formidable opposition from nonrail carriers,
Secretary of Commerce Weeks retreated. In what amounted to a
reversal, he suggested that the ICC should consider the effects
of minimum rates that would reduce competition, create a
monopoly, or destroy a competitor.

The Weeks reversal reflected the fundamental shift of railroads "from overlord to underdog" in the political arena. In the
mid-1950s the lobbying power of the American Trucking Associations, Inc., representing over thirty thousand trucking
companies, of the Teamsters' Union, of truck-minded farm

11. Meyer et al., *Economics of Competition*, pp. v–vi, 242–73.

organizations, such as the National Grange, and of 1,700 water carriers far outweighed railroad lobbying influence. Railroads had manipulated state legislators and influenced congressmen through political contributions and legal retainers, but by the 1950s these methods were neither in good repute nor a match for the vast numbers mobilized by truckers and their allies. The growing trucking industry, with votes diffused throughout the country, influenced politicians far more than did ebbing railroad power, concentrated in capital cities.

Though by 1958 railroads mounted a respectable counter-attack before the Senate Subcommittee on Surface Transportation, their effort proved only partly successful. The subcommittee, headed by George A. Smathers of Florida, praised the *New Automobile* decision and chided the commission for not allowing different modes to utilize their inherent advantages in rate-making, but conceded that the ICC should prevent unfair destructive practices. Thinking the only legislation necessary was an admonition to the commission to follow consistently "the policy enunciated in the Automobile case," the Smathers committee proposed an amendment requiring the ICC to ignore the effect of proposed minimum rail-rates on other modes. While the three shall-nots were dropped, their substance, it was feared by motor and water carriers, permeated the Smathers committee formulation. To hush these fears, the House committee came up with an ambiguous proposal acceptable to all transportation modes. The final "Janus-faced" version attacked umbrella rate-making—"rates of a carrier shall not be held up to a particular level to protect the traffic of any other mode of transportation" —but then retreated by adding "giving due consideration to the objectives of the national transportation policy." Railroads could stress the injunction to compete, while motor and water carriers could emphasize that umbrella rates had been approved to preserve—as national transportation policy directed—rail, highway, and water transportation systems. "The legislators," Judge Henry J. Friendly remarked, "had tackled a tough problem, had looked long and hard at it, and then, caught between conflicting pressures, had come up with a whimper."[12]

There were other sections in the 1958 Transportation Act. Reversing a trend since 1935, it reduced the number of regulation-exempted agricultural commodities transported by motor carriers. The act also authorized the ICC to guarantee repayment of $500 million in commercial loans to help railroads acquire new equipment, but by 1961 railroads had borrowed only $86 million. With traffic losses forcing them to curtail services, railroads were understandably reluctant to pay commercial-bank rates on debts for new equipment. Congress, in the new act, also made it easier for railroads to discontinue interstate and intrastate passenger service by giving the ICC, rather than community-minded state commissions, authority to make such decisions. Since the 1958 act allowed discontinuances upon short notice and placed the burden of proof upon rushed public agencies, it was widely criticized for letting the railroads, rather than the ICC, determine how the public would be served. On the other hand, the act removed unrealistic obstacles to discontinuances, allowed railroads to reduce their staggering passenger-service losses, and forced state and local agencies to assume responsibility for many commuter services. Had Senator Jacob Javits of New York not deleted a "net loss criterion" from the act, railroads would have discontinued even more trains; there were few profitable passenger trains in 1958 and virtually none after the post office adopted the zip code in 1963 and began phasing out the Railway Mail Service. Congress, as usual, gave the ICC wide discretion, but, lacking a net-loss criterion and forced to choose between enormous railroad losses

12. Friendly, *Federal Administrative Agencies*, pp. 131–35; Hilton, *Transportation Act of 1958*, pp. 28–34; Robert Bendiner, "The Railroads: From Overlord to Underdog," *Reporter* 19 (7 August 1958):19–24; Charles H. Hession, "The Mobile Motor Carriers: A Study of Social Mobility and Entrepreneurial Behavior in the Motor Carrier Industry" (1963; unpublished manuscript in the possession of Charles H. Hession, Department of Economics, Brooklyn College of the City University of New York), pp. 284, 287–97, 309–16.

and great public pressure against discontinuances, the commission reacted with inconsistent and vacillating decisions. Eschewing any rule, the ICC remained in its groove, used its traditional case-by-case approach, and balanced the losses of each train against the health of the railroad and the public clamor for the train's continuance. With nobody wanting to lose or use passenger service, the ICC was in a quandary. The sick bay it had been asked to administer had become a terminal ward. In effect, the commission let the railroads practice mercy killing on some passenger trains but insisted on prolonging the lives of other terminally ill ones. By September 1960 the ICC had allowed railroads to kill 116 interstate passenger trains and 20 intrastate trains, and by 1968 intercity passenger trains had been reduced by three-fifths, more than a third of passenger routes had been abandoned, and two states were without passenger rail service. Letting public pressure outweight railroad losses, the ICC salvaged a core of intercity trains for future operation by federal government subsidy (Amtrak).[13]

The key provision of the 1958 act, the new minimum rate-making rule, proved a monumental failure. Rather than eliminate the ICC's inconsistent minimum-rate policy, the new act added to the confusion. Consistently inconsistent, the ICC failed to affirm and maintain a minimum-rate policy. In the unanimous *Friendship* decision (1959), the full commission held that it would be guided by all the provisions and amendments to the ICA, rather than a single ratemaking provision, and typically prescribed fully compensatory minimum rates with a differential that would preserve the existence of motor carriers. In its *Tobacco* decision (1960), Division 2 of the ICC rejected as destructive rate-warfare compensatory rail-and-motor rate reductions, preserved existing rates and differentials,

13. *Landis Report*, p. 23; *Doyle Report*, pp. 573–76, 578; Clair Wilcox, *Public Policies Toward Business*, 4th ed. (Homewood, Ill., 1971), p. 387; Hilton, *Transportation Act of 1958*, pp. 34–43, 79–80, 97–154, 193–98; Robert B. Carson, *Main Line to Oblivion: The Disintegration of New York Railroads in the Twentieth Century* (Port Washington, N.Y., 1971), pp. 199–203, 215–22.

and clearly tried, as George W. Hilton observes, "to preserve a value-of-service rate structure in the face of competition among carriers that would have resulted in a cost-based set of tariffs." On the other hand, the full commission in *Paint and Related Articles* (1959) unanimously approved reduced rates—designed to regain traffic lost to motor carriers—that would cover long-run, out-of-pocket costs but not fully distributed costs. The *Paint* case indicated that the ICC veered toward constructing minimum rates on a cost-plus basis, but the decision, nevertheless, did equivocate. While it approved the reduced *Paint* rates, it left open the possibility that cost-based rates could be ruled unfair and destructive. Commissioner Charles A. Webb exclaimed that the *Paint* decision ignored the important question of how the 1958 Transportation Act affected minimum-rate policy.[14]

Testifying in 1960 before a subcommittee of the Senate Committee on Interstate and Foreign Commerce, ICC Chairman John H. Winchell confirmed the commission's irresolution. When asked how the 1958 act changed the ratemaking rule, Winchell responded, "I don't know that the 1958 amendment changed those portions other than writing into the act the rule of conduct which the Commission had previously followed [in *New Automobiles*]." Questioned further, however, Winchell said that the 1958 act resulted in bigger emphasis on service cost, "making it a more predominant factor in the consideration of the reasonableness of rates," but insisted that "there are many factors" to be considered in rate cases. "There is," Winchell confessed, "quite a difference of opinion as to how much emphasis should be placed on the upper part of 15a(3) [which rejected high rates to protect other competing modes] in proportion to the last statement, giving due regard to the national

14. Gasoline & Fuel Oil from Friendship to Va. & W.Va., 299 ICC 609 (1957), 305 ICC 673 (1959), Tobacco from N.C. to Cent. Territory, 309 ICC 347 (1960), Paint & Related Articles in Official Territory, 308 ICC 439 (1959), cited in *Doyle Report*, pp. 401–5, Friendly, *Federal Administrative Agencies*, pp. 136–37, and Hilton, *Transportation Act of 1958*, pp. 47–55.

transportation policy." By testifying first that the minimum-rate policy had not changed, then that it had changed, and finally that the meaning of the change was debatable, the ICC chairman added to the confusion.[15]

Mounting Criticism of the ICC

While this confusion prevailed, the nation in 1960 elected John F. Kennedy president. Seeking advice on regulatory commissions, Kennedy turned to James M. Landis, who had been Justice Louis Brandeis's law clerk, had served as chairman of the Civil Aeronautics Board, and had been dean of the Harvard Law School. In a December 1960 report for the president-elect, Landis criticized the regulatory agencies for their slow and costly procedures, for their piecemeal solutions, for their failure to develop broad policies and to plan for the future, for their inability to coordinate policy with other regulatory agencies, and for their weak personnel. Landis advocated an executive office to coordinate interagency activities; a permanent chairman for the ICC with power to appoint personnel and to reorganize the commission to give it positive direction; and, to cut the enormous workload at the commission level, that single commissioners, hearing examiners, or employee boards decide cases (subject to review) and that the full commission reconsider fewer division decisions.[16]

During the same month that Landis reported to Kennedy, John P. Doyle, staff director of the Transportation Study Group (created earlier by the Senate) submitted his draft report to the Senate Committee on Interstate and Foreign Commerce. Entitled *National Transportation Policy* and printed the following June, the Doyle report combined vast quantities of data with a critical yet constructive attitude and proved an informative source on the transportation industry and a powerful argument for overhauling its regulation. Regulatory policy, the Doyle report concluded, "has produced *a general program of preserving*

15. *Doyle Report*, pp. 405–7.
16. *Landis Report*, passim; *New York Times*, 27 December 1960.

the status quo which is in direct opposition to the overall objective of a dynamic transportation system which can best serve the economy and defense of the country." Predicting that the nation was headed for a transportation crisis, the report cited the relative decline of common as compared to contract and private carriers and, most significantly, the absolute decline in railroad traffic and revenue from 1956 to 1959. Railroads suffered, the report continued, from the great technological developments in competing modes; from enormous public investment in highways, airports, and waterways at a time when railroads had difficulty raising private capital; and from management bent more on obstructing competitors than on constructing bold measures. Both motor and rail common carriers had higher labor costs than nonregulated private and contract motor-carriers, who generally employed cheaper nonunion labor; and common carriers were subjected to "inequitable and destructive" ICC regulation. For example, the ICC regulated common-carrier minimum and maximum rates (but did not regulate private motor-carrier or bulk water-carrier rates), kept common carriers from acquiring facilities of other modes that would improve their service and efficiency, restricted consolidations of intramodal common carriers, and dictated the scope of motor-common-carrier service. These restrictions failed to recognize that railroads no longer monopolized transportation, that all common carriers faced stiff competition, and that consolidations of similar modes into larger systems and of different modes into integrated transportation companies would increase competition between regulated and unregulated carriers.

Railroad decline and the corresponding rise of other carriers resulted in the fantastic growth of public and private investment in transportation per ton-mile and passenger-mile. The investment was particularly apparent in the interstate highway system —"nontaxpaying belts of concrete," accommodating "more and more privately operated and lightly loaded automobiles and trucks," built on real estate often taken from "productive agricultural and commercial use." The Doyle report, however, predicted that private and contract carriers could not serve the nation's mass transportation needs and that railroads with their enormous capacity per train and their narrow roadbed would most likely expand by the century's end. These circumstances clearly indicated the need for a "basic revision of national policy."

The Doyle report suggested that Congress overhaul transportation laws, combine regulatory agencies into a federal transportation commission, and create a new executive department of transportation. Besides formulating and reviewing policy, the new department would execute the administrative functions of existing transportation agencies and would coordinate statistical collections and research projects with the proposed federal transportation commission. The report further suggested that Congress form a joint transportation committee and that it eradicate from transportation laws ambiguous phrases ("undue preference" and "*destructive* competition," for example) and eliminate inconsistencies and inequalities in the industry (such as exempting from regulation agricultural commodities and fish on highways, allowing the federal government reduced rates on common carriers, and taxing railroads and pipelines more heavily than motor, water, or air carriers).

The Doyle report regarded transportation regulation essential but insisted it be flexible and oriented to changing times. Motor-carrier regulation was particularly rigid, badly enforced, and unimaginative. To provide transportation service to sparsely populated areas, the report suggested a combined, single-vehicle service for passengers, mail, express, and freight. Pointing to "gross inadequacies of enforcement of economic and safety regulation" in highway transportation (in June 1960 illegal bootleg truckers, some utilizing "buy and sell" loopholes and fictitious leases, comprised 25 percent of truckers), the report called for a uniform, jointly developed federal-state enforcement program administered by state agencies. With ICC-issued motor-carrier certificates restricting commodities carried, routes traveled, and points served, highway transportation was

fragmented, confused, and wasteful. ICC-atomized grants required a new application for each new item a carrier wished to
haul. Thus, in 1959 a frozen-food carrier from the South to the
Northeast and Midwest was only authorized to carry frozen
hush puppies from High Point, North Carolina, despite the fact
that the shipper planned early production of other frozen-food
specialties. The Doyle report suggested that the authorization
program be reoriented toward economy and efficiency rather
than protecting other carriers.

The Doyle report advocated that the government do more
than regulate transportation. It recognized that to save commuter services and to solve metropolitan transportation problems the federal government must work with local authorities.
To save intercity passenger rail service, the report suggested a
national corporation "operating on existing facilities over routes
chosen by competent market survey," and, to increase and
fairly apportion freight cars, it suggested that Congress create a
national freight-car corporation.

The most important recommendations made by the Doyle
report concerned rates. Recognizing that devising a satisfactory
minimum-rate policy was troublesome, the report rejected the
traditional and prevailing concept of value-of-service rates,
which the railroads, the public, and the ICC had long espoused,
and concluded that "greater emphasis should be placed upon
cost as a factor in determining rates." Specifically, the report
advocated that long-run marginal cost (similar to long-run, out-
of-pocket costs which include appropriate costs but not all fixed
costs) be the floor for competitive ratecutting, that no carrier be
forced to maintain rates above long-run marginal costs to protect another carrier's traffic, and that service pricing below cost
was unfair in intermodal competition.[17]

Responding to the Landis and Doyle reports, the ICC in
early 1961 reorganized its structure and procedures. It strengthened the chairman by giving him authority to appoint personnel,

17. *Doyle Report*, passim, particularly pp. 1–28, 38, 70, 80, 92, 120,
534, and 549.

assign tasks, and control the budget, created the office of vice-chairman to supervise the bureaus, which had each been administered by an individual commissioner, and reduced ICC divisions to three. These improvements were negated, however, by retaining the annual rotation of the chairmanship and vice-chairmanship. Delegating its power further than it had in the past (despite enabling legislation dating back to 1933), the ICC assigned responsibility for important cases to individual commissioners, limited the right of full-commission appeal to general transportation issues, and increased the number of employee boards from four to twelve to handle the largely routine 28,000 annual nonadversary cases, which since 1933 had been handled usually by individual commissioners. In addition, Congress allowed employee boards to decide cases involving oral hearings.[18] Concentrating administrative responsibilities in the chairman and vice-chairman and delegating power to individual members freed the ICC to wrestle with postwar transportation problems. Wrestling neither vigorously nor capably with these problems and unable to direct its fragmented and delegated power, the ICC merely reinforced its dependence on its staff.

Mounting criticism of transportation policy in general and ICC practices in particular culminated with President John F. Kennedy's transportation message to Congress (5 April 1962). "A chaotic patchwork," Kennedy observed, "of inconsistent and often obsolete legislation and regulation has evolved from a history of specific actions addressed to specific problems of specific industries at specific times. This patchwork does not fully reflect either the dramatic changes in technology of the past half-century or the parallel changes in the structure of competition." Declaring that "current federal policies must be reshaped in the most fundamental and far-reaching fashion," Kennedy called for more competition and less subsidization and regulation of

18. I. L. Sharfman, *The Interstate Commerce Commission: A Study in Administrative Law and Procedure*, 5 vols. (New York, 1931–37), 4:62–64 (hereafter cited as Sharfman, *ICC*); *75th Annual Report*, 1961, pp. 1–6.

railroads, airlines, buses, trucks, and barges and urged massive federal aid for urban transit systems. Hailed as the most comprehensive transportation proposal a president ever submitted to Congress, Kennedy's plan would increase competition and lower rates by allowing railroads, buses, and airlines to cut passenger fares without ICC or CAB approval if fares covered service cost and by allowing railroads and trucks to cut bulk commodity rates and railroads and water carriers to cut farm commodity and fish rates, all without ICC approval. Although Kennedy wished the ICC to continue to regulate maximum rates, his plan to eliminate its control over minimum bulk-rates would benefit railroads enormously. Kennedy also proposed that the ICC encourage experimental freight rates combining services, varying classifications, and giving truck common carriers the same piggyback rates as shippers, that the federal government scrutinize its negative railroad-merger attitude, and that authority over emergency railroad loans be transferred from the ICC to the Department of Commerce.[19]

The *New York Times'* prediction that there was "no realistic prospect that Congress will act on the plan this year" proved accurate. White House and railroad pressure for legislation was offset by the hostility of water carriers, truckers, and the ICC. Hostile carriers, fearing traffic loss, and the ICC, fearing power loss, joined to prophesy that the legislation would bring "predatory rate discrimination by the railroads." These fears were based on the substantially lower rates—sometimes four times lower—that railroads charged when competing with other modes. It cost $4.39 to ship a ton of limestone 346 miles by rail from Baton Rouge to Bauxite, Arkansas, but only $2.40 to ship it the 735 miles from Baton Rouge to Prairie du Rocher, Illinois, a route with water competition. Although administration supporters reintroduced the legislation in the next Congress and Kennedy continued his support, the bill bogged down in committee and congressmen turned to the extreme alternative of extending ICC regulation to bulk shipments and agricultural

19. *New York Times*, 6 April 1962.

commodities. Such a move, desired by the ICC, would maintain the traditional value-of-service rate structure.[20] By November 1963, when Kennedy was assassinated, the legislation was dead; and hope for its resurrection died with him.

Minimum-Rate Policy in the 1960s

Since Congress failed in 1962 and 1963 to deny the ICC minimum-rate power over bulk and agricultural commodities, the commission and the courts continued to grope for a minimum-rate policy. Because that policy was unclear, different patterns have been observed. One view discerns that the ICC— desiring lower rates on bulk commodities—generally permitted railroads to cut rates to out-of-pocket costs to meet barge competition but would not allow railroads to reduce rates on high-value goods to compete with trucks. Others find that the commission insisted on "fully-distributed cost pricing" when another regulated mode objected, but when a regulated carrier competed with a nonregulated carrier the ICC did not object if the rates merely covered out-of-pocket costs. "The ICC protective umbrella," in short, "extends only to its perceived constituency, the regulated carriers."[21] While the ICC did seem to protect trucks more than barges from rail competition and did at times help regulated carriers attract traffic from unregulated carriers, we believe that the ICC's minimum-rate policy primarily aimed to preserve existing relationships and to prevent destructive competition. Content with the status quo, the ICC in the 1960s tended to maintain either differential or parity rates as an umbrella to protect competing modes (whether regulated or not) and avoided destructive competition, whether stressing that a proposed lower rate should cover out-of-pocket costs or

20. Ibid., 6 April, 16 September, 1 December 1962, 6 March, 19 May 1963; Friedlaender, *Dilemma of Freight Transport Regulation*, pp. 25, 62; Fellmeth, *Interstate Commerce Omission*, p. 167.

21. Friedlaender, *Dilemma of Freight Transport Regulation*, pp. 23–24; Meats, Fruits, Vegetables—TOFC Transcontinental, 316 ICC 585 (1962), in Fellmeth, *Interstate Commerce Omission*, p. 144, n. See also Hilton, *Transportation Act of 1958*, pp. 25, 66.

should meet fully distributed costs. Indeed, the ICC's protective umbrella hampered railroads—the commission's most important constituent—more than it did any other regulated or unregulated transportation mode.

Batted between the commission and the courts throughout the 1960s, minimum-rate policy remained hazy. The ICC lacked consistency, the full commission often reversed Division 2, district courts frequently reversed the commission, and the Supreme Court sometimes affirmed and sometimes overruled ICC decisions. In the 1960s the ICC's minimum-rate decisions were ambiguous. They failed to utilize consistently either out-of-pocket or fully distributed costs but rather, as Carl H. Fulda observed in 1961, created "the impression that the Commission selects whichever theory appears best to fit the case at hand." In the 1960 *Sea-Land* case, the ICC, following a hint in its 1959 *Paint* decision, ruled that compensatory railroad piggyback rates that would destroy coastwise water carriers were unfair, whether they covered out-of-pocket costs or fully distributed costs, and insisted on differentially higher rail rates. In 1961 the federal district court rejected the ICC's argument that water carriers had to be preserved for national defense (a curious argument since torpedoes destroy ships more effectively than bombs do railroads) and reversed the ICC's decision where the proposed lower rail-rates exceeded fully distributed costs.

The Supreme Court agreed in 1963 that the ICC could not cancel the compensatory piggyback rail rates, attempted to clarify minimum-rate policy, and remanded the case to the ICC for further consideration. The Court argued that a compensatory rate was not unfair or destructive simply because it would divert any or even all traffic from a higher-cost competing mode, that a carrier could not set rates to impair or destroy the inherent advantage of the low-cost mode, that national defense needs were—as the ICC contended—a part of the national transportation policy, and that the ICC failed to prove that the piggyback rate reductions would hurt water carriers and threaten national defense. Guided by this decision, the ICC reversed several prior reports which had prescribed differentials to protect water carriers and approved as just and reasonable proposed rail reductions which it judged would not destroy intercoastal water carriers. Clearly, the ICC could protect a low-cost carrier from destructive intermodal competition. To get this same protection, a high-cost carrier had to prove itself essential to national defense and its competitors destructive. Later in 1963, the Court upheld the ICC and refused to sanction a below-cost, barge-rail coal rate from West Virginia to Chicago, but Justice Hugo Black, with Justice William O. Douglas concurring, dissented and castigated the ICC for its "Sanskrit-like" opinions, for favoring large railroads (whose traffic the decision would protect), and for delaying decisions for as long as eight years.[22]

The celebrated *Big John* case illustrates both the ICC's predilection for umbrella ratemaking—despite the *Sea-Land* decision—and the stifling effect of ICC status quo policies on innovation. Strong competition, from trucks at one extreme and bulk carriers at the other, has impelled railroads to adopt technological innovations, such as truck trailers going piggyback on flat cars. Big John cars and unit trains are other examples of cost-saving innovations that have come despite ICC regulation and have begun to undermine value-of-service ratemaking. To compete with trucks and barges for grain shipments, the Southern Railroad invested $14 million in Big John aluminum hopper cars, which were double the capacity, half the weight, and cheaper and easier to load and unload than conventional box cars. Over the protests of water carriers, the Southern in 1961 applied for an up-to-60-percent rate reduction on grain. Early in 1963 Division 2 of the ICC approved the reduction, but a

22. Commodities—Pan-Atlantic S.S. Corp., 313 ICC 23 (1960), New York, N.H. & H. R.R. Co. v. United States, 199 F. Supp. 635 (D. Conn. 1961), Interstate Commerce Commission v. New York, N.H. & H. R.R. Co., 372 U.S. 744 (1963), in Friendly, *Federal Administrative Agencies*, pp. 138–39, Hilton, *Transportation Act of 1958*, pp. 55–60, and *76th Annual Report*, 1962, pp. 183–84; *77th Annual Report*, 1963, pp. 158–59; Garden Hose & Electrical Cable from N.J. or R.I. to Tex., 319 ICC 227 (1963), ibid., p. 68, and in *78th Annual Report*, 1964, pp. 22–23; *New York Times*, 23 April, 6 May, and 3 December 1963.

combination of grain-carrying truckers and barge operators, the Tennessee Valley Authority, which reflected barge views, and southern milling and grain elevator interests, fearful of eastern competitors, convinced the full commission to reconsider the reduction. In July 1963 the commission did not insist on rail rates covering fully distributed costs but preserved the barge lines' cost advantage by paring the Southern's reduction to 53 percent. In 1964 a federal district court overruled the ICC stating that the Southern's proposed rates were not prejudiced against certain Tennessee River points. After the Supreme Court in 1965 agreed and remanded the *Big John* case to the ICC for further consideration, the commission decided that the up-to-60-percent rate reduction would meet unregulated truck competition, would not ruin Tennessee River towns or barge lines, and was indeed legal. In its efforts to protect rival modes —in this instance unregulated ones—the ICC for four years deprived the Southern Railroad its full reward for developing a major cost-saving innovation.[23]

The ICC's rate policies also postponed for years the use of unit coal trains in the East. First used by the Railroad Administration in 1919, these trains, if used from 1958 to 1962, could have saved railroads up to $9 million annually. Typically composed of 100 cars, each carrying 100 tons, and forming a shipment of 10,000 tons, or approximately a fourth of a single barge tow, unit coal trains usually go from mine to utility and under proper conditions are competitive with barge operations. Although permitting discriminatory rates for similar services or commodities to meet certain competitive situations under existing technology, the ICC insisted that savings from innovations

23. Grain in Multiple-Car Shipments—River Crossings to So., 318 ICC 641 (1963), in *77th Annual Report*, 1963, pp. 69–70, and 325 ICC 752 (1965), in *79th Annual Report*, 1965, pp. 23–24; Cincinnati, New Orleans & Texas Pacific Ry. v. United States, 229 F.Supp. 572 (1964), in *78th Annual Report*, 1964, pp. 21–22; Arrow Transportation Co. v. C., N.O. & T. P. R. Co., 379 U.S. 642 (1965), in Hilton, *Transportation Act of 1958*, pp. 65–73; Friedlaender, *Dilemma of Freight Transport Regulation*, pp. 88–96, 120–26; Wilcox, *Public Policies Toward Business*, p. 386; *New York Times*, 19 January and 11 September 1965.

be applied nondiscriminately to all shippers using similar services. Since, with ICC approval, railroads had discriminated in coal shipments—charging interior cities higher rates than coastal cities serviced by competing pipelines and oil tankers— the introduction of nondiscriminatory unit trains, tying rates to costs, would have reduced railroad revenue from coal traffic. Because of ICC policy, the use of unit coal trains did not become profitable until 1962. Before that date, reductions on the discriminatory interior coal rates would have more than offset projected unit-train savings. By mixing discriminatory and non-discriminatory regulations, the ICC delayed an important cost-saving innovation.[24]

Despite their ultimate stunning victory in the *Big John* case, railroads emerged from the 1960s circumscribed by ICC minimum-rate powers. Hoping to seize the carriage of ingot molds from Pittsburgh to Steelton, Kentucky, the Pennsylvania and Louisville & Nashville railroads reduced their rate from $11.86 to $5.11 to match the barge-truck rate. Division 2 allowed the reduction, but after water and motor carriers protested that the railroad reduction deprived them—the low-cost mode—of their inherent advantage the full ICC insisted that railroad rates cover fully distributed costs ($7.59 per ton mile) rather than merely out-of-pocket costs ($4.69). The decision appalled railroads because their rates based on out-of-pocket costs (as in the *Big John* case) could compete with barge rates but heavy fixed charges made rail rates based on fully distributed costs high enough to amount to umbrella ratemaking. Although the federal district court reversed the ICC's stand, in 1968 the Supreme Court upheld the commission's right to determine what costs rates should cover, approved its setting of differential rates to reflect differences in service, and commended its efforts to prevent rate wars. If it wished, the ICC, with the Court's blessing,

24. Paul W. MacAvoy and James Sloss, *Regulation of Transport Innovation: The ICC and Unit Coal Trains to the East Coast* (New York, 1967), passim, particularly pp. 56–61, 116–19; Friedlaender, *Dilemma of Freight Transport Regulation*, pp. 48–49, 94–96.

could reject rates that fell below fully distributed costs, could engage in umbrella ratemaking, could prevent competition, could protect rival modes, could maintain the status quo.[25]

By 1968 the ICC had the semblance of a minimum-rate policy. It was the product of the commission's desire to maintain the status quo and the Supreme Court's contradictory attempts to define the ambiguous 1958 Transportation Act. The commission had protected existing carriers whether regulated or not, but the Court (in *Sea-Land* and in *Big John*—but not in *Ingot Molds*) made the ICC shift its emphasis from protecting other modes by maintaining differentially higher rail rates to allowing more competition through compensatory rates. The ICC in 1968 boasted that it permitted great latitude in meeting intermodal price competition through reduced rates, especially when traffic could be attracted from unregulated modes. The commission had moved from preventing competition in the early 1960s to meeting but not destroying it in the late 1960s. The ICC preferred that a low-cost mode (defined by fully distributed rather than out-of-pocket costs) not destroy a high-cost competitor. To meet competition, rates could be lowered to out-of-pocket costs, but if what proved to be the low-cost mode opposed these rates its inherent advantage would be protected by the commission. Charles S. Morgan, of the ICC's Bureau of Transport Economics and Statistics, had observed in 1953 that while the commission tried to maintain competition, "its more formidable task, particularly since 1935, has been to see that competition does not get out of hand, to the injury of carriers, shippers, and the public." Above all, the ICC consistently wished to avoid destructive intermodal competition.[26]

25. Ingot Molds from Pennsylvania to Steelton, Ky., 323 ICC 758 (1965), 326 ICC 77 (1965), American Lines v. L. & N. R.R., 392 U.S. 571 (1968), in *79th Annual Report*, 1965, p. 25, and *82d Annual Report*, 1968, p. 22; Wilcox, *Public Policies Toward Business*, pp. 386–87; Friedlaender, *Dilemma of Freight Transport Regulation*, p. 94; Hilton, *Transportation Act of 1958*, pp. 74–78.

26. *82d Annual Report*, 1968, p. 21; Charles S. Morgan, "A Critique of 'The Marasmus of the ICC: The Commission, the Railroads, and the Public Interest,'" *Yale Law Journal* 62 (1953):201.

Maximum Rate Policy Since the Late 1960s

Although minimum-rate policy dominated the ICC's problems during the two decades following World War II, in the late 1960s the traditional problem of maximum-rate raises (which usually also involved raising minimum-rate floors) reasserted itself. Minimum-rate policy affected only points and commodities involved in intermodal competition; maximum-rate questions affected everything. Yet the ICC was more willing to increase maximum rates, which hurt all consumers but left intermodal relationships intact, than to lower minimum rates, which benefited few consumers but disturbed differentials, intermodal relationships, and the status quo. Through the depression and World War II, maximum rates remained essentially constant. The ICC refused both to raise rates in 1931 when railroads asked for a 15 percent increase and to cut rates in 1933 at the behest of bulk-commodity shippers, but in 1938 it granted a 10 percent increase except for agricultural products. Postwar inflation, however, led the ICC from 1946 to 1949 to approve a series of increases amounting to more than 50 percent. Apart from increases in 1952 and in 1957, freight rates were relatively stable from the fifties into the mid-sixties.[27]

Beginning in 1966 carriers attempted to raise rates. Blaming inflation generally and higher wages and more expensive equipment specifically, motor-carrier rate bureaus that year proposed rate hikes but offered little data to prove that ton-mile costs had increased. Unless suspended by the ICC's Suspension Board pending a final commission decision, rates went into effect. In the late 1960s the board suspended less than half of protested proposals, and the ICC tended to approve motor-carrier and railroad-rate-bureau proposals. If a protested motor-carrier rate

27. Fifteen Per Cent Case, 1931, 178 ICC 539 (1931) and General Rate Level Investigation, 1933, 195 ICC 5 (1933), in Sharfman, *ICC*, 3B:161–221; *52d Annual Report*, 1938, p. 46; *62d Annual Report*, 1948, p. 34; *63d Annual Report*, 1949, pp. 29–30; *66th Annual Report*, 1952, pp. 46–47; *72d Annual Report*, 1958, pp. 31–32; *75th Annual Report*, 1961, p. 40.

were not suspended and the ICC in six or nine months deemed the increase unjustified, shippers would not be refunded their surplus charge unless the commission specifically required it. Rate increase proposals paid; most protested ones were effective for long periods, and, even if they were ultimately rejected, new ones could be proposed that might not be suspended.[28]

When in 1967 railroad officials joined truckers' plea for a general rate increase, shipper protests were more effective. They were aided by the new Department of Transportation (DOT), created by Congress at President Lyndon B. Johnson's request in October 1966. Despite its "few powers to enforce an overall and unified transportation policy," the DOT played an active role in selected rate cases before the ICC. The new department prepared briefs, demanded that the commission, before approving increases, require proof that the cost of moving a freight ton had increased, and presented statistics that frequently conflicted with rate-bureau data. Even when DOT evidence convinced the ICC to reject increased rates, those rates frequently had not been suspended and had already been in effect for months. By 1969, however, the new department's efforts, abetted by the ICC's awareness of growing consumer strength, had their effect. Finding that "evidence submitted in support of the proposed increases was deficient," the ICC denied general motor-carrier rate increases in the Middle Atlantic, New England, Pacific Inland, and Middlewest territories. The commission also began ordering refunds to shippers who had paid rates later judged unlawful. The ICC's new stance was not hostility to rate increases, but simply a closer look at them.[29]

The railroads justified their 1967 general-rate-increase request by anticipating a $320 million increase in labor costs. The

---

28. Fellmeth, *Interstate Commerce Omission*, pp. 181–84; *82d Annual Report*, 1968, p. 18.

29. *83d Annual Report*, 1969, pp. 39–41; Friedlaender, *Dilemma of Freight Transport Regulation*, p. 2, n. 2; Fellmeth, *Interstate Commerce Omission*, pp. 183–85.

Bureau of Accounts, however, reported in January 1968 that the increase was $53.5 million, and railroads failed to report their cost figures by 14 February 1968, as required by the ICC. While maintaining that in the future petitioning railroads would have "to make a more complete disclosure of the facts," the ICC allowed the "inaccurately explained" evidence to justify a 3 percent flat increase, pending investigation of the proposed specific increases ranging from 3 to 10 percent. In the follow-up case, the Department of Agriculture complained that railroads failed to submit cost-accounting figures which the ICC had demanded, but the commission granted the increase, arguing that railroads estimated costs correctly and that increased expenses since 1966 would not be met by revenue from both increases.[30]

Citing "significant wage increases" and inflationary pressures, the ICC granted further rate increases to railroads. In *Increased Freight Rates, 1969*, the commission responded to "an urgent need for additional railroad revenues" with a 6 percent increase and in *Increased Freight Rates, 1970 and 1971* granted a 20 percent increase in the East, 18 percent in the West, and 12 percent in the South. The ICC granted further increases in 1972, 1973, and 1974 and to better handle mounting requests worked out procedures for railroads in presenting evidence for general rate increases. The ICC insisted, however, that the roads use the 10 percent raise granted in June 1974 for long deferred maintainance and capital improvements. By November 1974 the railroads were back with a 7 percent freight-rate raise request. Fearing the wrath of consumers, the ICC rejected this increase in January 1975 but quickly reversed itself in March, when its initial decision appeared to have pushed the Rock Island and other lines over the brink into bankruptcy. A month later most eastern and western roads asked for 5 percent

30. Increased Freight Rates, 1967, 332 ICC 280 (1967), in *81st Annual Report*, 1967, p. 19, and *82d Annual Report*, 1968, pp. 20–21; Increased Freight Rates, 1968, 332 ICC 590 (1968), and 332 ICC 714 (1969), in *83d Annual Report*, 1969, p. 36; Fellmeth, *Interstate Commerce Omission*, pp. 185–88.

more in 45 days and were joined by southern roads, who requested an additional 2.5 percent by October 1975. Reasoning that rate increases would lose traffic and revenue rather than improve income, some lines—notably the Chessie System—did not take advantage of the 7 percent increase and did not file for the two other raises.[31]

Motor carriers suffered from the same inflationary pressures as railroads. During fiscal 1970, the ICC investigated and approved an application for increased motor-carrier rates in the southwestern states and allowed over 35 other general motor-carrier rate increases to take effect without formal investigation. These rate increases tended to be 9 percent for small shipments and 6 percent for volume shipments. Reporting in 1970 that less-than-carload rail service had been largely assumed by motor carriers, while rail piggyback service threatened motor-carrier truck-load service, the ICC revised motor-carrier rate structure by raising rates on shipments less than 500 pounds and lowering rates on shipments over 1,000 pounds. By approving higher rates for smaller shipments, which trucks virtually monopolized, and reducing rates on larger truck shipments, which could often go piggyback, the ICC essentially required small businesses to subsidize motor-carrier competition with railroads. Charging higher rates for small shipments may have reflected service cost, but reducing large-shipment truck rates to engender competition with a more efficient piggyback service robbed railroads of their inherent advantage. Motor carriers secured two rate increases in fiscal 1971, but subsequent increases were slowed by new ICC rules requiring "specific data concerning traffic costs, revenue need, and affiliates" to be filed with the request for the increase at least 45 days before rates

31. Increased Freight Rates, 1969, 337 ICC 436 (1970), in *84th Annual Report*, 1970, p. 35; Increased Freight Rates, 1970 and 1971, 339 ICC 125 (1971), in *85th Annual Report*, 1971, p. 18; Increased Freight Rates and Charges, 1972, 341 ICC 288 (1972), in *87th Annual Report*, 1973, pp. 15–16; *New York Times*, 2 September and 16 November 1974, 26 March and 29 April 1975.

went into effect. In 1972 the ICC refused increases in two territories because the new procedures were not followed.[32]

Rail and Motor Mergers

Although economists agreed that cost-of-service rates would better allocate transportation resources and help cure transportation ills, railroads and the ICC turned in the 1950s to the merger panacea. Having balked when Congress prescribed this cure in the 1920s, the ICC and railroads espoused it just when Meyer and his associates were discovering that mergers of large systems did not bring substantial savings. Reversing its traditional hostility, the ICC from 1955 to 1968 approved 33 mergers and rejected only five out of 38 applications. In mergers, the key commission figure was the hearing examiner who investigated a complicated proposal and made a recommendation, which the ICC usually approved despite frequent opposition from the Justice Department. Among ICC-approved mergers were the Chesapeake & Ohio and Baltimore & Ohio (1962), forming the Chessie System; the Norfolk & Western and Nickel Plate (1964); and the largest of all transportation mergers, the Pennsylvania and the New York Central (1966). Eliminating interrail competition in 32 urban centers, the Penn-Central merger was before the ICC and the courts six years before Supreme Court approval in 1968.

The ICC was castigated in the late 1960s for passively approving carrier-proposed mergers. It had not planned combinations despite the admonition of Justice William J. Brennan Jr. that "the ICC is not the prisoner of the parties' submissions. Rather, the agency's duty is to weight alternatives and make its choice according to the judgment how best to achieve and advance the goals of the National Transportation Policy." When in 1968 the ICC, reversing its earlier negative decision, approved the Northern Lines merger of the Great Northern; the

32. *84th Annual Report*, 1970, pp. 36–37; *85th Annual Report*, 1971, p. 23; New Procedures in Motor Carrier Rev. Proc., 340 ICC 1, in *86th Annual Report*, 1972, pp. 31–32; *87th Annual Report*, 1973, p. 30.

Northern Pacific; the Chicago, Burlington & Quincy; the Pacific Coast; and the Spokane, Portland & Southern, the state of Minnesota claimed that the ICC hearing examiner "parroted" the carriers' arguments and the Justice Department accused him of a "dismaying gullibility" and the ICC of "bodily" handing the "public trust" to the carriers. Two years later the Supreme Court reversed its 1904 *Northern Securities* decision and approved the Northern Lines merger, which eliminated rail competition in the Northwest as effectively as the Penn-Central merger did in the Northeast.

As the sixties drew to a close, the commission appeared to be taking a harder look at proposed railroad mergers. Although mergers were the rage in that decade, with few major lines untouched by the movement, predicted savings had not materialized, and the commission reported that merger applications had declined sharply. Ominously, the great Penn Central went bankrupt in 1970, only two years after the Supreme Court approved its creation. In fiscal 1970 the ICC denied the proposed merger of the Chicago & North Western and the Chicago, Milwaukee, St. Paul & Pacific because of an inequitable stock-exchange ratio and called for further investigation of the proposed Norfolk & Western and Chesapeake & Ohio merger to determine its effect on Penn-Central traffic. During that investigation, the principals withdrew their application. These mergers had been approved the preceding year by hearing examiners.[33]

In 1973 the ICC began playing a more active role in planning mergers. Though the ICC took a decade to decide the fate of the financially weak but strategically located Chicago, Rock Island & Pacific Railroad, it finally seized the initiative. In February 1973 Nathan Klitenic, an administrative law judge (formerly called a hearing examiner), suggested that huge savings would result if twenty-five midwestern and western lines were

33. *83d Annual Report*, 1969, pp. 22–28; *84th Annual Report*, 1970, pp. 28–30; *85th Annual Report*, 1971, p. 63; Wilcox, *Public Policies Toward Business*, pp. 387–88; Fellmeth, *Interstate Commerce Omission*, pp. 75–99; Carson, *Main Line to Oblivion*, pp. 190–99, 206–12.

consolidated into four strong systems. Twenty-one months later the ICC by a six-to-four vote allowed the Union Pacific to acquire the Rock Island and took steps toward implementing Klitenic's scheme by attaching conditions involving the sale of Rock Island trackage (particularly south of Kansas City) and indemnities to other railroads. Although the estimated savings and the wisdom of these unifications could be questioned, the ICC's action seemed a harbinger of the commission's awakening from its lethargy. ICC requirements, however, were so obnoxious to the Union Pacific that in March 1975 it rejected the merger, and the Rock Island, unable to get a $30 million federal emergency loan, went into bankruptcy and faced liquidation.[34]

Similar patterns emerged in motor-carrier consolidations. The ICC continued its policy "of handling each proceeding on an individual case basis." The commission denied only 30 motor-carrier mergers in 1968 and 31 in 1969, while granting 303 in each of those years. The ICC also granted most applications for transfer or lease of operating rights, with roughly ten requests to unify motor-carrier operations granted for each application denied. With several merger plans before the commission in fiscal 1972 involving unusually large motor carriers or motor-carrier complexes under common control, the ICC scrutinized the proposals more carefully and insisted before approving one of these mergers in the next fiscal year that a subsidiary guarantee the financial stability of the new system by selling specified properties for $6 million.[35]

As the seventies approached, carrier involvement in diversified activities became widespread. Accompanying and facilitating diversification was the rise of the noncarrier, conglomerate holding-company, which unified under one management transportation and nontransportation interests. By 1968 the ICC reported that conglomerates controlled 50 percent of Class I rail-

34. *87th Annual Report*, 1973, pp. 8–9; *New York Times*, 16 February 1973, 9 November 1974, 18 and 19 March 1975.
35. *83d Annual Report*, 1969, p. 29; *84th Annual Report*, 1970, p. 30; *86th Annual Report*, 1972, p. 30; *87th Annual Report*, 1973, p. 26.

road assets, that major oil companies controlled most pipelines, that water carriers, particularly large ones, were either diversified or subsidiaries of large corporations, and that even motor carriers were diversified and purchased by nontransportation companies. By investing in everything from chemicals to apparel, rail companies formed conglomerates to improve profits through diversification. It was possible for a conglomerate holding-company to shift investments from its railroad property to its nontransport enterprises and to use railroad tax credits to help offset the nontransport earnings of affiliates. Unregulated conglomerate holding-companies controlled the policies of the regulated common carrier it owned, and while common-carrier accounts had to meet ICC specifications, conglomerate accounts were not regulated.[36]

By 1970 conglomeratic ardor was dampened by stock-market fluctuations, tight money, high interest rates, the 1969 Tax Reform Act, and the failure in quick succession of three conglomerate-owned railroads. Nontransportation companies, however, stepped up their acquisition of motor carriers. In 1970 large companies, including B. F. Goodrich, Del Monte, and Pepsico, controlled over a hundred motor common carriers. Almost profligate in approving mergers and with little control over conglomerates—which it had sought unsuccessfully to control—the ICC ironically would not allow rail and motor carriers to form integrated transportation companies, which many economists suggested would provide shippers and passengers more efficient and less costly transportation.[37]

Despite its extensive power over common-carrier financial operations, the ICC did not wish to sift through complex arrangements to learn the identity of railroad owners. Even though the same interests might control competing lines, Ken-

36. *83d Annual Report*, 1969, pp. 32–35.
37. *84th Annual Report*, 1970, pp. 31–34; *85th Annual Report*, 1971, pp. 67–70; *86th Annual Report*, 1972, p. 4; *87th Annual Report*, 1973, pp. 50–51; Fellmeth, *Interstate Commerce Omission*, p. 111; Friedlaender, *Dilemma of Freight Transport Regulation*, pp. 155–59, 185–86.

neth Tuggle, chairman of Division 3 (handling carrier finances), opposed commission "snooping." Castigating the ICC for its ignorance about who owned the Penn Central, Justice William O. Douglas declared: "Only one of the largest stockholders is known. The remaining largest stockholders are brokerage houses and Swiss banks holding nominal title for their customers. The beneficial owners are unknown, and apparently of no concern to the Commission. The Commission was specifically requested to determine who are the beneficial owners of the stock and who would control the merged company. The Commission refused to accede to the request." Douglas also complained that the ICC was unconcerned both with the interlocking directorate of the Penn Central and corporations with which it dealt and with the increasing control over railroads by "banks, insurance companies, and other large financial interests." In 1967 out of 76 main railroads, 15 were owned by less than 10 persons, 25 by less than 50 persons, 37 by less than 1,000, and 48 by less than 5,000. Interlocking directorates further muted interrail competition. For example, the Illinois Central—largely controlled by the Union Pacific—did not protest when the Union Pacific wished to merge with the Rock Island even though the proposed combination would hurt the Illinois Central. In fiscal 1972 the ICC, apparently shaken out of its lethargy by criticism, ordered the Union Pacific to divest itself within ten years of its Illinois-Central holdings.[38]

Salvaging Northeastern Railroads

The commission also helped in efforts to resolve the plight of bankrupt railroads, including the Penn Central, Boston & Maine, Erie Lackawanna, Reading, Lehigh Valley, and the Central of New Jersey. At the behest of Congress, the ICC investigated and reported in March 1973 that northeastern railroads could not be reorganized and revitalized without federal aid. Congress utilized ICC suggestions as well as those of the

38. Fellmeth, *Interstate Commerce Omission*, pp. 99–106; *86th Annual Report*, 1972, p. 9.

DOT in writing the Regional Rail Reorganization Act of 1973 (passed in January 1974). That act established the United States Railway Association (USRA) to finance and plan—with the help of the DOT and a new Rail Services Planning Office of the ICC—an economically viable restructured northeastern railroad system, called the Consolidated Rail Corporation (Conrail). Congress set up an elaborate timetable calling for Conrail to be in operation by September 1975, but the Richard Nixon administration, preoccupied with the Watergate scandal, delayed four months in selecting the USRA board.[39]

In its preliminary plan, released in February 1975, the USRA proposed that Conrail abandon 6,200 miles of light density lines unless states and localities help shoulder losses, that it rehabilitate the remaining 15,000 miles over a 14-year period for $7.3 billion, that the federal government provide much of the funding needed by Conrail, a private corporation, that two solvent carriers—the Chessie System and the Norfolk & Western—take over portions of the bankrupt lines to compete with Conrail, and that high-speed passenger service be restored and increased among major midwestern and northeastern cities. The proposed abandonment of 30 percent of Conrail's freight trackage and additional reliance on trucks in the midst of an energy crisis outraged the affected communities and appeared absurd to many critics. In addition, the massive federal funding of a private corporation, organized for profit, seemed dubious to many, who demanded that the alternatives of nationalizing either the entire system or roadbeds and rolling stock be explored.[40]

Initially, both the DOT and the ICC seemed pleased with the plan, which they had helped influence. Following hearings enlivened by mounting public criticism, however, the ICC's Rail Service Planning Office in April 1975 raised "monumental new

39. *87th Annual Report*, 1973, pp. 10–11; U.S., Department of Transportation, *Rail Service in the Midwest and Northeast Region* (Washington, 1974), pp. 1–3.
40. *New York Times*, 27 February and 2 March 1975.

doubts about the plan's practicality" and "on every count" found "grave defects" in the USRA design for Conrail. In place of the USRA's regional plan, the commission's Planning Office advocated a nationwide five-year $12 billion program to rehabilitate roadbeds and equipment, which would be more than half financed by a federal two-cent-a-gallon fuel tax. By May 1975 the Gerald Ford administration seemed to be abandoning the USRA plan and confusion prevailed over the fate of Conrail. While protesting its continued support of the USRA plan, the DOT explored the sale of the bankrupt roads and the Justice Department suggested either "controlled liquidation" of the seven bankrupt roads or dissolving the Penn-Central merger. Penn-Central trustees countered by suggesting that Conrail become a holding company and manage the bankrupt roads as operating subsidiaries, while congressmen, aware that any feasible plan would cost the federal government billions, talked freely of nationalization. George Stafford, chairman of the ICC and member of the USRA, personified the confusion when, speaking of controlled liquidation, he admitted, "I don't know if I'm opposed to it or not." When spurred by public hearings, the ICC's planning office had found "grave defects" in the USRA's preliminary plan, yet in late August the commission, despite its misgivings about Conrail's extensive planned debt, attempted to save its own power by backing the USRA's basically unchanged final plan for Conrail. To oppose more effectively what it termed the Ford administration's "improper" attempt to tie the deregulation of rail rates to the launching of Conrail, the commission closed ranks with the USRA. That Conrail, the ICC declared, "would, in effect, be held hostage for the passage of this, or any other, highly controversial legislation should be unthinkable." With the USRA sticking to its plan, the Ford administration using the threat of abandoning northeastern rail service to force Congress to cripple the ICC, and the commission concentrating on saving itself rather than on improving the Conrail plan, the fate of the Penn Central and other bankrupt roads remained uncertain despite the energy crisis and the acknowledged need for improved rail service.[41]

The Embattled ICC

In recent years, two additional studies have offered their prescriptions to cure transportation's ills. Significantly neither the scholarly analysis by Ann F. Friedlaender (*The Dilemma of Freight Transport Regulation,* 1969, for a Brookings Institution conference) nor the muckraking attack by Robert C. Fellmeth (*The Interstate Commerce Omission,* 1970, a Ralph Nader group study conducted by Harvard and University of Pennsylvania law students) have had praise for the ICC. Friedlaender concluded that ICC regulatory policies resulted in "inefficient traffic allocations, excess capacity, stifling of technological change and innovation." Estimating that shippers would save $500 million annually if rate regulation ended, Friedlaender noted that since transportation costs affect nearly all prices the total cost of regulation was much higher. She recommended forming two or three competing integrated transportation companies in each region with a "competitive fringe of barge and trucking firms" to prevent price leadership by oligopolistic transportation companies. ICC approval of railroad mergers creating monopolies in the Northeast, Northwest, Middle Atlantic states, and Florida, however, virtually ruled out competing deregulated transportation companies because railroad mergers are almost impossible to unscramble. Considering the outlook bleak for radical changes in ICC regulatory policy, Friedlaender advocated that the ICC both prevent mergers that eliminate competition and relax piggyback regulations (by charging ramp-to-ramp, cost-based rates), freight forwarder restrictions, railroad abandonment policy in low-traffic areas, and minimum rates. These actions, she argued, would undermine value-of-service rates and help create a competitive-rate structure. Friedlaender, however, expressed little hope even for these marginal

41. Ibid., 28 February, 29 April, 9, 16, 21, and 30 May, 7 June, 29 July, and 26 August 1975.

changes as long as the ICC weighs losses to "a particular carrier or producer" more "than the social losses resulting from the inefficiencies created by the rate structure." While virtually all Brookings Institution conference participants agreed that "present regulatory policies are very costly to the United States economy," the ICC representative to the conference, claiming regulation worked fairly well, advocated the old panacea of extending regulation.[42]

Well-written, interesting, and sensational, the Fellmeth study, in the best muckraking tradition, appealed to a wide audience. Building on the work of Friedlaender, Meyer, Peck, and other economists, Robert C. Fellmeth and his associates investigated commissioners and their activities for a ten-year period (roughly covering the sixties); interviewed over 500 persons (ranging from a hundred ICC officials to truck drivers); surveyed shippers, ICC practitioners, and other affected persons through detailed questionnaires; and analyzed mountains of statistical data (including 1966 way-bill data collected in raw form by the ICC's Bureau of Accounts). Fellmeth and his investigators found that commissioners were unqualified political appointees with no clear idea of the public interest or how to serve it through regulation. Their intimate relations with the transportation industry resulted in a system of "deferred bribes" with nine out of the eleven commissioners who had left the ICC from 1958 to 1967 receiving lucrative positions in the industry.

Extreme conservatism dominated the high-level staff members who, in effect, ran the ICC. Their long tenure (that of bureau heads averaged thirty-one years) and predominating 1930s outlook made them defenders of the status quo. The passive, permissive stance of the commission led it to accept mergers and rate increases, to protect existing firms from new competition, to adhere to value-of-service pricing, to discourage innovations, and to ignore both the "massive violation of truck safety regulations" and the 5,000 yearly complaints from con-

42. Friedlaender, *Dilemma of Freight Transport Regulation*, passim, particularly pp. 163–74, 186–87.

sumers who had suffered outrages from home movers. While enforcing the ICA complacently, the commission seemed content to "preside over the funeral" of rail passenger service and did nothing to solve the boxcar shortage that plagued farmers. The Fellmeth study recommended that the ICC "should be abolished in its present form," that a new agency be "created from the ground up," that it encourage competition within the various transportation modes, that it concentrate on maximum, not minimum, rate regulation—particularly where monopolies exist—and that it gradually reduce rate discrimination and use cost as the rate base. Refusing comment on the Fellmeth study, the ICC's attitude, one high commission official admitted, was "Don't panic. If it just dies down, forget it."[43]

Though not abolished, the ICC was reorganized shortly before publication of the Fellmeth study. Beginning on 1 January 1970, the ICC chairman was no longer elected annually by fellow commissioners, but designated permanently by the president. This effort to provide the commission with a leader was similar to earlier practice, when the commission selected its permanent chairman. In May 1970 President Richard M. Nixon appointed Commissioner George M. Stafford as the first permanent chairman since Chairman Martin A. Knapp left the commission in 1910 to head the ill-fated Commerce Court. To lead and direct the ICC, a permanent chairman needed both political clout and deep understanding of the transportation problem. Stafford, who had been administrative assistant to Senator Frank Carlson of Kansas for seventeen years and a Kansas Republican party worker for five years before that, had political experience without political prestige and no regulatory or transportation expertise prior to his three years on the ICC.[44]

The postwar commission employed approximately 2,000 persons, while its budget almost quadrupled from 1946 ($8.7

---

43. Fellmeth, *Interstate Commerce Omission*, passim, particularly pp. 311–26.

44. *84th Annual Report*, 1970, p. 2; Fellmeth, *Interstate Commerce Omission*, pp. 2, 6.

million) to fiscal 1973 ($33.1 million) when the ICC received 8,500 formal cases, 9,000 informal proceedings, and 329,000 tariffs and schedules (one out of 26 were criticized and one out of 79 rejected). If opposed, a case could cost a litigant from $3,000 to several hundred thousand dollars. The enormous workload was handled by divisions of the ICC (Division 1, Operating Rights; Division 2, Rates, Tariffs, and Valuation; Division 3, Finance and Service); by sixteen boards of commission employees, each specializing in adjudicating a specific part of the ICA; and by the practice of assigning a commissioner or a board member responsibility for a case. Swamped by thousands of narrow cases, the commission rarely considered large transportation issues (approximately a dozen cases a year were important ex parte proceedings, complete with investigations and hearings) and was dependent on its staff for both decisions and policies. Its staff in 1973 was housed in five major offices and five bureaus. The Office of Proceedings was divided into sections on Operating Rights, Rates, and Finance to correspond to the three ICC divisions. Working with the commissioner or board member to whom a case was assigned, these sections helped draft opinions and did much of the ICC's legal work. The Section of Hearings, which conducted and reported hearings, was also in the Office of Proceedings until 1970, when it became the separate Office of Hearings. The managing director, the general counsel, and the secretary headed the other three major offices. The five major bureaus were Accounts, Enforcements, Operations (with a field staff five times larger than its Washington-office staff), Traffic (responsible for tariffs, rates, and suspensions), and Economics.[45]

In the absence of strong, experienced commissioners and in the presence of an enormous workload demanding technical skill and attention to detail, office and bureau heads and administrative law judges (hearing examiners) have assumed

45. *87th Annual Report*, 1973, pp. 107–11; Fellmeth, *Interstate Commerce Omission*, pp. 6–9, 11. Safety responsibilities had been transferred in 1967 to the Department of Transportation. *81st Annual Report*, 1967, pp. 5–8.

enormous importance. As the Fellmeth study emphasizes, in 1970 office and bureau leaders had been with the ICC for approximately thirty years, and half of the hearing examiners were eligible for retirement. The views of these important staff members were those of an earlier generation; they appeared convinced that regulation was working and that there was no need to disturb the status quo.[46]

Having always responded to pressure, the ICC began in the early 1970s to adjust to criticism advanced by everyone from economists to muckrakers, from *Fortune* to the *New York Daily News*. The commission had neither panicked nor reformed, but it had manifested some concern for consumers: it required more convincing proof before approving advanced rates, it attached more significant conditions to mergers (showing a new inclination to plan and shape), it permitted experimentation when it allowed 14,000 employees to purchase from a conglomerate the Chicago & North Western Railroad, it tightened regulations governing long-distance moving, it proposed new rules to improve service on interstate buses, and it both responsibly prescribed safety and service standards for Amtrak intercity passenger service established by the Rail Passenger Service Act of 1970 and held hearings drawing attention to the fact that Amtrak had not adhered to those standards.[47]

Overshadowing these adjustments are long-term parallel ICC investigations begun in 1971 of the railroad freight-rate structure (Ex Parte 270) and of its base or railroad net investment (Ex Parte 271). These investigations constitute the most searching look into freight rates the ICC has taken. While expending an enormous amount of its staff's resources in gathering

46. Fellmeth, *Interstate Commerce Omission*, pp. 13–15, 350. The Fellmeth study is particularly valuable for its information on the ICC and its workings.

47. *86th Annual Report*, 1972, pp. 9–10, 12–14; Dan Cordtz, "It's Time to Unload the Regulators: The Costs of Cushioning Competition Are Far Greater Than the Benefits to the Public," *Fortune* 84 (July 1971): 64–67, 143–45; *New York Daily News*, 18 July 1973; *New York Times*, 3 April, 1 and 18 May, and 15 July 1975.

data, the commission in June 1973 hired an outside expert, Leonard S. Goodman, to direct these projects. Awarding this contract to Goodman marked the first time since its appointment of Louis D. Brandeis in the *Five Percent* case (1914) that the commission had turned to outside counsel to assemble evidence. It is possible that these investigations will lead the commission to replace minimum-rate regulation and value-of-service ratemaking with cost-based rates that will engender competition and save consumers part of the estimated $16 billion which regulation annually inflates costs. These investigations recall Franklin K. Lane's studies of express companies and the commission's 1912 action which rationalized the express business and still remains "the most important single piece of work ever done by the Commission." Whether the present ICC will eclipse Lane's contribution depends on the quality of the investigations by Goodman and—given the commission's weakness—on the intensity of pressure mounted by transportation, shipper, and consumer interests. A May 1975 proposal by the Ford administration to allow railroads without ICC interference to increase or decrease their rates—by 7 percent the first year, 12 percent the second, and 15 percent the third—kept pressure intense by threatening to render the ICC powerless and Goodman's investigation of the railroad rate structure useless. If passed, the Ford proposal would nullify the ICC's basic power over maximum and minimum rates and reduce the commission to a hollow shell.[48]

Clearly, the ICC's independence is largely a myth. To survive, the commission must adjust, and the weaker the ICC is, the more susceptible it is to pressure. From time to time, the ICC has been swayed by components of the transportation industry, but the commission is part of the body politic and as

48. *85th Annual Report*, 1971, pp. 18–19; *86th Annual Report*, 1972, pp. 16–19; *87th Annual Report*, 1973, pp. 19–20; Lewis A. Engman, "Address of . . . Chairman, Federal Trade Commission, Before the 1974 Fall Conference, Financial Analysts Federation, Detroit, Mich., October 7, 1974" (Washington: Federal Trade Commission, 1974); Sharfman, *ICC*, 2:70, n. 141; *New York Times*, 20 May 1975.

such responds more quickly to political power than to industrial power. Commissioners are aware of political reality; to be re-appointed every seven years, they must be renominated by the president and reconfirmed by the Senate. When political leaders have been interested in transportation, the ICC has tended to reflect their viewpoints; when politicians have ignored transportation, railroads or trucks have had greater influence on the commission, and its staff, with its commitment to the status quo, has assumed more importance.

Indeed, maintaining the status quo appears to be the ICC's most persistent pattern. Having achieved the increased power it had agitated for, the commission used that power to preserve existing relationships. From its beginning, when Thomas M. Cooley instituted a case-by-case approach, the ICC chose a judicial rather than an administrative stance. Unlike "the vacuous and weasel-worded utterances characteristic of our day," however, Cooley's opinions set standards for adjudication and offered models to administrators and guides to carriers.[49] A brilliant lawyer and forceful leader who understood the railroad problem, Cooley remained on the ICC only a few years. In the hands of lesser men and women, the case-by-case approach led the ICC to drift aimlessly. It became a passive body reacting to specific problems rather than an aggressive policy-making group anticipating and coping with difficulties before they overwhelmed carriers, shippers, consumers, and the commission. Despite President Theodore Roosevelt's urgings to lead, despite the mandates of Congress to plan a national transportation system, and despite the exhortation of Justice William J. Brennan Jr. to break the confines of the case at hand to enunciate larger policy, the ICC remained a passive quasi-judicial body rather than an active administrative tribunal.

The policy of drift did not stem entirely from close ties with the transportation industry. Although in the post-World War II era those ties could be described charitably as shameful and more accurately as corrupt, the ICC's inertia has frequently

49. Friendly, *Federal Administrative Agencies*, pp. 29, 31.

harmed carriers. During the Progressive era when railroads needed rate increases, the ICC stubbornly clung to the status quo, and in the post-World War II years its confused minimum-rate policy, which maintained differentials and existing relationships between transportation modes, has dismayed railroads. On the other hand, in the twenties the ICC pleased railroads by neglecting to plan a national rail system.

Largely responsible for the ICC's inertia, commissioners have had varying degrees of strength, ability, and knowledge. Too often they have been weak nonentities. In its long history, the ICC has had only four outstanding commissioners: Thomas M. Cooley, Martin A. Knapp, Franklin K. Lane, and Joseph B. Eastman. Cooley's tenure was short; Knapp became isolated on the commission, particularly after the Hepburn Act gave the ICC genuine power over rates; Lane served less than seven years before leaving to join Wilson's cabinet; and Eastman, significantly, was known as a great dissenter. Without strong leaders or tending to ignore them when they were available, the ICC usually took the path of least resistance and hesitated when action might disturb existing rates or relationships. Weak commissioners responded to Congress in the Progressive era, railroads in the 1920s, truckers in the 1960s, and even a bit to consumer advocates in the 1970s; but these commissioners were most amenable to pressures which preserved existing relationships. In proportion to its weakness and inexperience, the ICC depended increasingly throughout the twentieth century on its long-time staff members, who had reason to protect a comfortable status quo and who seemed no more able than the commissioners to solve transportation problems. Although Congress and the executive intended the ICC to regulate the transportation industry, the commission, largely because of weak presidential appointments, has been regulated by its staff. The ICC has become a powerful commission composed of weak commissioners, superimposed upon an entrenched staff. The ICC's entrenched staff, however, is no match for an aroused public, Congress, and president.

Bibliographical Essay

THE LITERATURE on the ICC is extensive and impressive. Perhaps the best book to begin with is John F. Stover's *American Railroads* (Chicago, 1961), a readable, informative survey. For a concise, clear development of the economic background of the Interstate Commerce Act (ICA), Edward C. Kirkland's *Industry Comes of Age: Business, Labor, and Public Policy, 1860–1897* (New York, 1961) is unmatched. Kirkland is both appreciative and critical of railroads and their managers. The attitudes of railroad managers are revealed in Thomas C. Cochran, *Railroad Leaders, 1845–1890: The Business Mind in Action* (Cambridge, Mass., 1953).

Many groups have been praised for or accused of supporting the ICA. Solon J. Buck in *The Granger Movement . . . , 1870–1880* (Cambridge, Mass., 1913) and in *The Agrarian Crusade: A Chronicle of the Farmer in Politics* (New Haven, 1920) emphasizes the Grange's influence on railroad regulation, while George H. Miller's *Railroads and the Granger Laws* (Madison, 1971) contends that local merchants originated the antirailroad, antimonopoly, and antidiscrimination legislation in the Midwest and that the Grange was actually a moderating influence. Lee Benson's *Merchants, Farmers, & Railroads: Railroad Regulation and New York Politics, 1850–1887* (Cambridge, Mass., 1955) emphasizes the role of New York merchants in securing state railroad regulation and in formulating the ICA, while Gerald D. Nash in "Origins of the Interstate Commerce Act of 1887," *Pennsylvania History* 24 (1957):181–90, finds the germ of the ICA in the attempts of independent Pennsylvania oilmen to break the power of Standard Oil. Gabriel Kolko's hypothesis in *Railroads and Regulation, 1877–1916* (Princeton, 1965) that railroads wanted federal regulation and worked to secure the

ICA is novel, exciting, revealing, and misleading. Robert W. Harbeson in "Railroads and Regulation, 1877–1916: Conspiracy or Public Interest?" *Journal of Economic History* 27 (1967):230–42, accepts Kolko's notion that railroads wanted regulation but claims that Kolko "completely misunderstands the economic characteristics of the railway industry," that in fact the ICC did not conspire with railroads but served the public interest from 1887–1920. Edward A. Purcell, Jr., in "Ideas and Interests: Businessmen and the Interstate Commerce Act," *Journal of American History* 54 (1967):561–78, discredits theories that farmers, merchants, railroads, or even "the people" brought regulation. He credits diverse groups acting in self-interest, motivated by fear of the new national economy, and seeking protection from the federal government through the ICC. Finally, Albro Martin in "The Troubled Subject of Railroad Regulation in the Gilded Age—a Reappraisal," *Journal of American History* 61 (1974):339–71, argues that the ICA aimed at stripping railroads of their enormous power over the economy by prohibiting pools, while George W. Hilton in "The Consistency of the Interstate Commerce Act," *Journal of Law and Economics* 9 (1966):87–113, argues that the act inconsistently sought to stabilize railroad cartels while outlawing pools and suggests that the transportation industry would have been better off without the ICA.

The *Annual Reports* of the ICC are well organized and clear. I. L. Sharfman's *The Interstate Commerce Commission: A Study in Administrative Law and Procedure* (5 vols., New York, 1931–37) is both exhaustive and accurate and remains the indispensable work on the first fifty years of the ICC. Reflecting the ICC's prestige in the 1930s, Sharfman is sympathetic to regulation by independent commissions in general and the ICC in particular, but on occasion (particularly when reviewing the 1920s) he criticizes the ICC for failing to use its regulatory powers. Robert E. Cushman in *The Independent Regulatory Commissions* (New York, 1941) supplements Sharfman, particularly on the background of legislation. Emory R. Johnson's *Government Regulation of Transportation* (New York, 1938), Clarence Atha Miller's *The Lives of the Interstate Commerce Commissioners and the Commission's Secretaries* (Washington, 1946), and E. Pendleton Herring's *Federal Commissioners: A Study of their Careers and Qualifications* (Cambridge, Mass, 1936) are also useful supplements.

The effects of regulation are hotly debated. Gabriel Kolko argues in *Railroads and Regulation* (cited above) that during the late nineteenth century and the Progressive Era railroads dominated the ICC and utilized it to achieve their ends. Paul W. MacAvoy in *The Economic Effects of Regulation: The Trunk-Line Railroad Cartels and the Interstate Commerce Commission Before 1900* (Cambridge, Mass., 1965) presents statistical data showing that the ICC did stabilize rates until 1893. Albro Martin, however, in "The Troubled Subject of Railroad Regulation" (cited above) denies that the ICC cartelized railroads or stabilized rates, maintains that the ICC was "stillborn," and argues that MacAvoy's figures, based on published rates, are suspect because of rebates. Martin says that railroads cartelized themselves by consolidating after the ICA forbade pooling. In *Enterprise Denied: Origins of the Decline of American Railroads, 1897–1917* (New York, 1971), Martin not only insists that railroads did not dominate the ICC but blames the "palsied hand" of the ICC for the twentieth-century decline of railroads. Although Martin's prejudices are clear—he is fond of railroads and dislikes Progressives, shippers, and the ICC—his evidence is impressive. The mind of an outstanding commissioner is revealed in *The Letters of Franklin K. Lane, Personal and Political*, ed. Ann Wintermute Lane and Louise Herrick Wall (Boston, 1922). K. Austin Kerr in *American Railroad Politics, 1914–1920: Rates, Wages, and Efficiency* (Pittsburgh, 1968) untangles the various forces that impelled the Wilson administration to operate the railroads during World War I and the more complex maneuvers—in the name of scientific management—that led to the 1920 Transportation Act. For more on federal operation, see Walker D. Hines (director general of railroads, 1919–1920) *War History of American Railroads* (New Haven, 1928). Sharfman (cited above) is particularly full on the ICC during the 1920s and early 1930s. Earl Latham in *The Politics of Railroad Coordination, 1933–1936* (Cambridge, Mass., 1959) stresses the negative reaction of the ICC, railroads, and labor to Commissioner Eastman's efforts to coordinate and save railroads in the Great Depression. For more on Eastman—an outstanding commissioner—see Claude Moore Fuess's *Joseph B. Eastman: Servant of the People* (New York, 1952).

Whether written by a political scientist, an economist, a judge, a general, or a consumer advocate, the post-World War II literature on transportation regulation has been hostile to the ICC. Charles L. Dearing and Wilfred Owen, whose study *National Transportation Policy* (Washington, 1949) evolved out of their research for the Hoover commission, call for a department of transportation to plan and promote transportation while the independent agencies regulate it. Samuel P. Huntington, in "The Marasmus of the ICC: The Commission, the Railroads, and the Public Interest," *Yale Law Journal* 61 (1952):467–509, claims that the ICC identified with and supported railroads in their conflicts with motor and water carriers and that the commission was wasting away because its railroad allies were growing weaker. Marver H. Bernstein in *Regulating Business by Independent Commission* (Princeton, 1955) argues that the ICC has been too judicial and has failed to plan, that commissions have their life cycle, and that the postwar ICC was old and in a state of debility. Four years later, John R. Meyer, Merton J. Peck, John Stenason, and Charles Zwick in *The Economics of Competition in the Transportation Industries* (Cambridge, Mass., 1959) and James C. Nelson in *Railroad Transportation and Public Policy* (Washington, 1959) proposed a substantial reduction of ICC regulation and heavy reliance on competition to provide the most desirous combination of rates and service for the public. In 1961 General John P. Doyle, staff director of the Special Study Group on Transportation Policies in the United States, presented his report to the Senate Committee on Commerce (U.S., Senate Committee on Commerce, *National Transportation Policy*, 87th Cong., 1st sess., 26 June 1961, S. Rept. 445). The *Doyle Report* attacks the ICC for maintaining the status quo and suggests that greater emphasis be placed on innovation and on the cost and not the value of the service rendered by carriers. Judge Henry J. Friendly of the United States Court of Appeals for the Second Circuit in *The Federal Administrative Agencies: The Need for Better Definition of Standards* (Cambridge, Mass., 1962) focuses his attack on the ICC (and Congress, too) for inconsistencies and ambiguities, particularly in the area of minimum rates. George W. Hilton in *The Transportation Act of 1958: A Decade of Experience* (Bloomington, Ind., 1969) regards that act as an ineffective palliative and attacks the ICC as a wasteful cartel that should be abolished. In *The Dilemma of Freight Transport Regulation* (Washington, 1969), prepared for a 1967 Brookings Institution conference, Ann F. Friedlaender stresses that

ICC regulations have inefficiently allocated traffic, created excess carrying capacity, and stifled technological innovation. The ICC has been scathingly attacked by a Ralph Nader group study led by Robert C. Fellmeth and entitled *The Interstate Commerce Omission: The Public Interest and the ICC* (New York, 1970). Written in the muckraking tradition and researched by law students, the Fellmeth study maintains that the transportation industry has dominated the ICC but does not explain why railroads—obviously a very powerful component of the transportation industry—have suffered from ICC regulation. This study is valuable for data collected through questionnaires and for its emphasis on the consumer's point of view. Its conclusion that ICC regulation is enormously costly to the American people agrees with earlier studies by economists, but its plea that the ICC be abolished goes beyond the recommendations of most previous studies. Finally, Robert B. Carson in *Main Line to Oblivion: The Disintegration of New York Railroads in the Twentieth Century* (Port Washington, N.Y., 1971) argues that the ICC has usually befriended the railroads, that the railroads have had pretty much their own way (he largely ignores the ICC's minimum-rate policies which diverted traffic from railroads to trucks), and that railroad corporate policy—attempting to cope with excess capacity—has stressed mergers and abandonment of services and has dominated public policy with disastrous results for the national interest.

Index